THE PHILOSOPHY OF GIAMBATTISTA VICO

BENEDETTO CROCE

With a new introduction by Alan Sica

Translated by R.G. Collingwood

Transaction Publishers
New Brunswick (U.S.A.) and London (U.K.)

Copyright © 2002 by Transaction Publishers, New Brunswick, New Jersey. Originally published in 1913. Reprinted in 1964 by Russell & Russell, Inc.

This book is printed on acid-free paper that meets the American National Standard for Permanence of Paper for Printed Library Materials.

Library of Congress Number: 2001048081
ISBN: 0-7658-0869-2
Printed in the United States of America

Library of Congress Cataloging-in-Publication Data

Croce, Benedetto, 1866-1952.
   [Filosofia di Giambattista Vico. English]
   The philosophy of Giambattista Vico / Benedetto Croce ; with a
new introduction by Alan Sica.
      p. cm.
   Translated by R.G. Collingwood.
   Originally published: 1913. With new introd.
   Includes bibliographical references and index.
   ISBN 0-7658-0869-2 (alk. paper)
   1. Vico, Giambattista, 1668-1744. I. Title.

B3583 .C713 2001
195—dc21   2001048081

TO

WILHELM WINDELBAND

CONTENTS

APPENDICES

INTRODUCTION TO THE TRANSACTION EDITION

THE TWO NEAPOLITAN TITANS: CROCE'S REDEFINITION OF VICO

"The real revolutionary who, by putting aside the concept of probability and conceiving imagination in a novel manner, actually discovered the true nature of poetry and art and, so to speak, invented the science of Aesthetic, was the Italian Giambattista Vico"
—Croce, 1978, p. 220

"For Croce history was never mere antiquarianism; it was the record of human intelligence building up civilization in all its forms, social, intellectual, and artistic. All these activities were for Croce unintelligible save as an effort to realize ideals—the ideals of beauty, of truth, and of ethics—and history itself was unintelligible unless one assumed the capacity of human beings to be guided by ideals and even to sacrifice themselves for them."
—Orsini, 1961, p. 13

EVER since Edmund Wilson's enticing remarks which open *To the Finland Station* (Wilson, 1940, pp. 3-6), or certainly by the time Isaiah Berlin lectured on "The Philosophical Ideas of Giambattista Vico" at the Italian Institute in London during 1957-58, intellectual historians in the anglophone sphere have been aware that Vico's *The New Science* (1744) was a book that could not be ignored, any more than could Montesquieu's *Spirit of the Laws* (1748) or Rousseau's *Social Contract* (1762). As one expert put it, "*The New Science* is a book stuffed so full of ideas that it almost bursts at the seams" (Burke,

1985, p. 32). More recently, another Vichian opened his commentary with an ironic complaint: "It was Benedetto Croce, one of Vico's best admirers, who remembered that when Nicola Capasso first opened the *Scienza nuova,* he 'fancied he had lost his wits...by a joke hurried off to his Doctor Cirollo, to have his pulse felt.' We may still sympathize a little. Over and over we have heard it said that Vico was ahead of his time and that he anticipated nearly everything in our own" (Levine, 1991, p. 55). Karl Löwith's cherished survey, *Meaning in History,* is one of many such bits of expert testimony which point to Vico's anticipation of today's cultural and intellectual conundra (Löwith, 1949, p. 115).

After Berlin's opinion gained a much broader audience in 1976 via his *Vico and Herder* (reissued again in 2000), ritualized reference to Vico's name throughout the humanities and social sciences became as unremarkable as a close reading of Vico's thorny masterpiece was rare. Thus, perched on the broad hermeneutic shoulders of Sir Isaiah, modern readers have embraced Vico as if he were a distant relative of great wealth and personal charm who had suddenly surfaced, just in time to save the family from conceptual ruin. Yet like so many "ancient tomes," *The New Science* became a work with which everyone is vaguely acquainted, though few intimately familiar, since it shares with other "classics" the demand for concentrated explicative labor which becomes ever less likely in a world of high-speed distractions and cultural change. Still, when Gore Vidal tried to capsulize the meaning of the previous millenium in a short essay, he chose Vico (and Plato) for the fulcrum on which to set his lever: "What happens next? Vico calls the next stage Chaos" (Vidal, 1999, p. 39).

The general outline, as well as those theoretical "insights" of enduring value commonly attributed to Vico's masterpiece—hardly his sole writing worth remembering, it must be noted—have become well enough known through dozens of commentaries and précis that detailed recapitulation here is unnecessary. His fame is even such that a "Giambattista Vico Home Page" has existed for some time on the Web (see Vico, 2000), by means of which a ready grasp of his principal ideas, shorn of persuasive detail, can be gained without much effort. It goes without saying that sources such as these, listing quotable "bits" from Vico's texts, are quite literally "worlds removed" from Croce's intense dialogue with Vico's ghost. For as H. Stuart Hughes reminds us in his uniquely influential intellectual history of the period, "From Vico...Croce derived what was most vital and imaginative in his own theoretical work" (Hughes, 1977, p. 208), a viewpoint seconded by the nonpareil Italian historian, Arnaldo Momigliano: "Croce preferred Vico to all other philosophers" (Momigliano, 1966a, p. 358). This is not hard to understand when one considers Vico's concise style and innovative analysis; for example: "Men first feel necessity, then look for utility, next attend to comfort, still later amuse themselves with pleasure, thence grow dissolute in luxury, and finally go mad and waste their substance" (Vico, 1999, §241, p. 98; cited in Löwith, 1949, p. 133).

In any case, those of Vico's ideas that lend themselves to textbook summary have been endlessly restated with small variation: the three "ages" of human history (gods, heroes, and men) which repeat themselves ad infinitum, each producing, yet determined by, distinctive forms of language and myths; relatedly, the inevitable "barbarism of reason" or "of reflection" common to the "age of men" that undercuts tradition and civility through egocentric sophistication and rationalism, violently returning society to its primitive roots after destroying ethical consensus; poetry as humankind's first language, preceding rational thought; Homer's fictional identity and the cruel protagonists of *The Iliad* contrasted with the more subtle creatures in *The Odyssey*; the need for comparative linguistics and sociology to establish the role of "divine Providence" in historical change; the historical priority and primacy of poetry as humankind's road to truth and language; the associated limits of Cartesian epistemology, of the duplicitous *cogito*; methodological and ontological reasons for the distinction between the natural and the social sciences; plus Vico's pride at having demonstrated that the Twelve Tables of Rome could not have been borrowed from Greece, but were autochthonously created (for a modern appraisal of this claim, see Hutton, 1992, pp. 8-13). It was this stream of stunning and original ideas that caused no less a figure than Wilhelm Dilthey to "acclaim Vico's *New Science* as 'one of the greatest triumphs of modern thought'" (Ermarth, 1978, p. 376).

However, not all of these notions interested Croce equally, nor did he accept each of them uncritically. His approach to any text grew from what one eyewitness has termed his "personal modesty, punctilious discipline, [and] fear of moral weakness." Croce, so the portrait continues, "was by nature slow in forming his opinions and correspondingly slow in changing them. All the noise around him never distracted him from his rigid routine of scholarly work which, supported as it was by an exceptional memory, made him one of the greatest *érudits* of any time" (Momigliano, 1966a, pp. 358, 348). He was particularly taken, though, with Vico's critique of Cartesian mental experiments and the "modern" way of looking at the physical world which became Descartes' lasting gift to Western culture: "In his estimation, among the gravest faults of the Cartesians was their inability to appreciate the world of imagination and poetry. Of his own times he complained they were 'benumbed by analytical methods and by a philosophy which sought to deaden every faculty of soul which reached it through the body, especially that of imagination, now held to be the mother of all human error': times 'of a wisdom which freezes the generous soul of the best poetry,' and prevents all understanding of it" (Croce, 1978, p. 228). Already by April, 1901, Croce had accepted the general correctness of Vico's views about language and the roots of mythology in no uncertain terms: "Nor did he ever tire of repeating his views and forcing them upon the attention of his hostile contemporaries at every opportunity.... And what were these ideas? Neither more nor less, we may say, than the solution of the problem stated by Plato, attacked but not solved by Aristotle, and again vainly attacked during the Renaissance and afterwards: is poetry rational or irrational, spiritual or brutal? and, if spiritual, what is its special nature and what distinguishes it from history and science?" (Ibid., pp. 220-221).

Even though Croce ended his short explication of Vico's ideas with several pages of "corrections," his assessment is markedly complimentary, even admiring, which separates this critique from the dozens of others Croce produced. As he explains, clearly in an approving tone, "In all this, Vico is not only a thorough revolutionary, but is quite conscious of being so: he knows himself to be in opposition to all previous theories on the subject" (Ibid., p. 227). Overall, then, Croce had little to say about Vico that could be construed as unflatter-

THE PHILOSOPHY OF GIAMBATTISTA VICO

ing, even if, as many commentators now maintain, "Croce is prone to attribute to Vico ideas more characteristic of his own philosophical position than Vico's" (Gardiner, 1967, p. 251). But given the astonishing scope of Croce's protean mind and philosophical ambitions, this is hardly surprising, nor necessarily a fault. Croce was not the first scholar to become enamored of the Vichian universe, while at the same time trying to bring it within the orbit of his own purposes.

Thus, as Isaiah Berlin would have been the first to admit, his own enthusiasm for Vico's ideas was hardly original. Some prescient readers understood the importance of Vico's innovative worldview (a select group which did not include either Newton or Goethe, for both received copies of his *Principii di una scienza nuova* and had no idea what to make of it). These remarks from a "dedicatory letter" in 1760 by the Italian legal scholar Bernardo Tanucci (1698-1783) are typical:

> I must confess to your excellency the sin of having taken Vico's works in my hands a thousand times, and a thousand times turned away from them lest my talent should be taken captive. But then, whether by the exigencies of my profession, or by the surprising pleasure which overcame me whenever I succeeded in penetrating his thought to its depths, or whether by both together, I was led to banish from my sight all books but his, and I determined, in spite of every natural aversion, to drink the bitter drought until it coursed in my veins, and my mind renewed its youth with the joy of being able in good faith to glory in having grasped something of the truth. (Tanucci, 1760, p. 5; from Fisch, 1944, p. 64)

Tanucci unintentionally illustrates a common sociological phenomenon: the resistant acceptance of genius, or true innovation, when first apprehended too close to its point of origin. What becomes apparent is a "love-hate" relationship with a startling text, exemplifying Harold Bloom's important notion that all authors and thinkers endure the "the anxiety of influence" from predecessors whose works, they suspect, have more to offer a given literary tradition than do their own writings. This reaction to Vico's ideas became standard throughout the succeeding two centuries, first in his hometown, and then across Europe. Indeed, it exists even today.

However, one might almost expect a fellow countryman like Tanucci to write in terms of such unconstrained enthusiasm during an era when other nations could boast of genii far brighter than Italy's. Yet this kind of approbation crossed national boundaries, as documented in remarks made in 1839 by the great German historian of Roman law, Friedrich Savigny:

> Vico, with his profound genius, stood alone among his contemporaries, a stranger in his own country, overlooked or derided, although now the attempt is made to claim him as a national possession. Among such unfavorable circumstances his spirit could not come to full fruition. It is true that one finds in him scattered thoughts on Roman history resembling Niebuhr's. But these ideas are like flashes of lightning in a dark night, by which the traveler is led further astray rather than brought back to his path. *No one could profit from them who had not already found the truth in his own way.* Niebuhr in particular learned to know him only late and through others. (Savigny, 1850, IV, 217f; from Fisch, 1944, p. 70)

This is a begrudging acknowledgement of creativity, perhaps tinged with a share of nationalistic envy, yet is quite accurate in its larger meaning: that Vico's ideas came to his audiences via a haphazard network of influences and suggestions, and that *The New Science* was capable of provoking in its serious readers the widest possible range of reactions.

German scholars were not alone in their warm regard for Vico in the early nineteenth century. Paralleling Coleridge's enthusiasm in England, Jules Michelet was the most influential and outspoken Gallic writer to embrace a Vichian perspective. As Edmund Wilson explained in his classic formulation sixty years ago, "How was it then that the *Scienza Nuova* could come to a man of 1820 as an intoxicating revelation? Because Vico, by force of an imaginative genius of remarkable power and scope, had enabled him to grasp fully for the first time the *organic* character of human society and the importance of reintegrating through history the various forces and factors which actually compose human life. 'I had no other master but Vico,' he wrote. 'His principle of living force, of humanity creating itself, made both my book and my teaching'" (Wilson, 1972, p. 6). Wilson then allows Vico to speak for himself in what amounts to an extreme capsulization of his achievement. He claims to have illuminated the development of "the formation of human law" which grew through "the specific phases and the regular process by which the customs which gave rise to law originally came into being: religions, languages, dominations, commerce, orders, empires, laws, arms, judgments, punishments, wars, peace, alliances...in terms of these phases and this process of growth, the eternal propriety by virtue of which the phases and the process must be thus and not othewise" (Ibid.). Michelet accepted Vico's conceptual and historiographical holism and preached it as an inviolable creed to his students and followers: "All science is one."

Among the most extraordinary encomia from the twentieth century, which takes in not only Vico's own achievement but also contextualizes his intellectual growth, are these unforgettable images from Paul Hazard's standard intellectual history of the Enlightenment:

Naples! the sun! what joy to be alive! Hark to the shouting and the tumult! See, in the narrow, winding streets what swarms of people, the most mercurial people in the world! what vivacity! what zest! where shall we find their like? And how keen they are to learn, to improve their minds! How animated they are! How eagerly they converse! Look at their assemblies, their salons, where men, carrying the burden of profound learning with graceful ease, discuss the various questions that engage the attention of philosophers and men of science, consider the various schools of thought and weigh the facts. At Naples, which receives, because it always keeps its ears open, the latest tidings of all that is being said and thought in Europe, at Naples, the old, original, tumultuous Naples, which stands forth as the very embodiment of force and vitality, there was born into the world on the 23rd June, 1668, a certain Giambattista Vico. (Hazard, 1963, pp. 411-412)

And having set up the sociocultural stage for Vico's grand entrance, Hazard wittily illuminates his subject's personality, the sort capable of creating what became known generically as "the new science":

Every sort of hindrance that fetters the spirit he knew; yet he managed to evade them all. He might, for example, have been an infant prodigy—he escaped. He might have been one of those too docile disciples who meekly lap up everything their masters tell them; he escaped. He might have become a slave to his profession; he escaped. Finally, he might have become prosperous, one of the greatest perils a man of ideas can be threatened by. That, too, he escaped. He read Aristotle and all the Greeks, St. Augustine, St. Thomas, Gassendi, Locke, Descartes, Spinoza, Malebranche, and Leibniz without surrendering himself to any of them.... Solitary, majestic, melancholy, he determined to be himself; himself and none other. There are two sorts of intelligence, the intelligence which absorbs, and the intelligence which creates. Vico possessed them both. (Hazard, 1963, p. 412)

And if Hazard's boyish enthusiasm seems suspect today, by its style as much as its content, one might turn instead for an evaluation of Vico's enduring importance to the most austere and learned of all recent historians, Arnaldo Momigliano. Despite his Piedmontese origins, he held academic appointments in three countries simultaneously, and wrote often for English-language audiences: "Vico has survived even his English translators, as he has survived his idealistic interpreters. One of the few authentically great minds in the field of history, he still eludes his own historians" (Momigliano, 1966b, p. 253). Momigliano's restraint in allocating praise for intellectual achievement was famous, so in its own way echoes what Hazard declaimed thirty years before.

That Vico's book was far more perplexingly creative than, say, either Montesquieu's or Rousseau's, did not aid in the accurate dispersion of its various theoretical themes, even with the able assistance of secondary analyses such as Berlin's. As one of Vico's more talented interpreters observed twenty years ago, "Many of Vico's most brilliant interpreters hang like albatrosses around his neck, inhibiting open readings of his views. The practice of turning Vico's thought to one's own is a danger to which a great number of his commentators have succumbed, and Vico's ship has been sailed under many flags—absolute idealism, Catholicism, Marxism, historicism, particular conceptions of contemporary epistemology, and the methodologies of various contemporary schools of philosophy. Although Vico's thought can be found through such approaches, it is soon lost in the security of their shores" (Verene, 1981, p. 23). If the measure of a thinker's importance lies in the multifarious renderings of his work that follow his death, Vico posthumously has been as thoroughly "successful" as he was hopelessly frustrated while alive.

Sir Isaiah inspired a small, dedicated army of scholars (whose titular leader was Giorgio Tagliacozzo) which created the second renaissance of Vico studies. Yet he himself was following the strong lead Croce had already established in 1911 (ably disseminated by R. G.

Collingwood through translations and commentaries), a fact now generally conceded: "General studies of Vico include Isaiah Berlin's...written with the author's customary brilliance but remains [*sic*] essentially within the Croce tradition" (Burke, 1985, p. 97). Informed opinion about the utility and cogency of Croce's presentation of Vico is varied and ambivalent, as one would expect, considering the intrinsic difficulties of both men's ideas, and the titanic wills that set them on their unique courses of philosophic study. They were both by nature and conviction spiritual members of "the Academy of the *Investiganti*," that extraordinary seventeenth-century Neapolitan moveable feast of free-thinkers, who in their writings and speeches feared neither the Spanish Inquisition nor Papal dictates (Fisch, 1944, pp. 32-33). Still, nearly every informed source now agrees that Croce initiated the modern Vico renaissance when he published *La Filosofia di Giambattista Vico* ninety years ago, especially after translations of the work began to appear in other major languages. Already in 1953, Robert Caponigri announced that "The debt of all Vichian study to the work of Croce, it must be said at once, is immeasurable; singlehandedly, he has founded modern Vichian scholarship, and no step can be taken in Vichian studies without immediate recourse to his work" (Caponigri, 1953, p. 4). A generation later Peter Burke's verdict was still widely shared: "Benedetto Croce...read the *New Science* in the 1890s and in 1911 published a study of it which remains the most important and the most influential contribution to the subject" (Burke, 1985, p. 6).   Similarly, in her rigorous Vico monograph (a revised dissertation directed by Sir Isaiah), Cecilia Miller makes this point in typical fashion: "Croce's powerful and extremely persuasive pronouncements

regarding Vico, which referred constantly to the tran-
scendental aspects of history, are still a force to be reckoned with in Vico studies, both in the Italian-speaking
world and beyond...Croce's views are so pervasive that
an analysis of *Vico senza Croce* (Vico without Croce)
seemed to be in order. However far we have moved from
Croce's Idealism, his discussion of Vico and mythology
still maintains its relevance today" (Miller, 1993, pp. 6-
7). Miller's concise evaluation repeats in substance the
quaint sentiments of the Croce translator, Douglas
Ainslee, seventy years before: "I consider that the reading of Croce and a knowledge of his views on philosophy and literature is essential to a modern education
that aims at something above the ordinary curriculum
of petrified common sense" (Ainslie, in Croce, 1923, p.
xv). For although Vico had never been forgotten in Italy,
especially in his hometown of Naples, only after Croce's
inimitable reading of *Scienza nuova* had begun to circu-
late abroad was the idiosyncratic, Vichian way of analyz-
ing social, mythological, and historical spheres taken
seriously as a *modern* interpretation of continuing vitality. What the enthusiastic readings of Coleridge, Thomas Arnold, Comte, Michelet, and others had begun in
the first half of the nineteenth century (see Fisch, 1944,
pp. 61-107), Croce perpetuated in the twentieth.

   The other famous modernist writer most closely associated with Vico's name, of course, is James Joyce. But
even if Joyce had not found a kindred spirit in Vico on
his own (apparently soon after 1905 when he settled in
Trieste to teach languages for Berlitz), and used his ideas
to fashion "Mr. John Baptister Vickar, producer and
ubiquitous stage-manager of *Finnegans Wake*" (Litz, 1969,
p. 246), Vico's name would still have been resurrected
and reshaped through Croce's influence. Joyce not only

read Vico in the difficult original Neapolitan, but also apparently supplemented this investigation by means of Croce's own *Estetica* (1901), specifically the memorable chapter on Vico from the "History of Aesthetic" (Croce, 1978, pp. 220-234). And even if it is true, as some argue, that Joyce borrowed liberally from Michelet's *Oeuvres choisies de Vico* (1835)—especially the able editor's summarizing introduction—in order to grasp the useable drift of "the new science" (Atherton, 1960, p. 267), it is equally likely that Croce's interpretation guided Joyce as he fashioned an implicit theory of fictional composition which set twentieth-century literature on a new course (Ellmann, 1983, p. 340). It is therefore neither original nor shocking to hazard the claim that if *Ulysses* is agreed by critical acclimation to be the "most important" work of literature in the century just concluded, then Vico becomes by strong association modern literature's most important philosopher—at least as metamorphosed through the disparate lenses of Michelet, Croce, and Joyce. Harry Levin's classic account of Joyce's fiction evaluates Vico's broad appeal somewhat differently: "A philosophy which has room for such bedfellows [Michelet, Croce, Joyce] could only exist in the limbo between mysticism and empiricism, between traditional and modern thought" (Levin, 1960, p. 43).

Consider one supporting datum to this heterodox suggestion: In August, 1936, four years before his death, Joyce was in Copenhagen where he was practicing Danish, and bumped into a noted local writer in a bookshop. According to Ellmann, "Kristensen asked him for help on *Work in Progress* [later *Finnegans Wake*], and Joyce referred him to Vico. 'But do you believe in the *Scienza nuova*?' asked Kristensen. 'I don't believe in any science,'

Joyce answered, 'but my imagination grows when I read Vico in a way that it doesn't when I read Freud or Jung'" (Ellmann, 1982, pp. 691-692). Inflaming James Joyce's imagination would in itself serve as a worthwhile legacy for any abstract thinker, even if Vico's influence had gone no further than that.

Recall in this regard the opening sentence to Joyce's masterwork: "riverrun, past Eve and Adam's, from swerve of shore to bend of bay, brings us by a commodius vicus of recirculation back to Howeth Castle and Environs" (Joyce, 1959 [1939], p. 3). "Vicus" is "village" in Latin, and also hints at Vico Road in Dalkey, while even more strongly suggesting "*ricorsi storici* of Vico" (McHugh, 1980, p. 3). And later in the book: "The Vico Road goes round and round to meet where term begins" (p. 452). As Levin explains, "Joyce's book... actually bears out Vico's theories. The most far-reaching of these can be stated in three words: history repeats itself. It is, in Joyce's phrase, 'a theory none too rectiline of the evoluation of human society and a testament of the rocks from all the dead unto some the living' [*Finnegans Wake*, p. 73]. The pattern of repetition, as established by Vico and followed by Joyce, is a historical version of Dante's eschatology...The four sections of *Finnegans Wake* approximate Vico's periods of civilization (Levin, 1960, p. 144, 146-47). Using the tried-and-true tripartite division of history, Vico proposes that the divine period produces religion and piety, the heroic gives forth marriage and honor, and the civil, in its turn, creates burial rites and duty. Speech changes from inchoate to fabulous to historical; hieroglpyhs evolve into metaphors, and hence into profane vernaculars. Joyce made tragi-comic use of all this by means of his "time machine" in *Finnegans Wake*. the "wholemole millwheeling vicociclometer" (p. 614). Levin (Ibid., p. 145) points to another important passage: "his hero moves in vicous circles" (p. 134).

Since it is through "Croce's iridescent Italian—analytical, dramatic, rhetorical, and homiletic by quick turns" (Krieger, 1970, p. vii) that Joyce and so many other sophisticates learned about Vico, one must puzzle over the validity of those arguments today which accuse Croce's portrait of Vico as being more aligned with his own idealist agenda than with the latter's peculiar philosophy of history, mythology, and language. Though no longer argued with the same heat that it once was, the question of the precise relationship between Croce's portrayal of Vico's achievement and the "actual" work itself continues to inspire comment. This is particularly due to the cottage industry of Vichian studies that sprang up in the last third of the twentieth century, including since 1983 a journal, *New Vico Studies*, plus numerous monographs and symposia (e.g., see Tagliacozzo and White, 1969; Tagliacozzo and Verene, 1969; Tagliacozzo, Mooney, and Verene, 1980; Tagliacozzo, 1981; Tagliacozzo, 1983).

A relatively early sentiment about this delicate issue was Hayden White's, whose mastery of modern Italian intellectual history was already well demonstrated in 1959 when he translated into English the important Crocean work of Carlo Antoni, *Dalla storicismo alla sociologia* (Antoni, 1962). In his preface to that work he observed, "The man whose mission it was to synthesize all of these forms of historicism, to sort out what was living and what was dead in them, and to transform the living truth contained in them into a new, autonomous and self-justifying form of thought was Benedetto Croce. Croce's task was to free historical thought from its subservience to other forms of thought, not by denying that these forms of thought had their own function in contributing to the construction of a total vision of reality, but by rigidly defining the competence of each and showing that none had a right to usurp the place of historical thought itself" (White in Antoni, 1962, p. xxiv).

White throughout his penetrating remarks gives high praise to Croce's lifelong project of clarifying the epistemological relationship between various forms of knowing. In fact, it seems very much as if Carlo Antoni's skillfully drawn chapters about Dilthey, Troeltsch, Meinecke, and Weber (plus Huizinga and Wöfflin) all lead up to a kind of grandly conceived and executed synthesis within Croce's work—a viewpoint which White seemed at the time quite content to embrace. White ends his commentary: "Thus, Croce, in his most important book, *History as the Story of Liberty,* can conclude that his historicism is humanism raised to a level of philosophical self-consciousness. He does not hypostatize any given moment of the spirit nor deny the existence of any individual manifestation of it but finds each as precious and necessary as the other, here, now and forever, as moments of the one creative spirit which is the world" (Ibid., p. xxviii).

White was not the sole voice in singing Croce's praises as a hermeneutic practitioner. One specialist in modern Italian intellectual history, using terms that are probably uniquely unequivocal, refers to Croce as the "Critic Par Excellence":

> If the greatness of a critic consists in the quality, variety, and quantity of criticism, then perhaps no critic has ever been greater than Benedetto Croce: neither Voltaire nor Erasmus, neither Taine nor Coleridge nor Ruskin, neither Nietzsche nor Marx, neither Hegel nor Kant nor Hume nor Descartes, neither Jesus nor Socrates, who nevertheless can be said to constitute the criticism Hall of Fame in the history of man.

> In one respect, that of *quality,* Croce probably exceeds them all without possibility of comparison: his criticism was fully conscious of itself; the systematic articulation of this reflective awareness constitutes his theoretical philosophy, which provides both an understanding of the nature of criticism and criteria for its adequacy. In other words, Croce was a philosopher not merely in addition to being a critic but *because* he was a critic; his philosophy may be the first methodology of criticism in the history of thought. (Finocchiaro, 1988, p. 29)

Put another way, and in keeping with Dilthey's philosophy—

which bears strong similarities with Croce's in terms of inter-
pretative theory and practice—it could be argued that Croce's
idealism formed the interstitial step in the development of
hermeneutic philosophy before Gadamer's *Truth and Method*
arrived in 1960.

There is more than a little data to support Finocchiaro's
emphatic view when one examines the seventy volumes which
make up Croce's collected works in Italian. Unlike, say,
Bertrand Russell, whose sole book of analysis about another
philosopher is his early study of Leibniz, composed out of
necessity as lecture notes by the novice teacher (Russell,
1900), Croce seems to have considered it his hermeneutic
duty to publish pithy commentaries on an unequalled range of
thinkers. On Gioberti or Machiavelli, Hegel and Marx, Homer,
Terence, Virgil, Jesus, Petrarch, Cervantes, Shakespeare,
Goethe, Stendhal, Ibsen, or Calvin, the endlessly energetic
Croce committed essays and books to "everybody who was
anybody" in the history of the humanities (see Croce, 1966,
for English samples). As White explains, perhaps somewhat
dismissively, "As self-appointed arbiter of taste for European
humanism in its modern phase, Croce felt compelled to display his assaying abilities with more than normal frequency.
Ultimately, almost every major European thinker and writer
came to rest in a precise place on a hierarchy of accomplish-
ment where Croce's own philosophy provided the final test
of orthodoxy" (White, 1969, p. 379).

In view of this enthusiastic praise, which is hardly unique in
the pertinent literature, it is somewhat surprising a decade later
to read White's apparently revised opinion of Croce's Vico, his
contribution to what would become a highly influential volume
in the latest Vichian renaissance. White's new appraisal has
itself become something of an orthodoxy in the intervening years:
"Certainly his reading of Vico, as offered in his magisterial
The Philosophy of Giambattista Vico (1911), is little more

than an evaluation of the 'new science' in the light of its approximation to, or deviation from, the tenets of Croce's finished philosophy.... One of their aims (Croce's and Nicolini's [editor of *Scienza nuova*]) was to show Vico as a precursor of the Crocean 'philosophy of the spirit,' and, in order to do this they had to deny the legitimacy of Vico's attempts to found a science of society and to construct a philosophy of history" (White, 1969, pp. 383, 379). This view is now commonplace except in Croce's homeland (although not universally accepted; for an acute critique, see Roberts, 1987, pp. 345-49, 369-70), and was seconded by what might be called an "official" statement published two years before by Patrick Gardner: "A more arresting discussion is to be found in Benedetto's Croce's *La filosofia di Giambattista Vico* (Baris, 1911), but Croce is prone to attribute to Vico ideas more characteristic of his own philosophical position than Vico's" (Gardner, 1967, p. 251). More recent commentators, including a leading Vichian, have somewhat softened their criticism of Croce's alleged subsumption of Vico's ideas under the vast umbrella of his own brand of idealism: Croce's *La Filosofia* is "the initiator of modern Vico studies, involving a much disputed identification of Vico's 'Providence' with Hegel's concept of the cunning of reason" (Pompa, 1998, p. 606).

Only during the 1990s did English-language Vico studies begin to distance themselves insistently from the Crocean reading of *The New Science*. One interesting technical problem presented itself when Miller argued, on the basis of close textual scrutiny by two scholars in Italy, that the third edition of *La scienza nuova* of 1744, from which nearly all Vichean studies have worked, "clearly is inferior to that of 1730" (1993, p. 74). Until a translation of the second (1730) edition appears, most of the audience for Vico's ideas must content themselves with two extant translations of the third edition (including a new one by David Marsh for Penguin Books).

More broadly troubling in recent Vico studies is Mark Lilla's careful analysis, whose work Pompa characterizes as "a very detailed historical account of the whole of Vico's thought" (Pompa, 1998, p. 606):

> For many decades the dominant general introduction to Vico was that of the Italian idealist Benedetto Croce, who not only brought out the definitive edition of the *Opere* and amassed his *Bibliografia vichiana*, but also gave a particular direction to Vico scholarship with his *La filosofia*...Croce's book is a justificatory brief for Vico that promotes the *New Science* as the precursor of what is "living" in the Hegelian philosophy, without the embarrassing features Croce deemed to be "dead" (notably Hegel's view of science and his historical teleology). Croce saw Vico's early metaphysical writings in a purely epistemological light, claiming that Vico's equation of the known with the made anticipated the nineteenth-century German attempt to distinguish the natural and the human sciences. He then interpreted the *New Science* as an application of this epistemological principle. Though Croce recognized the existence of Vico's early theological and jurisprudential writings, he attributed little significance to them except as incubator for ideas conceived before their time.
>
> Croce's portrait of Vico as the prophet of a refined liberal idealism was immediately challenged by Catholic writers who laid great emphasis on precisely those religious and jurisprudential ideas that Croce wished to ignore.
>
> As it happened the Catholic interpretation had little influence in the twentieth century. The idealists' interpretation on the other hand, remained dominant in Italy long after the demise of Crocean idealism. That interpretation held that the *New Science* is Vico's most important and highly realized work, that it represents the application of a novel theory of knowledge to history, and that Vico's turn to science constitutes a rejection of his juvenile religious and jurisprudential reflections.... Isaiah Berlin's writings on Vico...offer the most significant recent interpretation of Vico's philosophy. Berlin's presentation of Vico as a figure in the "counter-Enlightenment" is extremely important and remains the most literate and sensitive interpretation of Vico in English today. But his almost exclusive emphasis on Vico's theory of knowledge and history, and his relative silence on questions of theology and jurisprudence, show the abiding influence of Croce and Collingwood [Croce's anglophone exponent and translator]. (Lilla, 1993, pp. 240-242)

Despite Lilla's commendably thorough analysis, his conservatism discovers in Vico what he hopes to see, as have so many earlier analysts (recalling Verene's remarks above). Anthony Grafton's lively review of the work in question says as much, pointing out that Vico, being "a baroque encyclopedist," is not unidimensional enough to be paraded comfortably under a single ideological flag:

> From Michelet on, modern readers of Vico have seen his historical enterprise as a form of liberation. His reading of the past, they have argued, freed men from the old providential history that denied human autonomy, and from the old classicism that revered the ancients as inimitable sages. His understanding of the differences between societies resulted in a new level of pluralism and tolerance—a new realization that no set of laws or values holds for all men and women at all times. In *To the Finland Station*, Edmund Wilson celebrated the sense of human power that peeped incongruously through Vico's old-fashioned terminology and imagery. In *Vico and Herder*, Berlin warmly praised Vico's historicism, his willingness to treat all societies as equal even as he underscored their radical differences in language and culture. Lilla will have none of this.... Lilla maintains that what lay at the center of his thought were tormenting theological problems. Man was fallen and ignorant...violent, brutal, and greedy.... Lilla, in short, sometimes oversimplifies Vico's goals and methods, much as earlier scholars often oversimplified his beliefs and assumptions. His treatment of Vico...is sharply illuminating. But it does less than justice to the antique and early modern components of Vico's scholarly arsenal. (Grafton, 1993, pp. 55-57)

As one can see, the Vichian interpretive thicket is lush and at points nearly impenetrable. Yet there is still another view, somewhat more subtle, which holds that Croce was too skillful, too self-aware as a critic of philosophic and literary texts, to allow himself the easy luxury of forcing Vico into a preformed Crocean worldview. What he did instead was to "test" Vico's ideas according to certain clearly delimited notions. His goal, then, was not to write a primer on Vico's *New Science*— Croce says quite bluntly that readers must study Vico first, and only then might find usefulness in his own remarks—but to extend a philosophical dialogue between himself and Vico, as equal interlocutors at the high table of thought. One critic in particular seems to have realized this:

These studies [in the so-called Anglo-American world] read Vico according to a certain interpretive key and in so doing highlight certain important aspects of Vico's work even though the claim each of them makes
that it also constitutes an overall reading of Vico's *Scienza nuova* to the
exclusion of other readings remains highly questionable. To a large extent,
these readings are predictable since it has already been preordained by
the text of Vico's *New Science* that he who reads the work transforms it
into the image that he has of it and in so doing knows it because he has
himself made it. The seductive power of the *verum factum*, whether it is
mentioned or not, accepted or not, is equally at work in a reading of the
Scienza nuova, whether we are conscious of it or not. This much is clear
from what Vico says...Reconstructive readings of Vico, therefore, risk
with their insights to fall in this blindness... It would seem that only the
type of criticism practiced by Croce, which most Vichians have de-
nounced and rejected, represents an alternative reading—which does not
mean to say that Croce was correct in his reading of Vico. Croce's reading
differs from others in that it does not aim at explaining Vico's philosophy
but confronts it and tests it for the epistemological claims it
makes...Croce's apparent critique of Vico's science is more the consequence of his method than of a desire to impose his philosophy on Vico
(Verdicchio, 1995, pp. 91-92).

One could spend a great deal of scholarly energy and printed
pages trying to disentangle the exact relationship between
Croce and Vico. But as Croce himself stated at the beginning
of his book, it is essential to read Vico first, and then to judge
his own interpretation of what importance *The New Science*
continues to have for modern readers. Croce let his thoughts
be known in blunt terms, for instance, when he characterized
Vico as "someone who was never quite in control of his subject matter, who wrote hurriedly and with confusion"
(Verdicchio, 1988, p. 45). To quote Croce himself,

[H]e was faulty in the arrangement of his books, because his mind did not
master all the philosophical and historical material it had accumulated; he
wrote carelessly because wildly and as if possessed by a demon: and
hence arise the lack of proportion and the confusion in the various parts
of his work, within single pages and single paragraphs... One idea while
he is expressing it recalls another, that a fact, and that another fact: he
tries to say everything at once, and parenthesis branches off into parenthesis in a manner to make one's brain reel.

Yet Croce cannot resist giving back with one hand what he has removed with the other: "But these chaotic periods, weighted as they are with original thoughts, are no less woven of striking phrases, statuesque words, phrases full of emotion, and picturesque images. A bad writer, if you will, but his is the kind of bad writing of which only great writers possess the secret" (Croce, 1913, pp. 257-258). Perhaps it is too obvious to observe that Croce realized he was likely dealing with the only abstract thinker native to modern Italy whose stature closely approached his own. This at least would explain some of his querulous ambivalence.

Or perhaps something more profound was at work that intervened between, then rejoined, the two Neapolitan titans. Momigliano, as always, provides the most telling insight into this strange, fertile relationship:

> Croce's intellectual world was limited to literature (poetry) and history. We can now see what connected literature and history so closely in his mind. Both 'represented' individual facts, 'expressed' individual situations. Beyond individual situations Croce saw nothing but mystery. It cannot be emphasized enough that Croce never believed that the human mind can understand the whole of reality. Mystery surrounds Man. We cannot even talk of ourselves as personalities, as individuals—each with his own destiny. Each of us in each moment finds himself as a fraction of the whole in a position he cannot change....In Croce's interpretation... you and I have to take what is given, do the best we can and never ask questions about ultimate meaning. (Momigliano, 1966a, pp. 356-57)

A willingness to be creatively uneasy about humankind's "destiny," about its peculiarly perplexed understanding of itself by means of its myths, languages, and religious sentiments, serves as a primary link between Vico's masterpiece from 1744 (or 1730) and Croce's intervention nearly two centuries later. The question facing worthy readers today is not whether either thinker was right or wrong in their views of history and language, but whether we can summon up enough mental strength and imaginative sensitivity to carry on from where they left off.

ALAN SICA

References

Antoni, Carlo 1962 (1940) : *From History to Sociology: The Transition in German Historical Thinking.* Foreword by Benedetto Croce; trans. and introduced by Hayden White. London: Merlin Press (originally published by Wayne State University Press, 1958).

Atherton, James S. 1960: *The Books at the Wake: A Study of Literary Allusions in James Joyce's Finnegans Wake.* New York: Viking Press (expanded and corrected ed., Mamaroneck, NY: P.P. Appel, 1974).

Benjamin, Walter 1969: *Illuminations.* Ed. and with an intro. by Hannah Arendt. New York: Schocken Books.

Berlin, Isaiah 1976: *Vico and Herder: Two Studies in the History of Ideas.* New York: Random House.

_____ 2000: *Three Critics of the Enlightenment.* Princeton, NJ: Princeton University Press.

Burke, Peter 1985: *Vico* (Past Masters Series). New York: Oxford University Press.

Caponigri, A. Robert 1953: *Time and Idea: The Theory of History in Giambattista Vico.* London: Routledge and Kegan Paul.

Croce, Benedetto 1966: *Philosophy Poetry History: An Anthology of Essays.* Tr. and with a monographic introduction by Cecil Sprigge. London: Oxford University Press. (Croce's own selection of representative works, originally published as *Filosofia-Poesia-Storia*, Milan and Naples: Riccardo Ricciardi, 1951, the penultimate year of his life when Croce was eighty-five.)

_____ 1970 (1923): *Goethe.* With an introduction and portrait by Douglas Ainslie. Port Washington, NY: Kennikat Press.

_____ 1978 (1901/09): *Aesthetic: As Science of Expression and General Linguistic.* Tr. by Douglas Ainslie. Boston: Nonpareil Books/David Godine.

Ellmann, Richard 1983: *James Joyce* (new and revised edition, with corrections). New York: Oxford University Press.

Ermarth, Michael 1978: *Wilhelm Dilthey: The Critique of Historical Reason.* Chicago: University of Chicago Press.

Finocchiaro, Maurice A. 1988: *Gramsci and the History of Dialectical Thought.* Cambridge: Cambridge University Press.

Fisch, Max Harold 1944: Introduction to *The Autobiography of Giambattista Vico.* Ithaca, NY: Cornell University Press.

Gardner, Patrick 1967: Giambattista Vico. *Encyclopedia of Philosophy*, ed. Paul Edwards, New York: Macmillan Company and the Free Press, Vol. 8, 247-251.

Grafton, Anthony 1993: Fear and Loathing in Naples (review-essay on Mark Lilla's *G. B. Vico*). *New Republic*, 209: 12/13 (September 20), 51-57.

Hazard, Paul 1963 (1935): *The European Mind: 1680-1715.* Tr. by J. Lewis May. New York: Meridian Books.

Hughes, H. Stuart 1977: *Consciousness and Society: The Reorientation of European Social Thought 1890-1930,* revised ed. New York: Vintage Books.

Hutton, Patrick H. 1992: The Problem of Oral Tradition in Vico's Historical Scholarship. *Journal of the History of Ideas,* 53:1 (Jan.-Mar.), 3-23.

Joyce, James 1959 (1939): *Finnegans Wake.* New York: Viking Press.

Krieger, Leonard 1970: Series Editor's Preface in Benedetto Croce, *History of the Kingdom of Naples.* Tr. by Frances Frenaye. Chicago: University of Chicago Press.

Levin, Harry 1960: *James Joyce.* Revised, augmented ed. New York: New Directions.

Lilla, Mark 1993: *G. B. Vico: The Making of an Anti-Modern.* Cambridge, MA: Harvard University Press.

Litz, A. Walton 1969: Vico and Joyce. Pp. 245-255 in Giorgio Tagliacozzo (ed.) and Hayden White (co-ed.), *Giambattista Vico: An International Symposium,* Baltimore, MD: John Hopkins University Press.

Löwith, Karl 1949: *Meaning in History.* Chicago: University of Chicago Press.

McHugh, Roland 1980: *Annotations to Finnegans Wake.* Baltimore, MD: Johns Hopkins University Press.

Miller, Cecilia 1993: *Giambattista Vico: Imagination and Historical Knowledge.* London: Macmillan.

Momigliano, Arnaldo 1977 (1966a): Reconsidering B. Croce (1866-1952). In *Essays in Ancient and Modern Historiography,* Oxford: Basil Blackwell, 345-364. (Reprinted from his *Contributo alla storia degli studi classici,* Vol. IV.)

_____ 1966b: Vico's *Scienza Nuova:* Roman "Bestioni" and Roman "Eroi." In *Essays in Ancient and Modern Historiography,* Oxford: Basil Blackwell, 253-276.

Orsini, Gian N. G. 1961: *Benedetto Croce: Philosopher of Art and Literary Critic.* Carbondale: Southern Illinois University Press.

Pompa, Leon 1998: Giambattista Vico. In Edward Craig (ed.), *Routledge Encyclopedia of Philosophy,* vol. 10, pp. 599-605. London: Routledge.

Roberts, David D. 1987: *Benedetto Croce and the Uses of Historicism.* Berkeley: University of California Press.

Russell, Bertrand 1992 (1900): *A Critical Exposition of the Philosophy of Leibniz.* London: Routledge.

Savigny, Karl Friedrich von 1850: *Vermischte Schriften von Friedrich Carl von Savigny...* (5 vols). Berlin: Veit und comp.

Tagliacozzo, Giorgio and Donald P. Verene (eds.) 1969: *Giambattista Vico's Science of Humanity.* Baltimore, MD: Johns Hopkins University Press.

Tagliacozzo, Giorgio (ed.) and Hayden White (co-ed.) 1969: *Giambattista Vico: An International Symposium.* Baltimore, MD: Johns Hopkins University Press.

Tagliacozzo, Giorgio, Michael Mooney, and Donald P. Verene (eds.) 1980: *Vico and Contemporary Thought.* London: Macmillan.

Tagliacozzo, Giorgio (ed.) 1981: *Vico: Past and Present.* Atlantic Highlands, NJ: Humanities Press.

Tagliacozzo, Giorgio (ed.) 1983: *Vico and Marx: Affinities and Contrasts.* Atlantic Highlands, NJ: Humanities Press.

Tanucci, Bernardo 1760: *Saggio di giurisprudenz universale.* Rome.

Verdicchio, Massimo 1988: Croce: Reader of Vico. *Italian Quarterly,* 29: 111 (Winter), 41-55.

_____ 1995: Vico Today in North American. *Italian Quarterly,* 32:125/126 (Summer), 83-92.

Verene, Donald Philip 1981: *Vico's Science of Imagination.* Ithaca, NY: Cornell University Press.

Vico, Giambattista 1999: *New Science.* Tr. by David Marsh. New York: Penguin Books.

_____ 2000: The Giambattista Vico Home Page: *http://www. connix.com/ ~ gapinton/index.html.*

Vidal, Gore 1999: Chaos. *The New York Review of Books,* December 16, 39-40.

White, Hayden V. 1969: "What is Living and What is Dead in Croce's Criticism of Vico." In Giorgio Tagliacozzo (ed.) and Hayden V. White (co-ed.), *Giambattista Vico: An International Symposium,* Baltimore, MD: Johns Hopkins University Press, pp. 380-389.

Wilson, Edmund 1972 (1940): *To The Finland Station: A Study in the Writing and Acting of History.* With a new introduction and ancillary materials. New York: Farrar, Straus and Giroux.

PREFACE

My reasons for believing that a new exposition of Vico's philosophy is required may easily be inferred from the observations on the effects of his work and the biographical notes which form respectively the second and fourth appendices to this volume.

Here I merely wish to state that my exposition is not meant for a summary of Vico's writings work by work and part by part. It rather presupposes an acquaintance with these writings, and, where that is lacking, is intended to induce the reader to procure them in order to follow better and to check the interpretation and estimate of them here offered.

On this supposition, though I have made free use of my author's actual words, especially in the chapters dealing with history, I have not thought it desirable to mark them as quotations except where it was important to emphasise the precise phrase of the original. I have in general combined such passages from fragments scattered over a wide field, sometimes abbreviating, sometimes amplifying, and always freely adding words and phrases of my own by way of commentary : and the continual use of quotation marks would merely have shown up in a manner more wearisome than valuable the reverse side of my embroidery, which any reader who so desires can study by the help of the references given at the end of the book.

In my anxiety to show in every detail of my work, so

far as I could, the veneration due to the great name of Vico, I have endeavoured to be brief with the brevity at which he himself aimed as the hall-mark of sterling scientific thought. With this in view I have refrained even from controversy with his various interpreters, and have either contented myself with mere remarks, or more often left my details to be justified by the coherence of my view as a whole. Some of the interpretations supported by me I believe to be the mature fruit of the investigations and controversies which form the greater part of the literature on Vico : all the rest, for which I am personally responsible, and the general idea of my book, I will defend against alternative and contradictory views when occasion arises, should it ever do so, in the detailed and direct manner which I have not thought it necessary to adopt in the course of my exposition. I hope, in fact, that the present work will rekindle rather than quench the discussion of Vico's philosophy : since in him we have, as Goethe calls him, the *Altvater* whom a nation is happy to possess, and to him we must hark back for a time in order to imbue our modern philosophy with an Italian feeling, however cosmopolitan it may be in thought.

The dedication of my book, besides being a token of respect to one of the greatest modern teachers of the history of philosophy, is intended to express the expectation and hope that the gap in this history to which I have called attention more than once, especially on page 277 of the present volume, may soon be filled.

B. C.

RAIANO (AQUILA),
September 1910.

TRANSLATOR'S NOTE

THIS volume represents the author's *La Filosofia di Giambattista Vico* (Bari, 1911) forming vol. ii. of his *Saggi filosofici* ; and also contains a paper read before the Accademia Pontaniana in March 1912 entitled " Le Fonti della gnoseologia vichiana," which figures here as Appendix III.   The whole of the translation has been revised by the Author.

R. G. C.

OXFORD, 1913.

CHAPTER I

THE earliest phase of Vico's theory of knowledge takes the form of a direct criticism of and antithesis to the Cartesianism which had guided European thought for more than half a century, and was to maintain its supremacy over mind and spirit for another hundred years.

Descartes, as is well known, had placed the ideal of perfect science in geometry, and endeavoured to reform philosophy and every other branch of knowledge upon this model. Now the geometrical method proceeds analytically till it reaches a self-evident truth, and thence by synthetic deduction it advances to more and more complex propositions. Accordingly, if philosophy were to adopt a rigorous scientific method, it also (thought Descartes) must look for a solid foundation in the shape of an elementary and self-evident truth from which to deduce all its subsequent statements, whether theological, metaphysical, physical, or ethical. Thus self-evidence— the " clear and distinct perception or idea "—was the supreme test : immediate inference—the intuitive connexion of thought with existence, *cogito* with *sum*— provided the elementary truth and the foundation of knowledge. By means of the clear and distinct perception, together with the systematic doubt which led him to the *cogito*, Descartes persuaded himself that he had once and for all made an end of scepticism.

But, by the same argument, all knowledge which had not been or could not be reduced to clear and distinct perception and geometrical deduction was bound to lose in his eyes all value and importance. This included history, as founded upon testimony ; observation of nature, when not within the sphere of mathematics ; practical wisdom and eloquence, which draw their validity from empirical knowledge of human character ; and poetry, with its world of imaginary presentations. Such products of the mind were for Descartes illusions, chaotic visions, rather than knowledge : confused ideas, destined either to become clear and distinct and so no longer to exist in their original nature, or else to drag on a miserable existence unworthy of a philosopher's consideration. The daylight of the mathematical method rendered useless the lamps which, while they guide us in the darkness, throw deceptive shadows.

Vico, unlike the other opponents of Descartes, did not confine himself to or waste time in scandalised outcries at the danger to religion entailed by the subjective method. He did not inquire, like the schoolmen, whether the *cogito* was or was not a syllogism, and if so whether it was or was not defective. He did not join in the protest of outraged common-sense against the Cartesian contempt of history, rhetoric, and poetry. He went straight to the heart of the question, to Descartes' criterion of scientific truth itself, the principle of self-evidence. While the French philosopher believed himself to have satisfied all the demands of the strictest science, Vico saw that as a matter of fact, in view of the need which he set out to meet, his proposed method gave little or no assistance.

Fine knowledge, says Vico, this of the clear and distinct idea ! That I think what I think is certainly an indubitable fact; but it has by no means the appearance of a scientific statement. Any idea, however false, may seem self-evident: that I think it so does not give it the force of knowledge. That " he who thinks, exists " was a fact well known to Plautus's Sosia, who expressed this conviction in almost the identical words of the Cartesian philosophy: " but when I think, I certainly exist " (*sed quom cogito, equidem certo sum*). But the sceptic will always reply to a Sosia or a Descartes that he has no doubt as to thought; he will even strongly maintain that whatever seems to him cogent is certain, and will uphold it against all objections; and that he has no doubt as to existence: in fact, he is seeking after it in the right way by suspending judgment and not adding to the obscurity of facts other obscurities arising from opinions. But while asserting all this he will still maintain that the certitude of his thought and of his existence is the certitude not of science but of consciousness, and of common consciousness at that. Clear and distinct perception is so far from being science that since, owing to Cartesianism, the principle has been applied to physics, our knowledge of nature has become no more certain. Descartes tried to leap from the plane of common consciousness to that of science: he fell back into common consciousness again without having touched his scientific ideal.

But in what does scientific truth consist, if not in immediate consciousness? How does science differ from simple consciousness? What is the criterion, or, in other words, what is the condition which makes science possible? Clearness and distinctness do not take us a step forward. The formulation of an elementary truth does not solve the problem. The question concerns not a primary truth, but the form which truth must have to enable us to recognise it for scientific or real truth.

In meeting this question, Vico justified his criticism
of the inadequacy of the Cartesian criterion by appealing
to a principle which at first sight may seem trite and
obvious. It is trite not because of the historic theory
with which Vico associated it, a theory later refuted by
himself : not, that is, because it belongs to one of the
earliest strata of Italian philosophy ; but in the sense
that it was common to and practically inseparable from
Christian thought. To a Christian who declares every
day his belief in a God Almighty, Omniscient, Maker of
heaven and earth, nothing is more familiar than the
assertion that God alone can fully know all things, because
he alone is their creator. The primal truth, Vico repeats,
is in God, because God is the primal creator. It is an
infinite truth because he is the maker of all things, and
absolute because it displays to him the internal and
external qualities of things, all of which he contains in
himself.

This same principle of religion and theology had been
already invoked in a philosophical context by certain
sceptics, as a weapon against the presumptuous claims
of human knowledge. Francisco Sanchez, for example,
in his *Quod nihil scitur* (1581), in discussing the difficulty
of knowing the nature and powers of the soul, had observed
that if man could have this knowledge in a perfect degree
he would be like God, or rather he would be God himself :
since it is impossible " that one should know perfectly
things which he has not created, nor could God have
created things of which he had not perfect foreknowledge,
nor ruled them when created : he himself therefore,
being alone the perfect wisdom, knowledge, and intellect,
penetrates all things, is wise concerning all things, knows
all things, and understands all things, because he is all
things and in all things, and all things are he and in him "
(*perfecte cognoscere quis quae non creavit, nec Deus creare
potuisset nec creata regere quae non perfecte praecognovisset :*

ipse ergo solus sapientia cognitio intellectus perfectus omnia penetrat omnia sapit omnia cognoscit omnia intelligit, quia ipse omnia est et in omnibus, omniaque ipse sunt et in ipso).[1] But Sanchez appeals to this thought only in passing, and without grasping its philosophical import or realising that his hand was resting upon a treasure ; while Vico for the first time drew from the praise of the infinite power and wisdom of God, and from their contrast with the limited faculties of man, the universal principle of his theory of knowledge, that the condition under which a thing can be known is that the knower should have made it, that the true is identical with the created : *verum ipsum factum.*

This, he explained, is precisely what is meant by saying that science is to know by causes, *per causas scire.* Since a cause is that which has no need of anything external in order to produce its effect, it is the genus or mode of a thing : to know the cause is to be able to realise the thing, to deduce it from its cause and create it. In other words, it is an ideal repetition of a process which has been or is being practically performed. Cognition and action must be convertible and identical, just as with God intellect and will are convertible and form one single unity.

Now once this connexion of the true with the created is recognised as the ideal, and indeed, since the ideal is the truly real, as the true nature of science, the first consequence of such a recognition must be that science is unattainable to man. If God created the world, he alone knows it *per causas*, he alone knows its genera or modes, he alone possesses scientific knowledge of it. Did man make the world ? Did he make his own soul ?

To man is vouchsafed, not science, but only conscious-

[1] In the appendix to his *Opera Medica* (Tolosae Tectosagum, 1636, p. 110). Windelband draws attention to this thought, *Gesch. der neueren Philosophie*, 3rd ed. i. p. 23.

ness, which merely traverses objects without being able
to show the genus or form whence they proceed. The
truth of consciousness is the human side of divine wisdom,
related to it as the surface to the solid : rather than
truth, we ought to call it certitude. For God, *intellegere*,
understanding ; for man only *cogitare*, thought, the
faculty that gleans elements of reality, but can never
gather them all. For God, true demonstration ; for
man, observations undemonstrated and unscientific, but
either certain through indubitable evidence, probable
through sound reasoning, or convincing because of a
plausible guess.

Certitude, the truth of consciousness, is not science ;
but it is not on that account false. Vico was careful
not to call the theories of Descartes false : his intention
was only to lower them from complete truth to fragmentary
truth, from science to consciousness. *Cogito ergo sum* is
very far from false. That we find it expressed by Plautus's
Sosia is an argument not for rejecting it, but for accepting
it ; only, as a truth of simple consciousness. Thought
is not the cause of my existence, and as such is not the
ground of scientific knowledge of that existence. If it
were, since man, as the Cartesians admitted, consists of
body and mind, thought would be the cause of the body :
a doctrine which would plunge us into all the mazes of
the controversy on the mutual effects of mind and matter.
The *cogito*, then, is a mere sign or indication of my existence,
and nothing more. The clear and distinct idea cannot
serve as a criterion even of the mind itself, to say nothing
of other things ; since the mind, though it knows itself,
does not create itself, and accordingly is ignorant of
the genus or mode by which it has this knowledge. But
the clear and distinct idea is all that is granted to human
thought, and, as the only wealth it possesses, is beyond
price. For Vico, too, metaphysic holds the highest place
among the human sciences, and all others depend upon

it ; but while for Descartes it can proceed by a method of absolute demonstration parallel to that of geometry, for Vico it must be satisfied with probabilities. It is a science not by causes, but of causes. And with probabilities it has been content in its greatest periods, in ancient Greece and in Italy at the Renaissance. Whenever, intoxicated by the arrogance that declares that " a wise man has no opinions " (*sapientem nihil opinari*), it has sought to abandon the probable, it has set its feet upon the path of confusion and decadence. The existence of God is certain, but not scientifically demonstrable ; and any attempt at such a demonstration must be considered a proof not so much of piety as of impiety, since to demonstrate God we must create him : man must become the creator of God. Similarly we must accept as true all that God has revealed ; but we must not ask how it comes to be true. That we can never understand. Human science bases itself upon revealed truth and the consciousness of God, and finds there its test of truth ; but the foundation itself is not science, but consciousness.

Just as Vico depreciated metaphysics, theology, and physics, the sciences upon which Descartes had bestowed honour and attention, so he reinstated those branches of knowledge which Descartes had in turn despised ; namely, history, observation of nature, empirical knowledge of man and society, eloquence and poetry. Or rather, he could vindicate them without reinstating them. Once he had shown that the lofty truths of a geometrically deduced philosophy were themselves brought down to mere probability, to statements having the validity of simple consciousness, the other forms of knowledge were *ipso facto* conclusively vindicated. All now found themselves upon an equality in the position, whether high or low, which we have described. The idea of a perfect human science, holding itself aloof from another science unworthy of the title, as founded not on reason but on authority, was shown to be illusory. The authority of observations and beliefs, whether one's own or others', public opinion, tradition, the consciousness of mankind, were restored to the position which they had always held : a position which they held even for Descartes himself, who, as often happens, despised the resources in which he was richest and of which he made the greatest use. A conspicuously learned man, he depreciated learning and scholarship, as one who has received nourishment from it might give himself the luxury of speaking with contempt of the common food which by now forms the very blood in his veins.

The Cartesian polemic against authority had proved in some respects beneficial. It put an end to the servile attitude, all too common, of continual appeals to authority. But this error was not more prevalent than that of private judgment, which presumed to reorganise knowledge from top to bottom on the strength of the individual conscious-ness : a tendency which ultimately, as in the case of Malebranche, leads to prophesying the immolation of all the ancient philosophers and poets, and a return to the nakedness of Adam. It is a fallacy, or at least an excess, which should be avoided by adopting a sound middle course. This course consists in following private judg-ment with due regard to authority ; in a true catholic union of faith with a criticism limited by and helpful to faith ; bearing in mind the necessary character of mere probability which is proper to human knowledge or science, and avoiding the tendency of the Reformation which elevates each man's inner consciousness into a divine guide in matters of belief.

To another group of the Cartesian sciences, however, Vico seems to grant a privileged position, one, that is, not of consciousness but of science strictly so called, in the sphere not of certitude but of truth ; namely, the mathematical sciences. These, according to him, form the only region in which man's knowledge is identical in character with God's, perfect and demonstrative. This is not due, as Descartes supposed, to their self-evident character. Self-evidence, when employed in physical science and in matters of action, does not yield truth of the same conclusiveness as in mathematics. Nor is mathematics in itself self-evident. What clear and distinct idea can lead, for instance, to the conception of a line as composed of points having no parts ? But the indivisible point which cannot be conceived in the world of reality, can be nevertheless defined. By defining certain names, man creates the elements of mathematics ; by the postulates, he carries them on to infinity ; by the axioms, he establishes certain eternal truths ; and, disposing these elements with the help of these infinities and this eternity, he creates the truth which he teaches. The validity of mathematics then arises not from the Cartesian principle, but precisely from Vico's other proposition, the conversion of knowledge with creation. " We demonstrate mathematics, because we create their truth " (*mathematica demonstramus, quia verum facimus*). Man assumes unity and multiplicity, points and figures, and creates numbers and quantities which he knows perfectly because they are his own work. Mathematics is a constructive science ; not only in its problems, but even in its theorems, which are commonly supposed to be mere objects of contemplation. For this reason it is a science which demonstrates *per causas*, in opposition to that other common view which excludes from mathematics the concept of causation. It is in fact the only one among all the human sciences which truly demonstrates by causes. Hence its extraordinary accuracy. The whole secret of the geometrical method lies first in defining the terms, that is, creating the concepts which are to be the subject matter of our reasoning ; secondly, in establishing certain common principles by mutual

consent of the disputants; and lastly, if required, in
making certain postulates of such a nature that they can
be granted, to enable us to proceed with our deductions,
which without such an agreement could make no progress ;
then, upon these principles, to advance by degrees from
the demonstration of the simplest truths to the most
complex, and not to affirm the complex propositions
before examining singly their component parts.

It might be said that, as to the validity of mathematics, Vico is in agreement with Descartes ; he differs
from him only in his reason for this validity. And,
admitting that Vico's reason must be thought the more
profound, this would only enhance and strengthen the
mathematical ideal which Descartes had set before science.
If mathematics is the one perfect form of knowledge
attained by the human mind, obviously we must found
the others upon it, and either remodel or condemn them
according to its pattern. Vico, in short, was hasty in
declaring Descartes wrong : he had found a better
argument whose existence the latter had not suspected.
But, however strongly this may appear at first sight
(and so it has appeared to some commentators), on a
closer examination it is seen that the high perfection
attributed by Vico to mathematics is more apparent
than real ; that the vaunted conclusiveness of its method
is by his own confession gained at the expense of truth :
in a word, that the stress of his theory falls less on the
truth of mathematics than on its arbitrary nature.

The fact is, that man, while occupying himself with
the investigation of the nature of things, and ultimately
realising his total inability to attain it, not having in
himself the elements of which they are composed, which
are indeed all external to his nature, is led by degrees to
the intention of profiting by this very fault of his mind.
By means of abstraction—not, be it remembered, abstraction from material things, for Vico is opposed to the

empirical origin of mathematics, but abstraction brought
to bear on metaphysical entities—he creates two fictions,
duo sibi confingit: the point in geometrical figures, and
unity in multiplication. Each is a fiction, *utrumque
fictum*, because the point when drawn is no longer a
point, and the unit when multiplied is no longer one.
Then, from these fictions, by his own arbitrary fiat,
proprio iure, he assumes an infinite process,¹ so that
lines may be produced or the unit multiplied *ad infinitum*.
Thus he constructs for his own purposes a world of forms
and numbers, all of which he embraces within himself;
and by lengthening, shortening, and combining the lines
and adding and subtracting the numbers, he performs
infinite operations and learns infinite truths. Since he
cannot define things, he defines names; since he cannot
reach the elements of reality he satisfies himself with
imaginary elements, the ideas arising from which admit
of no dispute. Like God, *ad Dei instar*, from no material
substrate and, as it were, out of nothing he creates the
point, the line, and the surface; the point, assumed as
that which has no parts; the line, as the locus of a point,
or as length without breadth or depth; and the surface,
as the meeting of two different lines in one point, that is,
length and breadth without depth. Thus mathematics
overcomes the failing of human knowledge, that its
objects are always external to itself, and that the mind
which endeavours to know them has not created them.
Mathematics creates what it knows; it contains in itself
its own elements, and thus forms a perfect copy of the
divine knowledge (*scientiae divinae similes evadunt*).

The reader of these and other similar descriptions
and praises by Vico of the processes of mathematics
seems to observe in them something like a tinge of irony;
which, if not actually intentional, certainly results from
the facts of the case. The brilliant truth of mathematics
arises, it appears, from despair of attaining truth; its

tremendous power from the knowledge of impotence. The similarity of the mathematician to God is not altogether unlike that of the imitator of an object to its creator. What God is in the universe of reality, man is in the universe of quantity and number,—a universe indeed, but one peopled by abstractions and fictions. The divinity which has been conferred upon man is only, so to speak, a Twelfth-night Godhead.

The different origin assigned by Vico to mathematics results in a correspondingly profound change in the validity of its truth. Mathematics no longer, as with Descartes, stands at the summit of human knowledge, an aristocratic science, destined to reclaim and to rule over the inferior sciences. It occupies a field as strictly limited as it is unique, beyond which if it ever attempts to pass it loses in a moment its magical virtue.

The power of mathematics is met by obstacles both *a parte ante* and *a parte post*, in its foundations and in the superstructure which in its turn it is to support. In its foundations, because if it creates its own elements, that is to say, the initial fictions, it does not create the matter of which they are formed, which is given to it no less than to the other human sciences by metaphysics, which while it cannot supply it with its true subject matter, supplies it with definite images of it. From metaphysics, geometry takes the point by drawing it, that is by annihilating it as a point, and arithmetic the unit by multiplying it, that is by destroying it *qua* unit. But since metaphysical truth, however certain it may seem to consciousness, is indemonstrable, mathematics itself rests in the last resort upon authority and probability. This is enough to expose the fallaciousness of any mathematical treatise which makes use of metaphysics. Vico seems to be involved in a kind of circle between geometry and metaphysics, of which the former, according to him, owes its truth to the latter, and after receiving it gives it back again to metaphysics, thus in turn supporting the human science by the divine. But this conception, the truth of which is more than doubtful, indeed we may frankly call it inconsistent and contradictory, recalls, whatever its value, the metaphysical or rather poetical or symbolic use made of mathematics by Pythagoras and other philosophers of antiquity and the Renaissance, and has no resemblance to a mathematically-treated philosophy like the Cartesian. Geometry in Vico's opinion is the one hypothesis by which metaphysics passes over into physical science. But while making this advance it remains a hypothesis, a probability, something intermediate between faith and criticism, imagination and reason ; which indeed is the eternal character of metaphysics and human science in general according to Vico's point of view in this first phase of his theory of knowledge.

Just as mathematics cannot be the basis of metaphysics, the science from which it is itself derived, so it cannot provide a foundation for the other sciences, although they follow it in order of derivation. All objects other than number and size are beyond the reach of the geometrical method. Physical science is indemonstrable : if we could demonstrate the physical world, we should be creating it (*si physica demonstrare possemus, faceremus*) : but we do not create it, and are accordingly unable to demonstrate it. The introduction of the mathematical method into natural science has not helped it. Without the mathematical method, science makes great discoveries ; by its means it has made none, whether great or small. The physical science of to-day is in fact like a house, sumptuously furnished by former owners, to which their heirs have added nothing, but have occupied themselves merely in moving and rearranging the furniture. Accordingly, we must reintroduce and maintain the experimental method in physical science, as opposed to this mathematical method; the English tendency as opposed to the French; the cautious use made of mathematics by Galileo and his school, as against the Cartesians' reckless and presumptuous employment of it. The English are right in not allowing physical science to be taught in the mathematical style. Such a style admits of progress only when the terms are defined, the axioms established, and the postulates granted. In physical science we have to define not terms but things : we can make no unchallenged statements ; and the complexity of nature forbids our forming any postulates. Thus in the more favourable instances this method results in a mere harmless verbalism. Observations of nature are expounded with the phrases : " By definition IV.," " By postulate II.," " By axiom III.," and concluded with the pompous abbreviation " Q.E.D. " But all this carries no demonstrative conviction. The mind retains as much freedom of opinion as it had before listening to such noisy methods. In these circumstances Vico could not refrain from satirical comparisons. The geometrical method, he says, in its proper sphere works unnoticed ; when it makes a noise, it shows that it is doing no work ; just as a coward's attack consists of much shouting and no blows, while a brave man holds his tongue and strikes home. Again, the man who upholds the geometrical method in subjects where it fails to carry conviction, when he pronounces this to be an axiom, or that to be a demonstrated truth, is like a man who draws amorphous pictures, quite unrecognisable without assistance, and then writes underneath " This is a man," or " This is a satyr," or " This is a lion," or the like. Hence it happens that the very same geometrical method served Proclus to demonstrate the principles of Aristotelian science, and Descartes to demonstrate his own, though totally distinct from, if not diametrically opposed to them. Yet each was a great geometrician, whom no one could accuse of inability to use the method. What ought to be introduced into natural science is not the method of geometry, but its conclusiveness; which is precisely what can never be done. Still less is it possible in other sciences, in proportion as they are more material and concrete; least of all in ethical science. For this reason, where the reality cannot be used, the name is misused instead; till, just as the title " Master," which Tiberius once refused as too haughty, is given to-day to the humblest man, so the name " demonstration," applied as it is to arguments at best probable, sometimes patently fallacious, has impaired the respect due to truth.

Even for mathematics itself Vico apprehends danger from the substitution of analytic for geometrical or synthetic methods. He doubts whether modern mechanics is really a product of analysis; for analysis blunts the inventive faculty or talent, and though infallible in its results (*opere*) is confused in its processes (*opera*); while the synthetic method is *tum opere cum opera* infallible. Analysis presents its grounds by inquiring whether the equations of which it is in search happen to be present; it appears to be an art of guessing, a kind of mechanism rather than thought. For similar reasons Vico attached no value to the more or less mechanical topics and arts of discovery and memory invented by Lulle and Kircher.

The sympathy with experimental methods which as we have seen estranged Vico from the French tendency of thought, that is from Cartesianism, and directed him towards the Italian and English schools of Galileo and Bacon, led him on the other hand to a hostile attitude towards Aristotelianism and scholasticism. Inculcating as he did the pursuit of the particular and the use of inductive methods, asserting that man possessed an inexhaustible wealth of physical knowledge which, thanks to fire, machinery, and tools, was able to issue in the creation of objects resembling the special products of nature, and praising his own metaphysic as one subservient to (*ancillantem*) the ends of experimental science, he was bound to realise how well deserved was the too universal discredit, as he calls it, into which Aristotelian science had fallen.   If he disapproved of the introduction by Descartes of physical forms into metaphysics, and of his resulting materialistic tendencies, he accused Aristotle and the schoolmen of the opposite error of introducing metaphysical forms into natural science.   Like Bacon he held that the syllogism and sorites produce nothing new, and only repeat what was already contained in their premisses.   He emphasised the many ill effects of the Aristotelian universal in every department of knowledge ; in jurisprudence, where empty generalities crush legislative wisdom ; in medicine, which aims rather at propping up systems than at healing the sick ; and in practical life, in which he describes the abusers of universals by the mocking title of " Thematists."   The use of universals results in homonymies or equivocations which cause all kinds of errors.   As against this distrust of universals in the sense of general or abstract conceptions, Vico showed a corresponding reverence for the Platonic ideas, the metaphysical forms, or as he also called them, kinds ; the eternal and infinitely perfect patterns of things.   A nominalist in mathematics, Vico was suspicious of nominalism in all other fields of knowledge.   He asserts the reality of the forms or ideas, and tells how from his youth up he was attracted by this doctrine, which he learnt from a teacher of his, who as a Scotist was a follower of the scholastic system most akin to Plato's.

Taken as a whole Vico's first theory of knowledge is neither intellectualistic, sensationalistic, nor truly speculative.   It contains all these three elements, harmonised to a certain extent, not by a hierarchical subordination

of any two to the third, but by the subjection of all three
to a recognition of the inadequacy of human knowledge.
Its intention may have been to meet by a tactical
manœuvre dogmatics and sceptics at once, the former
by denying that we can know everything, the latter by
denying that we can know nothing at all. But its
actual outcome is an assertion of scepticism or agnosticism, tinged, however, with a trace of mysticism. God's
knowledge is the complete sphere of knowledge, the
unity of which man's is but a series of fragments. God
knows all things because he contains in himself all the
elements of which he makes them : man tries to understand them by taking them to pieces. Human science
is a sort of anatomy of the world of nature ; it divides
man into body and soul, and soul into intellect and will :
from body it abstracts figure and motion, and from these
existence and unity. Of these metaphysics studies
existence, arithmetic unity and multiplication, geometry
figure and its measurements, mechanics the motion of
the circumference, physical science the motion of the
centre, medicine the body, logic the reason, and ethics
the will. But this anatomy meets with the same fate
as that of the human body. In the latter case, the
greatest physiologists doubt whether, owing to the
effects of death and of dissection itself, it is possible at
all to discover the true position, structure, and function
of the organs. Existence, unity, figure, motion, body,
intellect, and will are one thing for God, for whom they
coalesce into one, and another for man, to whom they
remain distinct. For God they live, for man they are
dead. The clear and distinct perception is a proof not
of the strength but of the weakness of the human understanding. Physical laws appear self-evident just until
they are subjected to comparison with metaphysical.
The *Cogito ergo sum* is absolutely conclusive when man
considers himself as a finite being ; but when he includes

himself in God, the one true being, he realises that in truth he does not exist at all. By means of extension and its three dimensions we believe ourselves to establish eternal truths ; but in fact *coelum ipsum petimus stultitia,* since the eternal truths exist in God alone. The axiom that the whole is greater than the part may seem eternal, but if we go back to the beginning, we find that it is false : we see that the centre of the circle contains in itself as much capacity for extension as the whole circumference. Wherefore, Vico concludes, " he has advanced in metaphysics who in the study of this science has lost himself."

To hold, as some have done, that these words show Vico a simple Platonist or a follower of the traditional Christian philosophy, would entail denying any importance whatever to his first theory of knowledge. It would be a confession of adherence to the fallacious method of philosophical criticism and history which looks only at the general conclusions of a system and ignores the particular content which alone gives it its true individuality. No doubt, any philosophy must always in its ultimate conclusions be either agnostic, mystical, materialistic, spiritualistic, or the like : in other words, it must have its place in one or other of the eternal categories in which thought and philosophical inquiry move. But to expound philosophers in this one-sided manner can only serve to perpetuate the mistakes repeated over and over again in the history of thought, when it passes fruitlessly from one error to another, leaving the old only to adopt the new, itself perhaps an old one born again or painted with the colours of youth. The Platonism, agnosticism, or mysticism of Vico is in the fullest sense of the word original, because it forms the accompaniment of doctrines not only not inferior to the average of contemporary thought, but greatly in advance of it.

The first of these doctrines is the theory of knowledge as the conversion of the true with the created, Vico's substitute for the otiose criterion of the clear and distinct perception. Though this conversion represents for Vico an ideal unattainable to man, it yet does not bring with it an exact definition of the condition and character of knowledge, the identity of thought and being, without which knowledge is inconceivable.

The second is the revelation of the nature of mathematics, as unique among the forms of human knowledge in origin, rigorous because arbitrary, wonderful but unfit to rule over and transform the rest of our knowledge.

Finally, the third doctrine is the vindication of the world of intuition, empirical knowledge, probability, and authority, all those forms of experience which intellectualism ignored or denied.

In these points Vico the agnostic, the Platonist, the mystic, was neither agnostic nor mystic nor Platonist. He achieved a threefold advance upon Descartes, and upon all these three heads criticised him conclusively.

The one thing in which Descartes was still in advance of Vico was precisely that dogmatism of which Vico would have none. Descartes, whether he succeeded or not, projected a perfect human science deduced from the internal consciousness. Vico, on the other hand, considering the French philosopher too confident and despairing of the success of his project, proclaimed the transcendent nature of truth, took his stand upon revelation, and contented himself with producing a metaphysic worthy of man's weakness, *humana imbecillitate dignam*. His was a philosophy of humility, as the Cartesian was one of self-confidence.

Now Vico could not advance even to this position without relaxing to some extent part of his humility, and taking over something of Descartes's confidence: without introducing into his Catholic turn of mind some trace of the leaven of that Protestantism he thought so dangerous, and venturing to conceive a philosophy rather less worthy of man's weakness and correspondingly more worthy of man, a creature at once strong and weak, at once man and God. This advance is to be seen in the next phase of his thought.

CHAPTER II

THE will to believe, which in Vico's case was very strong, and the complete sway which the Catholicism of his country and age held over his mind, bound him firmly down to the Christian Platonic metaphysic and theory of knowledge ; a theory whose inherent contradictions were prevented by the above psychological facts from coming explicitly before his mind. The idea of God at once dominated and supported him ; he neither had the audacity nor realised the necessity to probe to the bottom such problems as the validity of revelation, the conceivability of a God apart from the world, or the possibility of affirming the existence of God without in some sense demonstrating and therefore creating him. For Vico to open up and partially traverse a new path, which should lead the human mind to transcend that of the Christian Platonists, providence—to use for the moment an idea of his own which we shall explain later on—had perforce to deceive him ; to lead him by a long and circuitous way to the commencement of the new path without letting him suspect where it would end.

The writings in which Vico expounds his first theory of knowledge, *De ratione studiorum* and *De antiquissima Italorum sapientia,* together with the polemical works bearing upon them, belong to the four years from 1708 to 1712. In the following decade Vico was gradually led to devote

himself more and more to research in the history of law
and of the State. He read Grotius as a preparation for
writing the life of Antonio Carafa, and plunged into the
controversy on Natural Rights. He pursued his studies
of Roman law and the science of law in general, in order
to fit himself for a chair of jurisprudence at Naples University. He pondered upon the origins of languages,
religions, and states, out of dissatisfaction with his own
historical theories as set forth in the *De antiquissima* ;
perhaps also his convictions were shaken by a well-
directed criticism by the editor of the *Giornale dei letterati*.
His profession, the teaching of rhetoric, gave him continual opportunities for meditating upon the nature and
relations of poetry and the forms of language. Thus
even if it is inaccurate to say that Vico was led to his
later position culminating in the *Scienza Nuova* by a
philological, not a philosophical process (since clearly a
philosophical position can only come into being through
a process no less philosophical), it is at least certain that
the material and stimulus for his new thought were
supplied by philological studies.

These studies seem to have impressed upon him a fact
of great importance ; namely, that this subject-matter
could only be and had actually been worked over by his
thought through the aid of certain necessary principles,
appearing on every page of the history which he had
chosen for investigation. He had once believed that the
moral sciences, as compared with the mathematical
method, took the lowest place as regards certainty. But
now, in his daily acquaintance with these sciences, he had
come to hold the opposite view ; namely, that nothing
could be firmer than the foundation of the moral sciences.

This certainty was not the simple self-evidence of
Descartes, in which the object, however internal it is said
to be, remains extrinsic to the subject. It was a truly
internal certainty, reached by an internal process. In

the assimilation of historical facts, Vico felt himself to be making more truly his own something that already belonged to him ; to be entering into possession of what was his by right. He was reconstructing the history of man ; and what was the history of man but a product of man himself ? Is not the creator of history simply man, with his ideas, his passions, his will, and his actions ? And is not the mind of man, the creator of history, identical with the mind which is at work in thinking it and knowing it ? The truth of the constructive principles of history then comes not from the validity of the clear and distinct idea, but from the indissoluble connexion of the subject and object of knowledge.

The importance of this new discovery, the discovery of the truth which Vico now recognised in the moral sciences, lay in the realisation of a new implication of the theory of knowledge laid down by himself in the former period of his speculations ; namely, the criterion of truth consisting in the " convertibility of the true with the created." The reason why man could have perfect knowledge of man's world was simply that he had himself made that world. " When it happens that he who creates things also describes them, then the history is certain in the highest degree."

Connected as it thus was with his earlier view, the assertion of the possibility of the moral sciences did not, to Vico's own mind, present the importance and bring with it the consequences of a revolution entirely overthrowing the structure of his ideas, and compelling him to adjust them afresh. On the one hand, this assertion seemed to him a confirmation of his former doctrine, a new example to be added to those he had already collected of perfect knowledge ; namely, God's knowledge of the universe and man's of the world of mathematics. On the other hand, it seemed to be an extension of the field of knowledge, whose boundaries (for definite boundaries still existed) had at first been too narrowly drawn. Formerly he had described a small luminous sphere in the centre of a vast and dimly lighted field ; now the luminous sphere underwent a definite increase in size, and the penumbral region a corresponding diminution. This increase involved no sort of conflict with his religious beliefs ; in fact, it seemed to support them and to gain support from them in turn. For did not religion teach the liberty, responsibility, and consciousness which man has in respect of his own acts and creations ?

Thus Vico did not feel obliged to write a new treatise on metaphysics. It seemed enough to add a mere postscript to his former work, and to correct to some extent his earlier assertions. His new theory of knowledge, while adhering strictly to the criterion of truth enunciated by him in opposition to that of Descartes—the principle, that is, that only the creator of a thing can know it— divided the whole of reality into the world of nature and the world of man. But, while it laid down that the world of nature is created by God and that therefore God alone knows it, it restricted its agnosticism to this field. It asserted, on the other hand, that the human world, being man's creation, is known by man. In this way it raised the knowledge of human affairs, formerly considered merely approximate and probable, to the rank of perfect science ; and it expressed surprise that philosophers should so laboriously endeavour to attain to science of the world of nature, which is a sealed book to mankind, while passing over the world of man, the science of which is attainable. The cause of this error he traced to the ease with which man's mind, involved and buried as it is in the body, feels bodily things, and the labour and pains it costs it to understand itself, as the bodily eye sees all objects outside itself, but in order to see itself requires the help of the mirror.

In everything else his system remained unchanged.

Beyond the world of man lay the supernatural world, inaccessible to man, and the world of nature, itself also in a sense supernatural. Beyond the perfect knowledge which man could have of himself lay the metaphysic of Christian Platonism, now reduced to impotence, but continuing none the less to embarrass mankind. The natural sciences were now, as before, regarded as incomplete forms of knowledge : mathematics as a system of abstractions, absolutely valid in the abstract but in face of reality powerless. The Aristotelian syllogism, the Stoic sorites, and the Cartesian geometrical method were pursued with the same hatred as before ; and the same enthusiastic praise was lavished upon the induction advocated and illustrated in his *Organum* by Bacon, that " great philosopher and great statesman," and fruitfully employed by his countrymen in experimental philosophy.

Vico's frequent claim to have constructed the science of human affairs on " a strict geometric method " might seem to indicate a change of opinion as to the applicability of that method. But his continual warnings, during the same period and in the same works, against the use in physical and moral questions of the mathematical method, which, " where there are no figures either of lines or numbers, either gives us no conclusiveness, or else, instead of demonstrating the truth, may often give an appearance of demonstration to falsehood," would flatly contradict the supposed change of front were it not that we could interpret it so as completely to restore the coherence of Vico's thought. This interpretation is quite simple. Once the power of converting the true with the created is seen to attach to the moral sciences no less than to geometry, these sciences could and indeed must develop on a method analogous to the synthetic method of geometry, the method which proceeds from a truth to its immediate consequence. In this manner they follow the progress of the world of man from its ideal origin to its perfect development ; so that the student must not hope to be able to investigate these sciences *per saltum,* but must traverse them from beginning to end in detail, without refusing to accept unforeseen conclusions any more than he can refuse to do so in geometry ; but concentrating his attention on the firmness of the bond between premisses and conclusion.   Thus the method could be called geometric by analogy or synecdoche ; in fact, however, it was essentially speculative, and not to be confused with the application of mathematics to questions of morals, of which the Cartesians and Spinoza have left examples.

Nor can we agree without reservation to the opinion of certain commentators that Vico, in asserting the existence of a single science of man, to be studied in the modifications of the human mind, was retreating to the position of a follower of Descartes.   This opinion is often reinforced by another statement of Vico's, namely, that to conceive his New Science it would be well to return to a state of absolute ignorance, as if no philosophers, philologists, nor books had even existed in the world. It is true that with the new form of his theory of knowledge Vico himself joined the ranks of modern subjectivism, initiated by Descartes.   In a sense, indeed, he had already done so in his activistic doctrine of truth as the reconstruction of the created.   In this quite general sense Vico might himself be called a Cartesian.   Nevertheless, if he was still behind Descartes in making his subjectivism a principle not of the whole of knowledge but of the knowledge of the world of man only, in another way he was ahead of the French philosopher, in that for him the truth attained in the world of man was not static but dynamic, not a discovery but a product, not consciousness but science.

As for the advice that one should proceed as if there were no books, no philosophical or philological doctrines in the world, its meaning is merely the necessity of ridding oneself of all prejudice, of all common habitual assumptions, of all accretions of memory and fancy, in order to attain " the state of pure understanding, empty of every particular form," which is necessary for the discovery and apprehension of any new truth. So far removed is this advice from the Cartesian or Malebranchian renunciation of learning and authority, that—to mention one fact only—in the very passage to which we have just referred we find the warning that the New Science presupposes a comprehensive and varied mass both of doctrine and of learning, the truths of which it takes over as already known, and uses them as terms in its new propositions.

In a word, Vico in his new theory of knowledge became not more Cartesian but more Vician—more himself. Descartes seemed to him not even a serviceable path by which to attain proof of the possibility of constructing the science of mind by means of the mind. The true path was Vico's own criterion of truth, brought into relation with its author's observations made in the course of his historical studies. If we wish to look for precedents in the history of philosophy for Vico's theory of knowledge in its second form, the division between the two worlds of reality and the two spheres of consciousness, and the preference for moral as compared with natural studies, would lead us back to the position adopted by Socrates as against the " Physiologists " of his time, and the feeling of religious mystery which brought the Athenian philosopher to a standstill in face of the natural world and directed his efforts to the study of the mind of man. Again, as to the superior transparency of the moral sciences, as dealing with objects created by man himself, we might recall the Aristotelian division of the sciences into physical, treating of motion external to man, and practical and " poietic," which deal with man's own

creations. The distinction passed into the philosophy
of the schools : Thomas Aquinas speaks of nature as
" an order which reason contemplates but does not create"
(*ordo quem ratio considerat sed non facit*), and of the world
of human activity as "an order which reason creates
by contemplation " (*ordo quem ratio considerando facit*).
But no such reference is made by Vico, fond as he was of
expressing the debt of his own thought to the ancient
philosophers ; and admitting that the doctrine had some
force before his time, the divergence between this earlier
view and that of Vico on the knowableness of the world
of man is as great as that between the assertion of the
omniscience of God the Creator and the theory of knowledge which Vico was able to draw from it.

Of this theory, his doctrine of the moral sciences was
neither more nor less than the first legitimate application.
Both its author and the majority of his commentators
are using inaccurate language in describing it as a simple
extension of the previous applications—a second instance,
added to that of the mathematical sciences, already
examined.

In the mathematical sciences, the principle of the
conversion of the true with the created had been applied
in appearance only. The principle itself was original and
sound : so was the theory of mathematics. But the
connexion between the two truths was altogether artificial and false. What was lacking was, unless we are
mistaken, an effective relation between the concept of
God who creates the world and, as creating it, knows it,
and that of the man who arbitrarily constructs a world of
abstractions, and in doing so either knows nothing at all,
or else, when he ceases to be a geometer or arithmetician
and becomes a philosopher, when he is composing not
Euclid's Elements but the theory of knowledge in the
De antiquissima, knows merely that his procedure is
arbitrary. If the mathematical sciences construct

their concepts as they please, if they produce not truth but definitions, they are as a matter of fact not sciences at all, nor any form of knowledge, and cannot be compared with the divine knowledge, the knowledge of actual reality. In mathematics, says Vico, " man, holding within himself an imaginary world of lines and numbers, operates in this world by abstraction just as God operates in the universe by reality." It is a luminous comparison; but perhaps its light is that of metaphor rather than logic.

In the moral sciences, on the other hand, the comparison is so entirely logical that it should frankly be called co-incidence. Human knowledge is qualitatively identical with divine, and knows the world of man equally well; it is, however, quantitatively more restricted, and does not extend like the divine to the world of nature. In the human field we no longer find the expedients of weakness, definitions and falsifications; knowledge is here at its highest point of concreteness. Man creates the human world, creates it by transforming himself into the facts of society: by thinking it he re-creates his own creations, traverses over again the paths he has already traversed, reconstructs the whole ideally, and thus knows it with full and true knowledge. Here is a real world; and of this world man is truly the God.

It seems undeniable, then, that the application of the " *verum-factum* " made in the New Science is the only one which corresponds to the criterion previously formulated. The earlier attempt at an application of it to mathematics, though important in other respects and well calculated to free the mind from mathematical prejudice, cannot be considered a true or strict use of it. It is possible that Vico was sometimes vaguely conscious of the difference between the two applications, the strict and the metaphorical, which as a rule he confused and treated as identical. The science of the world of man, he says, proceeds exactly as does geometry, which while it constructs out of its elements or contemplates the world of quantity, itself creates it ; but with proportionately greater reality, since order has no connexion with human affairs, containing as they do neither points, lines, surfaces, nor figures. Another indication of his gradually dawning consciousness that he had now for the first time in his doctrine of the world of man discovered a true and proper knowledge, not a mere fiction of knowledge, may perhaps be seen in the much greater conviction, warmth, and enthusiasm with which he now uses the epithet " divine " : quite a different thing from the chilly, if not absolutely ironical, *ad Dei instar* of the *De antiquissima*. The proofs of the New Science, he says more than once, with fervour, " are divine in their nature, and should give thee, Reader, a divine joy : since in God knowledge and creation are one."

The conversion of the true with the created was bound to react upon the treatment of certitude in one, perhaps the chief, of the various meanings in which Vico uses the word, namely, historical fact : the *peculiare, certum,* as opposed to the *commune* or *verum*. This forms the other important section of Vico's second theory of knowledge. In the former theory these cognitions were, as we saw, legitimised and protected by being put on a level with all other kinds of knowledge, all of them equally weak or equally strong, being all alike founded on probability or authority, whether of the individual (autopsy) or of mankind.

But now that the knowledge of the human mind and its laws was rescued from the region of authority and probability, historical fact, although still in a sense, by its very nature, founded upon authority, was placed in a new light. The certain must enter into a new relation, confronted as it now was not by another certainty, that is, mere probable knowledge of the human mind, but by a truth, a piece of philosophical knowledge.

This relation is also called by Vico the relation between philosophy and philology : the former dealing with necessities of nature, *necessaria naturae*, and contemplating the reason from which issues the science of truth ; the latter with decisions of the human will, *placita humani arbitrii*, and following the authority whence comes knowledge of the certain. The one considers the universal, the other the individual ; the one, as Leibniz would have said, the *vérités de raison*, the other the *vérités de fait*. With Vico the distinction is not so clearly expressed : in fact, authority as opposed to reason sometimes, according to him, becomes a part of reason itself, or is confused with the knowledge of the human will as opposed to that of rational volition ; but the general sense is none the less quite plain. By philology Vico means not only the study of words and their history, but, since words are bound up with the ideas of things, he means also the history of things. Thus philologists should deal with war, peace, alliances, travels, commerce, customs, laws and coinage, geography and chronology, and every other subject connected with man's life on earth. Philology in a word, in Vico's sense, which is also the true sense, embraces not only the history of language or literature, but also that of events, philosophy, and politics.

It is true that philology, the truth of fact or certitude, had not always been so brutally treated as it was by the Cartesians. Grotius had given evidence of immense historical learning employed on behalf of his doctrine of natural right. Gravina, Vico's contemporary and fellow-countryman, demanded as necessary to the student of law not only " the art of reasoning " (*ratiocinandi ars*) but " skill in the Latin tongue " (*Latinae linguae peritia*) and " knowledge of history " (*notitia temporum*). And Leibniz, whom we have just named, reasserted the value of learning as against the Cartesians, and extended his patronage, *en grand seigneur*, to the varied collection of historical anecdotes which he scattered freely over his pages. But Vico observed that the philosophy and philology of his time always remained external to one another, as they had been almost entirely in Greece and Rome. All the quotations from historians, orators, philosophers, and poets accumulated by Grotius were a mere embellishment. Perhaps Vico would have passed the same judgment upon the liberal use made of history by Leibniz, if he had known of it and expressed his opinion. In reading the works of philologists he was conscious of such a sense of vacuity and weariness in the unintelligent jumble of historical observations, that he was almost led to agree with Descartes and Malebranche in their hatred of scholarship : for a time, in fact, he did entirely agree with them. But these two philosophers—so his later thought ran—ought, instead of despising erudition, rather to have asked whether it were possible to reclaim philology to philosophical principles ; and the philologists for their part, instead of marshalling facts for a display of learning, ought to strive to make them the aim of science. Philology must be reduced to a science. This was Vico's idea of the relation of certitude to truth, or philology to philosophy.

What was the meaning of reducing philology, or history, which is the same thing, to a science or philosophy ? Strictly speaking, the reduction is impossible : not because they deal with subject-matter different in kind, but because their subject-matter is in point of fact homogeneous. History is already essentially philosophy. It is impossible to make the most insignificant historical statement without moulding it with thought, that is with philosophy. But since the existence of this philosophical basis of philology was not at that time realised, indeed it was none too often realised in later times, and in consequence easily denied ; and since most people, as we have seen, imagined either an aristocratic geometrical philosophy, hating and avoiding the " profane mob " of facts, or else, as at first Vico did, a philosophy and a history equally devoid of cogency, and merely matters of opinion : for these reasons Vico, after the change of his philosophical point of view, now that he had attained to the consciousness of the speculative method in the science of man, and understood more deeply the human mind, was bound to see how much current history stood in need of reform and extension ; to feel the lack of an improved philology as a consequence of the improved philosophy, and to express it in terms of the theory of knowledge by the formula reuniting philology to philosophy : " that this second science, as is fair, should be the consequence of the first " (*ut haec posterior, ut par est, prioris sit consequentia*). He was bound, in other words, to rescue history from its condition of inferiority, where it was a mere slave to caprice, vanity, moralising and precept-making, and other irrelevant aims, and to recognise its own true end as a necessary complement of eternal truth. Philosophy nowadays is full of and intimate with historical fact : and this gives it greater breadth and a more lively sense of dealing with concrete reality. This is no doubt one meaning of Vico's formula concerning the union of philosophy and philology, and the reduction of the latter to a science.

It is, however, certain that in propounding this formula he had in view a further and, as often happened, a different meaning. This other meaning might be most simply illustrated by comparing it, as Vico himself did with Bacon and his " more certain method of philosophising " : that method which Bacon expressed in the title of his work by the words *Cogitata et visa*, and Vico proposed to " transfer from the natural to the human or political world." In a word, he demanded the construction of a typical history of human society (*cogitare*) which was then to be discovered in the facts (*videre*). Thus the ideal construction would acquire certainty from the facts, and the facts truth from the ideal construction : authority would be confirmed by reason and reason by authority. He demanded a science which should be at once a philosophy of man and a universal history of nations. Now this structure which he required—something intermediate between *cogitare* and *videre*, thought and experience, this mixture of the two processes—is intrinsically different from the unity of philosophy and philology, in so far as that is a philosophical interpretation of factual data. Such an interpretation is living history : the other is neither philosophy nor history, but an empirical science of man and society, drawing its materials from schemata which are neither the extra-temporal categories of philosophy nor the individual facts of history : although it can never be constructed without philosophical categories and historical facts. It is an empirical science ; and as such, neither exact nor true, but only approximative and probable, and subject to verification and correction from the side both of philosophy and of history.

It would be impossible to decide either which of these two meanings of philology reduced to history is that of Vico himself, since both are included in his thought : or which is the prevailing one, since in point of fact now one, now the other prevails : although the second, or empirical, signification is the more often formulated. We might even say that when Vico entitled his treatise *Scienza Nuova*, the principal meaning he attached to this " invidious " name referred precisely to this empirical science, the science, that is, which was to be at once a philosophy and a history of man : the ideal history of the eternal laws which govern the course of all nations' deeds in their rise, progress, points of rest, decline and fall. The fact is, Vico did not and could not unify the two different meanings ; he maintained the duality which, simply because it was never made explicit,

presented an appearance of unity. Thus each of the
tendencies shown by his interpreters is partially justified :
one group of whom maintain that Vico laid down and
employed the speculative method; another, that his procedure was both in intention and in effect empirical,
inductive and psychological : the former believing that
he aimed at a systematic philosophy of man, the latter
that he was bent upon a scheme of sociology or social
psychology. Both views are one-sided, but the second
more so than the first. If there actually were in Vico
elements both of Bacon and of Plato, of the empiricist and
the philosopher, yet when we look at his intellectual
personality as a whole, when we penetrate into the depths
of his mind and share in his difficulties and his colossal
labours, we must recognise that whatever he meant and
believed Vico was of the stuff of a Plato and not a Bacon :
that even the Bacon of whom he speaks is in part his own
invention, a Bacon tinged with Platonism : and that the
New Science seemed so new to him fundamentally, not
because it was an empirical structure on Bacon's lines—
indeed in that case no science could be older : we need
only cite Aristotle's *Politics* and Machiavelli's *Discourses*,
—but because it was impregnated throughout by a new
philosophy, which did in truth break into it on every
side, through all his empiricism.

CHAPTER III

THE lack of clearness on the relation of philosophy to philology, and the failure to distinguish between the two quite different ways of conceiving the reduction of philology to a science, are at once the consequences and the causes of the obscurity which prevails in the " New Science." By this name we refer to the whole mass of research and theory which Vico was producing from 1720 to 1730, elaborated above all in three works, the *De uno universi iuris principio et fine uno* and the first and second *Scienza Nuova* ; it attains its maturest and most developed form in the last of these, and this is the most important for reference.

The New Science, agreeably to the various meanings of the terms philosophy and philology and of the relation between them, consists of three groups of investigations, philosophical, historical and empirical. Altogether it contains a philosophy of mind, a history, or group of histories, and a social science. To the first named belong the ideas expressed in various axioms or aphorisms scattered up and down the work, on imagination and the imaginative universal, on the intellect and the logical universal, on myth, religion, the moral judgment, force and law, certitude and truth, the passions, providence, and all the other determinations affecting the course or development of the thought or mind of man. To the second, namely history, belong the sketch of a universal history of primitive peoples from the time of the Flood, and of the origins of the various civilisations : the description of the ancient barbaric or heroic society in Greece and especially in Rome, with regard to religion, customs, law, language and political constitution : the study of primitive poetry, concentrating upon the determination of the genesis and character of the Homeric poems : the history of the social struggles between the patricians and plebeians and the origin of democracy, also studied chiefly in Rome : and the description of the return of barbarism or the Middle Ages, also studied in all aspects of life and compared with primitive barbaric society. Finally, to empirical science belongs the attempt to establish a uniform course of national history, dealing with the succession both of political forms and of other correlative manifestations of life both theoretical and practical, and the series of types successively drawn by Vico of the patriciate, the plebs, feudalism, the patriarchal family, symbolic law, metaphorical language, hieroglyphic writing and so forth.

Now if these three classes of inquiry and theory had been logically distinct in Vico's mind and united and compressed within the limits of a single book for literary reasons alone, the result might have been confused, ill-proportioned, out of harmony, and therefore fatiguing to the reader, but not obscure. But in point of fact it cannot be said that the *Scienza Nuova*, at least in its second form, the final exposition of his thought given by Vico, lacks a general plan, well enough conceived. The treatise is divided into five books. The first is intended to summarise general principles, that is, philosophy. The second, in addition to a short note on the most ancient universal history, describes the life of barbaric society, to which the third, on the discovery of the true Homer, the most conspicuous example of barbaric poetry, forms an appendix. The fourth is meant to sketch the empirical science of the movement of national history : and the fifth to exemplify the movement of " reflux " in the particular case of the Middle Ages. And yet, in spite of this fine architectonic scheme, the second *Scienza Nuova* is the most obscure, just as it is the most rich and complete of Vico's works. If on the other hand, while keeping his ideas clear in his mind, Vico had used an unfamiliar terminology or a style of exposition either too compressed or too full of allusions or implicit presuppositions, he would certainly have been a difficult writer, but in this case, as in the other, not obscure. But such a hypothesis does not suit the facts. Vico is very sparing of scholastic language ; he prefers living and popular terminology. He is not compressed : in fact, he is fond of repeating his ideas, emphasising them by repetition with great insistence. And he lays all his cards on the table : that is to say, he shows all the material by which his doctrines have been suggested. Finally, it amounts to very little to say that Vico was not fully conscious of his own dis-coveries : such consciousness is more or less deficient in every thinker, and in fact none could have it more fully. The obscurity, the real obscurity which we find in Vico is not superficial. It does not come either from merely general or from secondary causes. It really consists in the obscurity of his ideas ; in his insufficient under-standing of certain connections, and the substitution for them of fallacious ones ; in the arbitrary element, that is, which he introduces into his thought, or to put it more simply in his own downright errors. One might re-write the New Science, recasting the order and changing and elucidating the terminology—the present writer has made the attempt for himself—and still the obscurity would remain, or even increase ; for in such a translation the work in losing its original form would lose also the turbid but powerful strength which may at times take the place of clarity, and, while it does not illuminate, stirs the reader's mind and generates waves of thought as it were by sympathetic vibrations.

That Vico's obscurity, his mistake or mistakes, is due to the confusion or lack of distinction in his theory of knowledge mentioned above, on the question of the relations between philosophy, history and empirical science—a confusion which exists no less in his actual thought on the problems of the mind and history of man —that this is so can be seen by observing how philosophy, history and empirical science pass into each other by turns in Vico's mind, and vitiating each other in turn produce the perplexities, ambiguities, exaggerations and hasty statements which perturb the reader of the New Science. The philosophy of mind masquerades now as empirical science, now as history : empirical science now as philosophy, now as history : and historical propositions assume the universality of philosophical principles or the generality of empirical schemata. For example, the philosophy of man undertakes to determine the forms, categories or ideal moments of mind in their necessary succession, and in this aspect it well deserves the title or definition of " eternal ideal history " according to which particular histories proceed in time ; while no fragment however small of actual history can be conceived in which this ideal history is not present. But, since ideal history is also for Vico the empirical determination of the order in which the forms of civilisations, states, languages, styles, and kinds of poetry succeed one another, it comes about that he conceives the empirical series as identical with the ideal series, and as deriving validity from it. Hence he asserts that this series must always be exactly reproduced in the facts, " even if infinite worlds were produced from time to time through eternity " : an assertion which is plainly false, since there is no reason why the empirical fact of Greek or Roman aristocracy should be repeated for ever, with a " must have been, must be now, must be hereafter " ; or why civilisations should rise and fall precisely as did those of antiquity. And this very treatment of the empirical course of events as absolute threw a shadow of empiricism over their ideal course ; since the latter once identified with the former took over its empirical and temporal character instead of the eternal and extra-temporal character which it had as originally conceived. The same must be said of the various forms of mind which, as ideal and extra-temporal, are always all present in every fact ; but Vico, by confusing them with the real and concrete facts which empirical science splits up into its schemata, destroyed them in their ideal form and distinction as soon as he had stated them. It is true that the moment of force is not that of justice ; but the empirical type of barbaric society founded upon force, precisely because it is a representative and approximative determination, and is referred to a concrete and total state of things, contains not only force but justice as well ; and when this ideal moment and this type of society are interchanged and treated as identical, on the one hand the philosophical concept of force is confused with that of justice and becomes impure, contradictory and incoherent, and finally annuls itself : on the other, the empirical type of barbaric society becomes exaggerated and unduly rigid. The confusion between the philosophic and the empirical is clearly expressed in Vico's aphorism defining the nature of things. " Nature of things is nothing else than their production at certain times and in certain manners : and whenever these latter are of such a kind, then the things produced are of such a kind and no other." Here we see the confusion between time and manner, between ideal and empirical genesis. Similarly, it is perfectly true that history ought to proceed in harmony with philosophy, and that a philosophical absurdity can never be a historical event : but, since the distinction between philosophy and empirical science was not drawn by Vico, when evidence was lacking and philosophy therefore inapplicable he felt no less sure of attaining truth. He merely filled the gap with a conjecture supplied by the schema of empirical science, and persuaded himself that he had fallen back on a " metaphysical proof." Or again, if he found himself faced by uncertain facts, instead of patiently waiting till the discovery of further evidence should dispel the doubt, he cut the knot by accepting the facts, as he put it, in conformity with laws : which always means the empirical schema. A legitimate method, doubtless, when treated as hypothetical. But this hypothesis became in its turn, for Vico, a " truth meditated in the idea " : so that the comparison with facts, which none the less he recommends for the sake of confirmation, became strictly speaking superfluous : or, if the comparison showed that the facts disagreed with it, the facts, as mere appearance, must be in the wrong, rather than the hypothesis, which is laid down as philosophical truth, and therefore indubitable. Hence arises the tendency observed in Vico to do violence to the facts.

These examples are enough to indicate the deep-seated fault in the structure of the New Science, and to establish one point in our exposition and criticism of Vico's thought, in the course of which many other examples of the same point will arise of themselves, and those already given will become more clear. But another point which must be well established is that this fault is the fault of an organism in the highest degree healthy, and that the different species of inquiry between which Vico failed to distinguish were composed of investigations of extraordinary originality, truth, and importance. It is in fact the fault often found in highly original and inventive intellects, which seldom work out their discoveries in accurate detail, while less inventive minds are generally

more precise and logical.   Depth and acuteness do not
always flourish equally side by side : and Vico, however
much he fell short in acuteness, was always profoundly
deep.

Light and shade, truth and error, which alternate and
interweave at almost every point in the New Science, are
variously distinguished according to the various temperaments of readers and critics : and in conspicuous cases,
like that of Vico, such variations assume the most sharply
defined form.   Some minds are self-willed and suspicious,
quick to mark any trifling contradiction, merciless in
demanding proof of every statement, and indefatigable in
wielding the forceps of dilemma to dismember an unfortunate great man.   For them Vico's work, like many
others of the same kind, is a closed book.   At most, it will
provide them with a theme for what is known as a " refutation": an easy and congenial task, yet hardly a successful
one, since the man they have demolished generally emerges
from the slaughter more alive than before.   But there
is another type of mind, which, at the first word which
reaches the heart, at the first ray of truth which dawns
upon the eyes, opens its whole self in desire, abandons
itself in faith, and grows wild with enthusiasm ; which
refuses to hear of faults and never sees difficulties, or
the difficulties at once vanish, and the faults find the
easiest of justifications : and when it commits itself to
writing, its writings appear in the guise of " defences."
For such a mind we fear that the New Science is a book
all too open.   No doubt, if these two attitudes were the
only alternatives, if no third choice were open, one would
have to choose the fault of love rather than that of cold
indifference ; the excess of faith, which may yet enrich
us by one or two aspects of the truth, rather than the
absence of faith which never lets us realise one.   But a
third attitude is possible to, and indeed incumbent on
the critic ; namely, that which never takes its eyes off

the light, but yet does not conceal the shade; which transcends the letter to attain the spirit, yet not ignoring the letter, but always returning to it, always endeavouring to play the part of a free but not a fanciful interpreter, a warm lover but not a blind one.

The two points above established, the strength and weakness essential to Vico's intellect, his tendency to confusion or his confusion of tendencies, supply us with a kind of general canon of interpretation; namely, that of separating analytically at every step his pure philosophy from the empiricism and history with which he mixes, and in which so to speak he embodies it, and on the other hand separating the latter from the former: and of observing, in the process, the causes and effects of the mixture. The dross cannot be treated as non-existent, bound up as it is with the gold in its natural state: but it must not hinder us from recognising and purifying the gold. Or, to drop the metaphor, the history must be indeed a history, but that it can only be if guided by intelligence.

CHAPTER IV

THE IMAGINATIVE FORM OF KNOWLEDGE
(POETRY AND LANGUAGE)

THE chief, almost indeed the only, forms of the mind studied by Vico in the New Science are the inferior, individualising activities to which he gives the general name of " certitude." These are, in the region of theoretic mind, imagination : in that of the practical mind, power or will : and in the empirical science corresponding to the philosophy of mind, the barbaric society and poetic wisdom whose examination occupies, in his own words, " almost the whole bulk of the work."

His deep interest in these lower forms, and in the primitive societies and barbaric histories which display them, is further illustrated and explained, among his external circumstances, by the studies he undertook in Roman law and its expressions and rhetorical figures : by the still living tradition of Italian humanism : by the recently stimulated pursuit of the archaeological sciences : by his own desire to investigate the earliest civilisation of Italy, and so forth. But many of his contemporaries and countrymen were handling the same materials without acquiring any of his taste for and comprehension of imagination, simplicity and force : indeed Vico himself, when he wrote the *De antiquissima,* had the taste for these things but as yet no comprehension of them. The full reason for this interest is seen when we consider the development of Vico as a philosopher, without losing sight of the complexity of his nature in all its opposition to the Cartesian type of mind. Cartesianism, with its attention confined to the universalising and abstractive forms, ignored the individualising : and this necessarily attracted Vico all the more towards them as towards a mysterious problem. Cartesianism shrank in horror from the tangled forest of history : Vico plunged eagerly into that very department of history where the historical flavour, so to speak, is strongest ; namely, that which is furthest and psychologically most different from civilised periods. Cartesianism extended the psychology of civilisation to all periods and nations : Vico was led to investigate in all their profound divergencies and contradictions the modes of feeling and thought proper to various times.

The great effort which had to be made, and actually was made by Vico, in order to penetrate through modern intellectualism and recapture the point of view of primitive psychology, is expressed in his language about the " grave difficulties " entailed by his " labour of fully twenty-five years " in the attempt to "stoop from these civilised natures of ours to those absolutely wild and savage minds, which we cannot picture to ourselves at all, and can only understand with great toil." It is expressed again, rather differently, by his insistence on the impossibility, now that, even with the common people, the mind of man is too completely separated from the senses, accustomed to the free use of abstract terms, sharpened by the art of writing, and spiritualised so to speak by the employment of numbers,—the impossibility of entering into the chaotic fancy of primitive man, whose mind was the very reverse of abstract, acute or spiritual; but rather sunk in the senses, blunted by passion, and buried in the body : and of grasping such ideas as that of the " sympathy of nature." This necessary effort

—a painful one, but successful—was another reason for
his feeling that his science was " new." He says indeed
that this study of the ideal form and the historic period
of certitude was entirely lacking to Greek philosophy as
a whole. Plato had attempted it in the *Cratylus*, but
unsuccessfully, because he knew nothing of the language
of the first legislators, the heroic poets, and was deceived
by the altered and modernised forms under which the
laws existed in his time after continual revision at Athens.
Among the moderns, J. C. Scaliger, Francisco Sanchez
and Gaspar Schopp had fallen into a similar mistake
when they attempted to explain language by the principles
of logic, and indeed of Aristotelian logic, in spite of its
having arisen centuries after language itself. Grotius,
Selden, Puffendorf and the other writers on natural rights
also studied human nature as civilised by religion and
law ; so that in retracing the course of history they began
in the middle: that is to say, they confined themselves to
the intellect, ignoring the imagination, and to the will
under moral restraint, passing over the undisciplined
passions. Vico himself, while he had shown his interest
in this problem by undertaking to investigate the " most
ancient wisdom of Italy," was yet led astray in his study
by following the lead of the author of the *Cratylus*.

In its philosophical aspect, the New Science might,
owing to this prominence given to the study of the individualising forms, above all the imagination (since the
doctrine that primitive man is a poet and thinks in poetic
images is in Vico's words the " master key " of the work)
be called, without undue paradox, a philosophy of Mind
with special attention to the Philosophy of Imagination
or Aesthetic.

Aesthetic may in fact be considered as a discovery of
Vico's, though with the reservations to which the determination of discoveries and discoverers is always subject ;
and although he did not deal with it in a separate treatise

or give it the happy title with which Baumgarten christened it ten years or so later. It is interesting however to notice that the terminology of the New Science lights upon a name similar to one of the equivalents for Aesthetic which Baumgarten passes in review; namely that of " the Logic of Poetry." But ultimately the name matters little : what does matter is the fact : and the fact is that Vico adopted a theory of poetry which was then and was still for a time to be a bold and revolutionary innovation. At that time, as is well known, the old practical or didactic theory held the field : the theory which, starting late in the history of the ancient world, persisting through the Middle Ages, and transplanted into the Renaissance, regarded poetry as an ingenious disguise for the popularising of lofty philosophical and theological ideas. Beside this theory, though inferior in authority, stood another, which considered poetry as the product of or means to diversion and pleasure. These views had come to alter the original meaning of the Aristotelian treatise on poetry, so as to be at last introduced into it and discovered there as if Aristotle himself had held and written them. Nor was this mistake corrected by Cartesianism, which, as we should expect from its general direction, rather tended to enfeeble and annul the very object of these definitions, as a thing of no value, or practically none. At a time when philosophers were trying to reduce metaphysics and ethics to a mathematical form, and despised concrete intuition : when men were devising a literature and a poetry suited to disseminate science among the common people or the world of fashion : when experiments were being made in the construction of artificial, logical languages, superior to those of past or present usage : when, finally, it was thought possible to lay down rules for composing musical airs without being a musician, and poems without being a poet : in this atmosphere of detachment, coolness, hostility and mockery, only a miracle could arouse a

different and indeed opposite feeling—a warm and vivid
consciousness of the real nature of poetry in its original
function : and this miracle was worked by the keen, restless
and stormy mind of Giambattista Vico.

He criticised at once the three doctrines of poetry as a
means of adorning and communicating intellectual truth,
as merely subservient to pleasure, and as a harmless
mental exercise for those who can do it.   Poetry is not
esoteric wisdom : it does not presuppose the logic of the
intellect : it does not contain philosophical judgments.
The philosophers, in finding these things in poetry, have
simply put them there themselves without realising it.
Poetry is produced not by the mere caprice of pleasure,
but by natural necessity.   It is so far from being superfluous and capable of elimination, that without it thought
cannot arise : it is the primary activity of the human
mind.   Man, before he has arrived at the stage of forming
universals, forms imaginary ideas.   Before he reflects
with a clear mind, he apprehends with faculties confused
and disturbed : before he can articulate, he sings : before
speaking in prose, he speaks in verse : before using
technical terms, he uses metaphors, and the metaphorical
use of words is as natural to him as that which we call
"natural."   So far from being a fashion of expounding
metaphysics   poetry is distinct from and opposed to
metaphysics.   The one frees the intellect from the senses,
the other submerges and overwhelms it in them : the one
reaches perfection in proportion as it rises to universality,
the other, as it confines itself to the particular : the one
enfeebles the imagination, the other strengthens it.   The
one takes precautions against turning the mind into body,
the other delights in giving body to the mind.   The judgments of poetry are composed of sense and emotion, those
of philosophy are composed of reflection, which if introduced into poetry makes it frigid and unreal : and no one
in the whole course of history has ever been at once a

great poet and a great metaphysician. Poets and philosophers may be called respectively the senses and the
intellect of mankind : and in this sense we may retain as
true the scholastic saying " there is nothing in the intellect
which was not first in the senses." Without sense, we
cannot have intellect : without poetry, we cannot have
philosophy, nor indeed any civilisation.

Almost more miraculous than this conception of poetry
is the fact that Vico saw into the true nature of language,
a problem much less canvassed and investigated, and
no more satisfactorily solved, by ancient and modern
philosophy down to the present day. Language was
as a rule alternately confused with logic and debased into
a mere external and conventional sign, or else in despair
referred to a divine origin. Vico realised that the divine
origin was in this case a mere refuge of indolence ; that
language is neither logic nor convention, and, like poetry,
is neither esoteric wisdom nor due to a decision or agreement. Language arises naturally. In its first form, men
express themselves " by mute actions," or by signs, and
" by bodies having natural connexions with the ideas
which they wish to indicate," *i.e.* by means of symbolic
objects. But in the case both of articulated languages
and of common speech, all philologists have, " with an
excess of good faith," which means a deficiency of insight,
accepted the view that meanings are decided at pleasure :
whereas at the so-called origin of language meanings
must have been natural, and every common word must
certainly have started from one single individual of one
nation, and been derived from the primitive language
of gestures and objects. In Latin, as in other tongues,
it is to be noticed that almost all the words are formed
to express natural properties, or used by transference :
and the greater part of every language, in every nation,
is metaphorical. The opposite opinion was due to the
ignorance of grammarians, who, meeting with a great

number of words expressing confused and indistinct
ideas, and not knowing their origin, which had formerly
made them lucid and distinct, invented for their own
peace of mind the conventional theory ; and dragged in
Aristotle and Galen as against Plato and Iamblichus.
The serious objection generally brought against the natural
origin of language and in favour of the conventional,
namely the variations in the common speech among
different nations, is solved by considering that owing to
diversities of climate, temperament and custom nations
looked at the same useful or necessary objects in different
aspects, and hence produced different languages.   This
is also seen in the case of proverbs ; which are substantially identical maxims of human life, but expressed in
as many different forms as there are, or have been, different
nations.   The insistence, then, with which Vico claims
to have discovered the true origin of languages " in the
principles of poetry " is of especial importance.   On the
one hand, it entails the assertion of the spontaneous and
imaginative origin of language, and on the other it tends
implicitly if not explicitly to suppress the dualism between
poetry and language.

In these principles of poetry Vico found not only the
origin of languages, but also that of letters or writing.
He pronounced the separation of the two origins, connected
as they were by nature and appearing, in the primitive
dumb language of signs and objects, as identical, to be a
mere mistake of the grammarians.   Here again, it is no
case of esoteric wisdom or convention.   Hieroglyphics
were not invented by philosophers as a means of concealing
the mysteries of their lofty thoughts: they were a universal
and natural necessity to all primitive peoples : and only
the alphabetic scripts arose among nations by a free
agreement.   In other words Vico drew a distinction
(though in a confused manner) within the so-called scripts,
between those which are true scripts and therefore con-

ventional, and others which are directly expressive and are therefore language, story-telling, poetry and painting. These expressive scripts or languages are characterised by the inseparability of content from form. They are poetical just in the sense that the story and its expression are one and the same thing, namely a metaphor common to poetry and painting, so that it could be depicted by a dumb man without verbal expression. As examples, Vico quotes traditional anecdotes ; for instance, the five " real words " (the frog, the mouse, the bird, the ploughshare and the bow) sent by Idanturas king of the Scythians to Darius when the latter had declared war on him : and the parable of the tall poppies which King Tarquin enacted before the eyes of his son Sextus's ambassador, concerning the means of ruling Gabii—methods of expression parallel to practices still found among savages and the lower classes :—and in addition to these, heraldry, flags, and the emblems upon medals and coins. There is a frivolous legend which belittles and degrades the true value of heraldry by asserting it to have been invented in German tournaments as a custom of gallantry by young men seeking to win the love of noble maidens. But in the Middle Ages heraldry was a serious thing. It was, so to speak, the hieroglyphic script of the period : a wordless language to eke out the poverty of ordinary speech and alphabetic writing. It was only later, in times of culture, that it became a sport and a pleasure, and gallant and learned blazonings were adopted which had to be enlivened by means of mottoes because their own meaning was now merely analogical ; while primitive and natural heraldry was dumb, or rather spoke without needing an interpreter. Even in the days of culture a few such expressive forms retained this simplicity and naturalness. Flags or ensigns for instance form a kind of armed language with which nations, as if deprived of speech, make themselves understood in the wider affairs of the natural rights of peoples; wars, alliances and commerce.

Thus in the light of Vico's aesthetical idea poetry, words, metaphors, writing and graphic symbols are all illuminated and spring to life : great things and small, epic poetry and heraldry. The doctrine of imaginary forms was quite a new departure in the history of ideas : for while Vico opposed his own conceptions to those of the contemporary schools, especially the Cartesian, he by no means attached himself to any other more or less remote school or tradition. He himself felt that he was opposed not to a particular school but to all who had ever formulated doctrines on the subject. He says that he has " overturned " all the theories about poetry held by Plato, Aristotle, and so on down to Patrizio, Scaliger and Castelvetro in modern times, all of whom had lost themselves in ineptitudes which " even to mention makes one ashamed." Patrizio made poetry begin with the songs of birds and the whistling of the wind ! As regards language, he had been ultimately dissatisfied both with Plato and with the moderns Wolfgang Latius, Scaliger and Sanchez. As regards writing, once the theory of divine origin supported by Mallinkrot and Ingewald Eling was refuted, or rather interpreted in his own way, which came to the same thing, he made an attempt to discredit the futile, vague, ill-founded, mis-shapen, pompous and absurd opinions which derived it from the Goths and through them from Adam and personal instruction from God, or more directly from the Earthly Paradise, or from a Gothic Mercury as inventor. Finally, as to heraldry, he remarks that the writers on the subject have never understood anything about it, and have only by a mere random guess let fall a hint of the truth in calling it " heroic."

In fact it would be hard to find real and true precedents for Vico's aesthetic conceptions. At most, we might indicate vague suggestions contained in various scattered statements which he collects : a certain immediate stimulus in the discussions of the seventeenth century on the distinctions between intellect and genius, reason and imagination, dialectic and rhetoric: and a certain convergence of external particulars, such as the collection of rhetorical subtleties expressed in subtleties of language, made by Tesauro, a rhetorician of the time.

These conceptions, however, produced as they were by a remarkable stroke of originality, no sooner passed from general outline to particular determinations, from the first idea or inspiration to concrete development, than they appear to become confused, fluctuating and unstable. We may set aside the various opinions successively held by Vico, and bound up with the historical growth of his mind, upon the subjects of poetry, language or metaphor, beginning with his academic orations, passing thence by way of the *De ratione* and *De antiquissima* to the *Diritto universale*, from these to the first and thence to the second *Scienza Nuova* : a study of these might supply subject-matter for a special essay, but does not come within the scope of our treatise. But even in the final form of his aesthetic thought, contradictory doctrines exist side by side. He is not content with saying, as he does say, that poetical form is the primary activity of the mind ; that it is composed of feelings of emotion ; and that it is entirely imaginative and devoid of concepts and reflection. He goes on to add that poetry, as opposed to history, " represents reality in its best idea," and therefore fulfils the justice and gives every man the reward or punishment which he does not always get in history, governed as the latter often is by caprice, necessity and chance. Again, he says that the end of poetry is " to give life to the lifeless," since its most sublime task is the attempt to give life and sensation to insensible objects.

He says that poetry is " nothing but imitation " ; that children, with their great imitative powers, are poets ; and that primitive races, the children of mankind, were also sublime poets. He says that poetry has for its special subject-matter " the impossible made credible " : for instance, it is impossible that body should be mind, and yet it was believed that the thundering sky was Jupiter. Hence the miracles performed by magicians by means of incantations were a favourite subject of poetry. He says that poetry is due to " poverty," that is, that it is a pathological product of the mind. Since uncivilised man is of low brain-power and cannot satisfy the thirst he feels for the general and the universal, he fills their place by inventing imaginary genera, poetical universals or characters. Consequently the truth of the poet is identical with the truth of the philosopher : the one abstract, the other clothed in images : the one a metaphysic of reason, the other a metaphysic of feeling and fancy, suited to the understanding of the people. From poverty also, that is from inability to articulate, arises song, and therefore mutes and stammerers utter sounds which are songs : and metaphor arises from inability to express things in an accurate manner. He says, finally, that the aim of poetry is to teach the people to act virtuously.

These sayings indicate very various ideas about poetry, of which some are compatible with the central doctrine but thrown out in a disconnected manner and therefore not in fact reconciled with it : others are quite incompatible. Vico might have been cited in turn, on the testimony of single passages, as a supporter of the moralistic theory of art, the didactic theory, the abstract or typical theory, the mythological theory, the animistic theory, and so on. And if he neither falls back into the old theories he hated, nor loses himself among the new fallacies which followed him, it is due to the fact that all these waverings and inconsistencies were continually submerged by the thought that poetry is the primary form of the mind, prior to intellect and free from reflection and reasoning.

Just as he was unable by the use of his leading principle to distinguish and reconcile the other theories on the nature of poetry which already existed or had been invented by himself, so he did not succeed in escaping from the tyranny of old or new empirical classifications. He struggled to reduce these in their turn to philosophical form, and tried to deduce successively the various kinds of poetry, epic, lyric and dramatic : the kinds of verse and metre, spondaic, iambic and prose : the kinds of figurative language, metaphor, metonymy, synecdoche and irony : the parts of speech, onomatopoeism, interjection, pronoun, particle, noun and verb : the moods and tenses of the verb (in which connexion he refers to a case of aphasia observed by himself in Naples, "a gentleman seized with a severe apoplexy, who utters nouns but has completely forgotten verbs ") : the kinds of writing, hieroglyphic, symbolic and alphabetical : and of languages, according to their increasing complexity, from monosyllables to compound words and from a preponderance of vowels and diphthongs to a preponderance of consonants. In the course of these attempts he frequently offered new and sometimes correct interpretations of isolated facts : but he did not and could not connect them into a scientific system. Moreover he never realised the relation between poetry and the other arts. On the one hand, he unites them, as when he considers painting and poetry to be fundamentally identical and notes a number of analogies between the poetry and painting of the Middle Ages : on the other, he separates them sharply, as when he asserts that delicacy in art is the outcome of philosophy, and that painting, sculpture, casting and intaglio are the most delicate arts because they are compelled to abstract the surface of the material objects they represent.

These inconsistencies and errors which we have briefly reviewed are due partly to Vico's insufficient power of distinguishing and elaborating, partly—and this is the greater part—to that fundamental fault which we have already seen to exist in the structure of the New Science. In this case the fault is, more precisely, Vico's confusion between the philosophical concept of the poetic form of the mind, and the empirical concept of the barbaric form of civilisation. " This earliest age of the world," as he himself says, " can be truly said to have concerned itself exclusively with the primary activity of the mind." But the earliest age of the world, composed as it was of men of flesh and blood, not of philosophical categories, cannot have been concerned with one solitary activity of the mind. This single activity may have preponderated, as we generally say : the very word reveals the quantitative and approximative nature of the conception : but all the others must have been at work simultaneously, imagination and intellect, perception and abstraction, will and morality, song and arithmetic. Vico could not shut his eyes to this obvious fact, and introduced into this phase of civilisation not only the poet, but also the theologian, the physicist, the astronomer, the *pater-familias*, the warrior, the politician, and the lawgiver ; but he tried to regard the activities of all these as "poetical" in character, as he called it, by a metaphor drawn from the alleged preponderance of the imaginative form of the mind ; and the whole system he called " poetic wisdom." The metaphorical nature of the terminology is suggested, in fact leaps to the eye, in certain characteristic passages, as where the "arts," that is, the mechanical crafts which produce objects of practical utility, are called " poetry with a certain kind of reality," and where ancient Roman law, because of the abundance of formulae and ceremonies with which it was adorned, is said to be a "serious dramatic poem." But the metaphors are dangerous, since, as in the case of the New Science, they light upon a soil favourable to their growth into concepts : and in point of fact the historical phase of barbarism, metaphorically expressed as poetic wisdom, soon turned in Vico's mind into the ideal phase of poetry, and transferred all its own attributes to this ideal phase. The former included theologians, and accordingly Vico regarded poetry as theology, but an imaginative theology : teachers, and poetry became a teacher, but of the common people : natural scientists, and it became science, but the science of an imaginary world. And since these barbarians, uncultivated as they were and confined to the world of images, could not think in concepts, the imaginations of poetry, individualised and particular, and its judgments, always expressed in material form, were falsely interpreted as " imaginative universals," supposed to be something intermediate between the individualising intuition and the universalising concept. Poetry, which ought to represent sense and nothing else, came to represent a sense already intellectualised ; and the saying that nothing is found in the intellect that has not already been in the sense, acquired the meaning, that the intellect is nothing but the sense clarified, and the sense nothing but the intellect confused. Thus there was no further need for the added caution " except the intellect itself " (*nisi intellectus ipse*). Conversely, barbaric civilisation became a kind of mythological or allegorical representation of the ideal phase of poetry, and primitive tribes were transformed into crowds of " sublime poets " just as, in the ontogenesis corresponding to this philogenesis, children had been made into poets. The concept of the " imaginative universal " unites in itself the double contradiction of the doctrine ; since to the imaginative element must be joined, in this mental construction, the element of universality which taken by itself would be a true and proper universal, rational and not imaginative. Hence arises a *petitio principii* by which the origin of the rational universal, the point requiring explanation, is already presupposed. On the other hand, if the imaginative universal is interpreted as freed from the element of universality, that is, as a mere imagination, Vico's aesthetic doctrine would certainly become once more consistent : but his " poetic wisdom " or barbaric civilisation would be deprived of an indispensable portion of its organism in parting with every kind of concept : for concepts are, so to speak, the skeleton of the body.

To resolve the contradiction it was necessary to separate poetry from poetic wisdom : and we do find some signs of this separation in Vico. He sometimes admits, almost against his will, the lack of correspondence between the philosophical category and the type of society, and in dealing with the latter is compelled to fall back upon such phrases as " very nearly " and " more or less." He says, for instance, that primitive man consisted " exclusively of strong imagination, with no, or very little, reason " : that he was " almost all body, with hardly any reflection " : or again, after making a show of philosophical distinction between the three languages of gods, heroes and men, he goes on to observe that " the language of the gods was almost all dumb, and very little articulate ; the language of heroes was composed of equal quantities of articulation and dumb-show ; the language of men was almost all articulated, and very little in dumb-show." He admits again in a fine simile that poetic speech outlived poetic wisdom and survived far into the historic and civilised period, " as great and rapid rivers run far out into the sea and keep their waters fresh as they bear them along with the force of their flow." Even in modern times we cannot afford entirely to neglect imaginative speech : " to describe the operations of the pure mind, we must avail ourselves of poetic language, of metaphors drawn from the senses." It appears that poetry does not end with barbarism, for poets arise even in civilised times : and if it is said that the poets of the earliest times were naturally imaginative, those of later days artificially so, that is, according to Vico, by deliberately forgetting the proper use of words, freeing themselves from philosophy, filling their minds with childish and vulgar prejudices and submitting to the bondage of conventions like the use of rhyme—all these restrictions, besides being easily refuted, are merely an unsuccessful attempt to diminish the weight of the fact above mentioned, namely that poetry belongs to all ages, not merely to that of barbarism : it is an ideal category, not a historic fact. But the restrictions prove, as also do the infrequency and the unemphatic nature of the passages quoted, that Vico was not in a position to effect the separation of poetry from poetic wisdom, hampered as he was by the hybrid character of the concept and of the actual method of the New Science.

If, on the other hand, the idea of poetry as pure imagination had not remained firmly at the foundation of Vico's thought, in spite of all the confusions and inconsistencies in which it became involved, and had not been at work underground, so to speak, in the New Science, it would have been difficult or perhaps impossible to understand the leading conception which dominates his philosophy of mind, closely connected as it is with that idea. This is the conception of the mind as a development, or, to use Vico's own words, a progress or unfolding (*corso, spiegamento*) ; a conception which improved upon, though it did not explicitly contradict, the ordinary view which was almost exclusively confined to the enumeration and classification of the mind's faculties. The doctrine of imaginative universals as spontaneous mental products, rudimentary universals but not without an element of truth in them, was at least an adequate weapon against the empirical theory which made civilisation the outcome of a highly developed and rational practical wisdom and the personal labour of God or of wise men who must have sprung from the earth or fallen from heaven in some unaccountable manner.

Vico clearly stated the dilemma between the two, and only two, possible explanations of the origin of society. Either it came from the reflection of wise men, or from a certain human feeling and instinct among brutish men. He accepted the latter solution, that of " brutes " which gradually became human : the theory, that is, of the evolution of thought from the imaginative to the rational universal, and the progress of social relations from force to equity. But was this an adequate foundation for " ideal history " or the philosophy of mind ? In the philosophy of mind, it could be translated into a similar if not identical view—the doctrine which, owing to Cartesianism and a certain recrudescence of the Scholasticism of Duns Scotus, lasted down to Vico's own times and expressed the life of the mind by the successive stages of the concept, obscurity, confusion, clarity and distinctness. Leibniz, as is well known, made a special study of obscure and confused perceptions, the *"petites perceptions."* The doctrine was essentially intellectualistic, since the concepts, however confused or obscure, were never anything else than concepts : and hence it was unable to account either for poetry or even for mental development, the dialectic of which cannot be understood if it is regarded as consisting of merely quantitative differences. Such differences are in reality not differences at all, but identities and therefore the negation of change : and in fact the whole of this school of thought was anti-aesthetic and static, devoid both of a true theory of imagination and a true theory of development. Vico's thought, on the other hand, was averse to intellectualism and in sympathy with imagination: it was entirely dynamic and evolutionary. For Vico, mind is an eternal drama : and since drama demands antithesis, his philosophy of mind is rooted in antithesis, that is in the real distinction and opposition between imagination and thought, poetry and metaphysic, force and equity, passion and morality ; although he seems sometimes, for the reasons given above, to mistake its nature ; or rather, although he actually does sometimes confuse it with empirical inquiries and doctrines, and with the determinations of history.

CHAPTER V

THE SEMI-IMAGINATIVE FORM OF KNOWLEDGE
(MYTH AND RELIGION)

VICO's doctrine of mythology, while no less original and profound than that of poetry, is also, like the latter, not entirely lucid : for the relations between poetry and myth are so close that the shadow cast upon the one must of necessity extend to some degree over the other.

In proceeding to inquire, as we have hitherto done and shall continue to do, into the state of contemporary knowledge of the several sciences and problems with which Vico set out to deal, we may briefly recall *à propos* of the study of mythology not only the great literary collections of myths formed during the sixteenth and seventeenth centuries, of which Boccaccio had already given an example in the fourteenth century, but also the learned defences of the two explanatory theories, already known to classical antiquity and not entirely unknown in the Middle Ages. These were, first, the theory of myth as allegory of philosophical truths (moral, political and so forth), and secondly, the theory of myth as the history of actual persons and events, adorned by the fancy which made heroes into gods (Euhemerism). The former tendency inspired among other works the *Mythologiae sive explanationis fabularum libri decem* of Natale Conti (1568) and Bacon's *De sapientia veterum* (1609) ; in which, however, this system had been advanced with a certain hesitation, and with the explicit caution that, even if it were not valid as historical interpretation, it would always be of value as moralisation (*aut antiquitatem illustrabimus aut res ipsas* : " we shall explain either antiquity or the facts themselves "). The latter was authoritatively represented by John Leclerc (Clericus), the learned Dutch Genevese for whom Vico expressed so much respect and gratitude for the attention he had deigned to bestow upon his *Diritto universale*. His edition of Hesiod's *Theogony* marked an epoch in the study of mythology, and he was followed among others by Banier, author of the work *Les Fables expliquées par l'histoire* (1735). A third system, also not without some ancient precedent, derived myths from particular nations, the Egyptians or the Hebrews, or from the original works of individual philosophers and poets. This view, when it neither resolved itself into a pure and simple historical supposition as to the origin of some or all myths, nor appealed to divine revelation, clearly involved the theory that myth is not an eternal form but a contingent product of the mind, born at a certain time and capable of dying or already dead.

Vico strongly opposed the first and third of these views of mythology, namely the allegorical theory and that of historical derivation. On the allegorical view, he mentions Bacon's treatise, which had stimulated him to the study of the subject, but which he considered " more ingenious than sound " : on the other school, which regarded myths as sacred history altered and corrupted by the Gentiles and especially by the Greeks, he refers to Vossius's *De theologia gentili* (1642) and to a dissertation by Daniel Huet. Myths or fables do not contain esoteric wisdom, that is to say, rational concepts, subtly concealed by the veil of fable : hence they are not allegorical. Allegory implies on the one hand the concept or thing signified, on the other the fable or medium of concealment, and between the two, the art by which both are kept in equilibrium. But myths cannot be split up into these three moments, nor even into a thing signified and a thing which signifies it : their meaning is univocal. The theory also implies that a believer in the content does not believe in the form : but the makers of myths believed fully and ingenuously in their own work. Once, for instance, that first divine fable was created, the myth than which none greater was ever afterwards invented, that of Jupiter, king and father of gods and men, in the act of thundering, the very men who had invented him believed in him, and with their religion of terror feared, reverenced and worshipped him.

Myth, in a word, is not fable but history of such a kind as could be constructed by primitive minds, and strictly considered by them as an account of actual fact. The philosophers who arose later made use of myths to expound their doctrines in an allegorical manner ; or deceived themselves into thinking that they found them there owing to the feeling of veneration which attaches to antiquity, and increases as our comprehension of it diminishes ; or thought it expedient to make use of such things for political purposes, like Plato Homerising, and at the same time Platonising Homer : and in doing this they turned the myths into fables, which they were not originally, and are essentially not. Thus we may say that the philosophers and students of mythology who indulged in such strange fancies about the legends were the real poets, while the primitive poets or myth-makers were the true students, and intended to narrate the actual facts of their time. For the same reason, namely, because myth is an essential part of poetic or barbaric wisdom, and, as such, a spontaneous product of all times and places, it cannot be attributed to one single nation as its inventor, from which it passed to others ; as if it were a particular discovery of a particular man or the object of revelation.

This doctrine, superior as it is to the allegorical and historical theories, is another aspect of Vico's vindication of the non-logical forms of knowledge as against the intellectualism which denied them and merely represented them either as artificial forms or as due to supernatural causes. Nor does the opinion seem acceptable which attaches Vico to the Neo-Euhemeristic school. He does not indeed explicitly combat this school, and we may even grant that he presents certain superficial resemblances to it : but together with the resemblances there is this radical difference, that for Vico the stories are not alterations of actual history, but are essentially history ; their supposed alteration is the actual truth as it appeared to the primitive mind.

Vico did not and could not give a more precise determination of the nature of myth, precisely because owing to the fluctuating character of his concept of poetry itself he was not in a position to lay down the boundary between the two forms. He talks generally of poetry and myth as distinct things, but he does not establish the distinction. And yet Vico was familiar enough with the concept which supplies this distinctive criterion, and had enunciated it : but instead of using it for his doctrine of mythology, he had made of it one or more of his various definitions of poetry. That " poetic character," that " imaginative universal " whose introduction into aesthetic as the explanatory principle of poetry causes so many insuperable difficulties, is really the definition of mythology, and as such provides the science of mythology with the true principle that is required. If the concept of accomplishing great labours for the common welfare cannot be disengaged from the idea of a particular man who accomplished one of these labours, this concept becomes for instance the myth of Hercules : and Hercules is at once an individual man who does individual actions, and kills the Lernaean hydra and the Nemean lion or cleanses the stables of Augeas, and also a concept : just as the concept of beneficent and glorious labour is at once a concept and Hercules : a universal and an imaginary idea : an imaginative universal.

Again, that sublime task which Vico declared proper to poetry, the task of giving life to inanimate objects, belongs properly not to poetry but to myth.   Mythology, embodying its concepts in images, which are always individual things, at last animates them like living beings. Thus primitive man, ignorant of the cause of lightning and therefore not possessing the scientific definition of it, was led by the mythological tendency to conceive the sky as a vast living being, who, like man himself when, in the grip of his fierce passions, he shouted, muttered or roared, spoke and meant something by his speech.   It is mythology again, not poetry, whose origin must be traced to " poverty," to the weakness of men's minds and their inability to deal with the problems they would solve, in their incapacity for thinking in rational universals and expressing themselves in accurate language, whence arose imaginative universals and metonymy, synecdoche and metaphor of all kinds.   The contradictions we have seen in the imaginative universal which make it incapable of acting as the foundation of an aesthetic doctrine are quite in keeping in the doctrine of myth : for myth consists precisely of these contradictions : it is a concept trying to be an image and an image trying to be a concept, and hence a kind of poverty, or even of powerful impotence, —a contrast, a mental transition where white no longer exists and black has not yet come into being.   Finally, poetic wisdom, that is, the theology, science, cosmography, geography, astronomy and the whole system of other ideas and beliefs of primitive nations as Vico describes them, was really mythology, not, as he says, poetry, for the good reason, given by himself, that these things were their history : and poetry is poetry and not history, even more or less imaginary history. The Homeric poems are poetry in so far as they express the aspirations of Hellenism : the same poems, in so far as they were recited and heard as accounts of actual facts, are history : the two things being forms of mental products which, though they seem to be materially united in a single work, are not for that reason to be identified.

All this was both seen and not seen, or rather, sometimes realised and sometimes overlooked, by Vico : and hence he cannot be said to have succeeded in determining satisfactorily the distinction, and solving the problem of the relation, between mythology and poetry. Another problem of importance relating to the science of mythology, and still the subject of controversy, namely, the question whether myth belongs to philosophy or to history, might be supposed to have been decisively solved by Vico : since he repeats over and over again that myths contain the historical judgments of primitive peoples, not the philosophical. But in reality when we examine the point closely it appears that he neither solved the problem nor even propounded it. The historical judgments of which Vico is speaking are contrasted strictly not with philosophical judgments in general but with the " mystical judgments of the earliest philosophy " and the " judgments of analogy " which the writers criticised by Vico found in mythology. Thus on the one hand his words repeat the criticism of the allegorical theory and, on the other, controvert that fallacious method of historical interpretation which ascribes the ideas and customs of to-day to the nations of antiquity. The fact is that Vico's theory is just as much in agreement with the theory connecting myth with philosophy as with that which connects it with history ; and as much with the eclecticism which admits both these elements as with the speculative

view which also admits them both, but because philosophy
and history both in themselves and as constituents of
myth are at bottom one and the same.

Considered as " poverty," myth must be superseded.
In the natural effort of the human mind to rejoin God,
the true One, from whom it has come, and its inability
owing to the exuberant animal nature of primitive man
to make use of the faculty, buried as it is beneath his
too keen senses, of abstracting from subjects their properties and universal forms,—in these circumstances, it
constructs for itself fanciful unities, imaginary genera
or myths : but in its subsequent progress and development, it gradually resolves the imaginary genera into
intelligible genera, poetic universals into rational, and
sets itself free from mythology. Thus the error of myth
passes into the truth of philosophy. Vico knew and
employed a concept of error, error properly so called,
which proceeds from the will, not from thought, which
is never in error as regards itself, " for the mind is
always put under compulsion by truth, since we can
never lose sight of God " (*mens enim semper a vero urgetur
quia numquam aspectu amittere possumus Deum*) ; the
error which consists in the arbitrary conjunction of un-
meaning words, " but words very often, by the will of
him who is lying, escape the force of truth and desert the
mind, or even do violence to the mind and turn away
from God " (*verba autem saepissime veri vim voluntate
mentientis eludunt ac mentem deserunt, immo menti vim
aciunt et Deo absistunt*) ; the error, in a word, which
exists when, in his own powerful language, " though men
speak with their mouth, they have nothing in their minds ;
since within their minds there is falsity, which is nothing."
But he also knows that error is never pure error, simply
because there is no such thing as a false idea and falsity
consists only in the wrong combination of ideas, and
therefore it always contains truth, and every fable has

a certain element of truth. Hence, far from despising
fables, Vico recognised their value as embryonic forms
so to speak of stored-up knowledge or of what will one
day develop into philosophy. The poets (which means,
in Vico's new sense of the word, myth-makers) are the
senses (that is, in its new meaning, rudimentary and
imperfect philosophy) : the philosophers are the intellect
of mankind, that is the more highly developed philosophy
which derives from the former. The idea of God evolves
by degrees from the God who strikes the imagination of
the isolated man, to the God of the family, *divi parentum*,
the God of a social class or country, *divi patrii*, the God
of nations, and finally to the God " who is Jupiter to all
men," the God of humanity. The fables stimulated
Plato to understand the three divine punishments which
not men but only gods could inflict, oblivion, infamy
and remorse : the passage through the lower world
suggested to him the concept of the purgatorial journey
by which the soul is purified of passions, and the arrival
in Elysium suggested the journey of union by which the
mind comes to unite itself with God by the contemplation
of the eternal divine ideas.

From the similes and metaphors of the poets Aesop
drew the examples and fables by which he gave advice :
and the instance founded upon a single case which satisfies
an untutored mind developed into induction, drawing
its validity from several similar cases, as taught dialectic-
ally by Socrates, and thence the syllogism invented by
Aristotle, which cannot exist without a universal. The
etymologies of words reveal the truths observed by
primitive man and deposited by him in his language :
for instance the fact, laboriously proved by modern
philosophers, that the senses themselves create the so-
called sensible qualities is already suggested in the Latin
word *olfacere*, which implies the idea that the sense
of smell " makes " the odour. Vico attaches such im-

portance to this connexion between poetic universals and
rational universals, between myth and philosophy, that
he is led to assert that such judgments of philosophers
as cannot find parallel or precedent in poetic and popular
wisdom must be wrong.   Here we have another meaning
sometimes assigned by him to the relation of philosophy
to philology: namely, a reciprocal confirmation of common
wisdom by esoteric wisdom and *vice versa*, both of
which are united in the idea of an everlasting philosophy
of man.

Simultaneously with his theory of myth and its
relation to philosophy, Vico expounds his theory of
religion, and the relation it bears to philosophy.   Two
thoughts on this subject are to be found up and down
the New Science.   The first is, that religion arises in the
phase of weakness and savagery from the mind's need
to allay its desire to understand more or less the
phenomena of nature and man; for instance, to explain
lightning.   The second is, that religion is produced in
the mind by fear of the person who threatens by lightning.
We might describe these two views as theories respectively
of the theoretical and practical origin of religion ; and
since according to Vico's doctrine man consists of nothing
but intellect and will, clearly religion can have no other
origin than these two.   Now, setting aside religion in its
practical aspect, to be discussed later, religion in its
theoretical aspect is surely nothing else than the imaginative universal, poetic animism, or myth.   To it belongs
the institution which Vico calls divination ; that is, the
methods of collecting and interpreting the language of
Jupiter, the " real words," gestures and signs of God,
formed as imaginative universals and created by the
animating fancy.   And as from myth come science and
philosophy, so in like manner from divination comes the
knowledge of ground and cause, philosophic or scientific
prediction.

In this way Vico escaped the prejudice which was beginning to prevail in his time—we may recall Van Dale's history of ancient oracles, popularised by Fontenelle, and Banier's book already mentioned—and was to be so powerful for a century, of considering religions as " some one else's imposture " : whereas, he says, they were really due to " one's own credulity." The man who refused to admit the artificial origin of myth could not admit it of religion. But just as he denied no less the supernatural or revealed origin of myth, so at the same time he proclaimed neither more nor less than the natural, even the human, origin of religions ; and—a fact especially worthy of notice—placed this origin in an inadequate form of the mind, namely the semi-imaginative form identical with mythology. Nor need we attach weight to certain brief and incidental remarks which seem to contradict this theory, as when he says that religion precedes not only philosophy but language itself, which presupposes the consciousness of some community between man and man : such equivocations are due to the invariable confusedness of his method and his habitual lack of clearness. The identification of religion with myth, and its human origin, are ideas not only emphatically expressed, but essential to Vico's whole system. It is a human origin which in his own words does not exclude a different concept of religion, namely as revealed and hence of supernatural origin. In fact he always separates poetic theology, which is mythology, and natural theology, which is metaphysics or philosophy, from revealed theology. But this last concept is admitted by him not because it is connected with the others and derived from a principle common to them, but simply because Vico asserted its existence no less than theirs. The human origin, poetic theology, followed by metaphysical theology, is the form valid for the Gentile portion of mankind, that is the whole human race except the Hebrew people with its privilege of revelation. The motives that led Vico to maintain this dualism and the annoying inconsistencies in which it compelled him to rest will be seen later on in their own place. But precisely because Vico left this dualism without mediation, we must in expounding his thought hold fast both terms of the dualism : and for the time being we will confine ourselves to the merely human origin—religion as a product of the theoretical needs of man in a condition of comparative moral poverty. This conception has only an indirect connexion with Bruno's view of religion as a thing necessary to the ignorant and undeveloped mob, and with Campanella's theory of natural or permanent religion, an eternal rational philosophy coinciding with a Christianity freed from its abuses. Its parallels in contemporary authors are few and distant : even when they mention it in passing, they grasp it only in a superficial way and propound it without connecting it at all with their other ideas : they attack religion as a form of ignorance, and omit the wisdom of the ignorance, or religion as truth.

CHAPTER VI

THE MORAL CONSCIOUSNESS

VICO's other doctrines on the theoretical reason, that is to say on the logic of philosophy, of physical and mathematical science and of historical study, have been expounded above in the statement of his theory of knowledge, and are drawn almost entirely from his early works, since in the New Science the phase of the " completely developed mind " hardly appears except as a limit of the field of study. Here it will suffice to mention that he also touches upon the problem of the relation of poetry to history : but, still because of the confusion of philosophy with social science, he fails fully to solve it. From one point of view it seems to Vico that history is prior to poetry, because the latter, as he says, presupposes reality and contains an " imitation of the second degree " : from another, poetry is the primary form, because among primitive peoples history is poetry, and the first historians are poets. At any rate he insists upon the poetic element essential to history : of Herodotus, the father of Greek history, he observes that not only are " his books full, for the most part, of fables," but " the style retains a very great Homeric element, a feature which all subsequent historians retained, using as they did a phraseology intermediate between the poetic and the colloquial " : " almost the words of the poets," *verba ferme poetarum,* as he says elsewhere in a phrase borrowed from Cicero.

73

Nor are the relations between theory and practice, intellect and will, explained in detail by Vico, although on the whole he suggests the general idea that as in God intellect and will coincide, so it is in man, God's image ; whose mind is not divided into thought and will—thought proceeding according to one method and will according to another—but his thought and will interpenetrate and form one single whole : a view far superior to that of the contemporary philosophy of Leibniz, which retained the idea of a divine arbitrament and therefore of irrationality. Another view, peculiar to Vico, might be taken by a hasty interpreter to imply the priority of practice to theory. He says that philosophers arrive at their conceptions thanks to experience of social institutions and laws in which men agree as a kind of universals : that Socrates and Plato, for instance, presupposed the Athenian democracy and law-courts.   But the succession of religions producing republics, republics producing laws, and laws producing philosophical ideas, which he calls " a fragment of the history of philosophy philosophically narrated," is really a theory of sociological, not of philosophical value.

As regards his doctrines of practical reason, which we are here beginning to consider, it might be thought that Vico, unlike his attitude with regard to the theoretical reason, did not stand in sharp opposition to the thought of his time, but actually united himself with a contemporary movement, namely the school of natural rights. The head of the school and leader of the movement, Hugo Grotius, was called by Vico one of his " four authors," together with Plato, from whom he had drawn his aspirations towards an idealistic philosophy, Bacon, who had aroused in his mind the idea of a positive and historical science of society, and Tacitus, his debt to whom, or at least the debt which he believed he owed him, we shall examine later on.   Along with Grotius he frequently mentions the other chief authorities on natural rights, Selden and Puffendorf, omitting their innumerable followers, whom he considers less as scientific authorities than as " adorners "of the Grotian system.

His adherence to the school, in a certain sense, is clear, and is admitted and proclaimed by Vico himself. But it is also beyond doubt that he was no mere adherent : he was not a follower of the kind that retains the general or leading ideas while developing and correcting details. He was a follower in the dialectical sense only, that is, in so far as he thought it necessary to contest the primary theses, or to accept them only in a profoundly modified form. Natural right offered him not solutions but problems: and of these, while some came before him already clearly formulated, others, and these were the more important, arose only in his own mind : problems either unsolved or unrealised, till Vico propounded and in part solved them.

Natural rights presented many aspects and many tendencies : and it would be well to begin by distinguishing and enumerating these. In the first place, the school taken as a whole and in its essential character expressed the social progress by which Europe, on emerging from feudalism and religious warfare, acquired a new consciousness, distinctively bourgeois and non-clerical in character ; and it observed that the growth of this consciousness was contemporaneous with the anti-clerical and bourgeois institution of " masonry." The word "natural" meant, among other things, "not supernatural": and hence implied hostility or indifference towards the supernatural, the institutions representing it, and the social conflicts resulting from it. It was not by accident that Grotius was an Arminian ; that Puffendorf went to law with theologians ; that Thomasius is remembered as one of the champions of freedom of conscience. The protestations of respect for religion and the church, habitually and liberally inserted by these publicists in their works,—which are draped, so to speak, with a veil of piety,—were merely politic safeguards, enabling the author to threaten the enemy unobserved and to strike from under cover. This caution is praised, in Grotius's case for example, by a follower of the school (the author of *Pauco plenior iuris naturalis historia*, 1719), who extols the master as "the instrument of divine providence," coming like Messiah to redeem the "natural light" from its bondage to the "supernatural," and as such gifted with all the power and ability he could need : so that after tasting the persecutions of Scholasticism, "he behaved with caution, to avoid further irritating the jealousy against his natural and reasonable prudence that had issued forth from its lair at his threats" (*caute versabatur . . . ne maius bilem adversus prudentiam naturalem et rationalem ex latebris productam tam minis irritaret*), and in proceeding to separate human from divine laws, did not execute a frontal assault on the theological school when he attacked its fundamental errors, but even praised it in the preface to his work. The word "natural" also denoted what is common to individuals of different nations and ranks : and hence from a practical point of view provided an admirable war-cry for uniting the bourgeoisie of different countries in definite common aspirations and struggles. The treatises of natural rights were for the bourgeoisie of the seventeenth and eighteenth centuries what the "Manifesto of the communists" and the cry "Proletariates of the world, unite" attempted to be for the working classes of the nineteenth.

In so far as this school and this publicism were signs of a practical movement, the philosophical interest held in them a secondary place and discharged a function of minor importance : so that, secondly, the works on natural right, philosophically considered, did not as a rule rise above a simple popular empiricism. The principles on which they rest are not examined and often

not even superficially reconciled : the concepts which
they use are less concepts than general representations :
and the form of the writing is systematic in appearance
only. Some of these writers endeavoured to harmonise
their doctrines of natural right with the Platonic, Stoic
or Cartesian philosophies, or appealed to logical or metaphysical axioms, or made use of deduction and the mathematical method. But all this was mere aggregation,
not fusion; ornament, not reinforcement : at most, it
was of value as a proof of diligence and earnest intentions.

The philosophy, however, which was more or less
implicit in the pamphleteers of natural rights, and explicit
in the philosophers who set out to elaborate the doctrine,
agreed with the spirit of the time, whose general characteristics are well known. Thus arose the third or ethical aspect
of natural right, namely its utilitarianism ; sometimes
more or less concealed, sometimes openly declared, and
worked out from time to time by a philosophy of mathematical or sensationalistic methods, and of materialistic
or rationalistic tendencies : or else, what comes practically
to the same thing, an abstract and intellectualistic
morality, threatening at any moment to fall into utilitarianism. From this intellectualism and utilitarianism,
combined with the practical and revolutionary character
of this mental movement,—which was bent rather upon
bringing about the triumph of an abstract system of right
than upon recognising that which really develops in
history, in all the complexity of its many forms and
vicissitudes—derived its fourth characteristic, the lack of
historical sense, or the anti-historical attitude of the school,
which set up the abstract ideal of a human nature apart
from human history instead of fused with and living
in it.

Finally, bourgeois, anticlerical, utilitarian and materialistic as it was, the movement of natural right had a fifth
important trait, namely its aversion to transcendence

and its tendency towards an immanental conception of man and of society.   This characteristic is neither fully explained nor fully worked out in the doctrines, but is none the less easily recognised among the total views of the school.

Now Vico's genius was truly and indeed exclusively theoretical, and not at all practical or reformatory : his method was profoundly speculative and contemptuous of empiricism, his mind idealistic and opposed to materialism and utilitarianism : his theory of knowledge eager for the concrete, for " certitude," and, as such, of historical sympathies.   Consequently his doctrine of the practical reason, though deriving its impetus from the theory of natural rights, was bound to emerge in a shape different from or even contrary to that theory in all the first four characteristics enumerated above.   And if it did in one respect coincide—which it only does in the conclusion, not in the path by which the conclusion is reached—it did so in the very point in which Vico would least have wished it : in its immanental or anti-religious tendency.

But since our subject is not the criticisms and modifications which the theory of natural right received from Vico's thought, but rather that thought itself, it is time to pick up the thread of the exposition, following an order somewhat different from that in which we have summed up the various characteristics of the theory, and beginning by observing Vico's opposition to the professed or implicit utilitarianism of the school, and the ethical doctrine by which he replaced it.

The two chief representatives of utilitarianism in the seventeenth century, whom Vico always keeps in view, are Hobbes and Spinoza : but in addition to them, he refers to Locke and Bayle and, in the preceding century, Machiavelli ; and going back to the ancients, the Stoics with their conception of faith and the Epicureans with that of chance, Carneades and his scepticism, and finally the

unconscious theory contained in the saying " *Vae victis* "
attributed to Brennus, chief of the Gauls who took Rome.
He admired Hobbes's splendid attempt to enrich philosophy by a theory which had been lacking to the greatest
days of Greece, the theory of man considered in the
whole society of the human race : but he pronounced the
result unsatisfactory, and the attempt, whose outcome,
like that of Locke's system, was hardly distinguishable
from Epicureanism, a failure.   Hobbes did not observe
that he could never have propounded his problem of the
natural rights of mankind had not his motive been supplied
by the Christian religion itself, which commands not
indeed justice but charity to all mankind.   With the Stoics
on the other hand, with the fatalism and determinism
which made it impossible for them to reason soundly about
the state and laws, with the so-called " Spinozists of
antiquity," he ideally united Spinoza ; the uniqueness of
whose utilitarianism, equally removed from the Lockian
spirit and the Hobbist, since Spinoza " judges of the truth
of things by the mind, not by sense " (*mente non sensu de
veris rerum diiudicat*), did not escape Vico's notice.   But
unique though it was, it led Spinoza to think of the state
in a somewhat undignified way " as of a mere society of
shopkeepers."   These utilitarian doctrines, with their
libels upon human nature, seemed to Vico only fit for men
without hope, too insignificant ever to have a share in
the state or proud enough to believe themselves repressed
and denied access to the positions of which in their arrogance they thought themselves worthy.   Among these he
counted the unfortunate Spinoza, who, he thinks, having
as a Jew no country of his own, was moved by envy to
devote himself to the construction of a metaphysic
" intended to overthrow all the nations of the world."
He passes stern judgment upon the state of contemporary
ethics, which was all that it could be on the basis of a
mechanistic and materialistic metaphysic without a gleam

of finalism. Descartes produced nothing at all in this field, since his few written remains on the subject do not amount to a doctrine, and his treatise of the Passions belongs rather to medicine than to morals. Malebranche and Nicole were equally sterile, and Pascal's *Pensées*, the one exception, are " but scattered lights." Of the Italians, Pallavicino's treatise *Del bene* offers no very profound depths of ethics : and Muratori's attempt in his *Filosofia Morale* was a very unsuccessful one.

Utility is not the explanatory principle of morality, because it proceeds from man's bodily nature, and on that account is subject to change, while morality, *honestas*, is eternal. To derive morality from utility is to confound the occasion with the cause, to confine oneself to the surface and to offer no explanation at all of the facts. None of the various modes in which philosophers have successively called the utilitarian principle to life, fraud or imposture, force, desire,—none of these accounts for differentiation, that is, for the social organism. What fraud could ever have seduced and deceived the supposed simple and frugal first owners of the land, living as they did perfectly contented with their lot ? What force could have succeeded, if the rich, the alleged usurpers, were few, and the poor, the robbed, were many ? Such explanations are ridiculous, and unworthy of a serious problem. These strong and powerful men were really powerful with something other than mere strength : thus they became protectors of the weak and enemies of destructive and anti-social tendencies : their rule was one of force, it is true, but " imposed by a more powerful character " (*a natura praestantiori dictata*) ; a fact which the barbarian Brennus may be pardoned for not knowing, but not so a philosopher. The force which created and organised the earliest states was nothing but " noble human nature," to which states must always hark back, although they may have been won by fraud and force, in order to

subsist and maintain themselves : which agrees with
Machiavelli's advice to hark back to the beginnings,
but with the implication that the deepest beginnings are
to be found in mercy and justice.   Men are held together
by something stouter than utility.   Human society cannot
originate and endure without mutual trust ; unless people
accept each other's promises and take each other's word for
facts they cannot examine.   Could this trust be perhaps
ensured by strict penal laws against falsehood ?   But
laws are a product of society, and this mutual trust is
necessary that society may arise.   It may be said, as it
is by Locke, that we are dealing with a psychological
process, by which men gradually acquired the habit of
believing when some one spoke to them and promised to
tell the truth.   But in that case these men already understood the idea of a truth which by mere disclosure compelled assent without any personal teaching ; and the
psychological principle of habituation is transcended.

The true cause of human society then is not utility,
which only assists the action of the cause as its occasion,
and brings it about that men, with all the weakness
and poverty of their nature, and the divisions among
them due to original sin, are led to extol their social
nature " under compulsion of facts " (*rebus ipsis dictan-
tibus*), in the phrase of the jurist Pomponius, quoted with
approval by Vico.   Objects, facts and circumstances in
morality change, though morality itself does not change :
and hence arises the illusion of the utilitarians, who cling
to the external, confine themselves to the appearance and
see the change but not the permanence.   Murder is forbidden : but the approval, bestowed upon the man who
when his life is threatened and he cannot otherwise save
himself kills his unjust aggressor, does not imply that the
moral judgment upon homicide varies ; since in these
particular circumstances the case is really one not of
homicide but of capital punishment inflicted by the

unjustly attacked person finding himself alone : a power
tacitly delegated to him so to speak by society.   Theft is
forbidden : but the man who in order to preserve his life
steals a loaf from another does not violate morality because
he is exercising a right founded upon equity.

The only philosophy which carries with it a true ethic
seems to Vico to be the Platonic, resting as it does upon
a metaphysical principle, the eternal idea which draws
out of itself and creates matter : while the Aristotelian
ethic is founded upon a metaphysic leading to a physical
principle, that of the matter from which particular forms
are drawn, a principle which makes God a potter shaping
objects external to himself.   The ethic of the Roman
lawyers was doubtless rich in fine aphorisms : but it was
nothing but a mere art of equity, conveyed by means of
endless minute maxims of natural justice, sought for by
the writers in the reason of the laws and the will of the
lawgiver.   Hence it cannot be regarded as a moral
philosophy, in which the best method is to proceed from a
very small number of eternal truths, established by ideal
justice in the fabric of metaphysic.   For analogous
reasons Vico could not rest satisfied with Grotius and the
school of natural rights : of which in general he makes
the perfectly just remark that their ponderous tomes, in
spite of the impressive titles they bear, contain nothing
that is not universally known.   If Grotius's principles be
weighed in the accurate balance of criticism, they are all
found to be probable or plausible rather than necessary
and incontestable.   In dealing with the question of utility,
Grotius missed the exact point by failing to distinguish
the occasion from the cause : nor did he " nail down "—
that is, he did not end—the ancient dispute as to whether
right is a question of nature or of human opinion only,
the same controversy as that carried on by philosophers
and theologians with Carneades the sceptic and Epicurus :
he advances the hypothesis of primitive men who were

" simpletons," but quite omits to give reasons for it. And since these " simpletons " of his, after suffering injuries from their beast-like isolation, initiated a sociable life, a step to which they were determined by utility, Grotius himself slipped unawares into utilitarianism and Epicureanism.

Vico on the other hand answered the question, whether right is natural or conventional, by the grave aphorism " except in their natural condition, things neither progress nor endure." To the question, whence society arises, he replies by mentioning the common feeling of humanity, the conscience, the need which man feels of escaping from the internal enemy, which tortures his heart. The origin of society certainly lies in fear, but it is fear of oneself, not of another's violence : it lies in the agonies of remorse, the shame whose tinge suffusing the cheeks of the earliest men lit the first beacon of morality upon earth. Shame is the mother of all virtues, honour, frugality, honesty, loyalty to the pledged word, truthfulness in speech, abstention from others' property, and chastity. In extolling society, man is extolling human nature.

Shame or the moral consciousness, translated into terms of the corresponding empirical science, becomes that common consciousness of man upon matters of human necessity or utility which is the source of the natural right of nations. This common consciousness, says Vico, is an unreflective judgment, felt in common by a whole class, a whole people, a whole nation and the whole of mankind. An unreflective judgment is not strictly a judgment at all, since reflection is inseparable from judgment : it is not judgment, because it is felt and not thought. But on the other hand it is not what is called a " feeling,"—a vague term unknown to Vico, as it is to traditional philosophy. It is rather a practical attitude of mind, similar on the whole in persons living in similar conditions and producing similar customs in the various social groups, from the customs of a particular class to those of all mankind,   The attitude is quite spontaneous, and for this very reason unreflective ; so that customs arise from within, not from without, and their similarity does not depend upon imitation (" without one nation taking example from another "). Through this *sensus communis* the moral consciousness embodies itself in compact and unyielding institutions : and thus the *sensus communis* reduces to certitude the free will of man, which is in itself quite uncertain.

CHAPTER VII

MORALITY AND RELIGION

BUT this internal fear, shame or moral consciousness is
aroused in man by religion. The fear is the fear of God,
the shame is abasement before his face. Primitive man
wanders over the earth alone, wild, fierce, without articulate
speech, without a permanent mate, at the mercy of his
unbridled and violent passions, a " brute " rather than
a man. What can restrain him ? what can rescue him
from at last destroying himself ? Wise men cannot
direct him, for we cannot say whence or how they
can reach him. The intervention of God cannot
save him : God has withdrawn himself to his chosen
people, and has no dealings with the rest of mankind,
the Gentiles. But this " brute " is still a man : God,
while abandoning him, has left a spark of his own essence
at the bottom of his heart. See ! the sky lightens : the
wild creature stands awestruck and afraid : in his mind
arises the shadowy idea of something greater than he,
something divine. So he conceives or rather imagines
a first God, a Sky-god, a thundering Jupiter : and to this
deity he turns to appease his wrath or invoke his aid.
But in order to conciliate him and secure his help, he must
shape his own life conformably to his purpose : he must
humble himself before his God, overcome his own pride
and arrogance, abstain from certain actions and perform
others. Thus the conception of a deity lends power to

85

that peculiar possession of the human will, the attempt, that is, the liberty, to control the movements communicated to the mind by the body and to annul or to redirect them simultaneously. With these acts of self-control, with freedom, morality comes into existence : the fear of God has laid the foundations of human life. Altars arise all over the earth : the caves of her mountains, whither the man now bears the woman, ashamed as he is of gratifying his desires before the face of the sky, which is the face of God, preside at the first marriage-rites and shelter the first families : her bosom opens to receive the sacred trust of the bodies of the dead. The first and fundamental ethical institutions—worship, wedlock and burial—have arisen.

This social and ethical power of the idea of God appears again in the course of subsequent history : since when nations have relapsed into savagery through warfare, and human laws have no more power over them, religion is the only means of subduing them. It reappears again in the individual development of human life : children indeed cannot learn piety except through the fear of some deity ; and when all natural help fails him man requires a superior being to save him, and this being is God. All nations believe in a divine providence : tribes living in a society without any consciousness of God, for instance in some parts of Brazil, among the Kafirs, and in the Antilles, are travellers' tales, an attempt to increase the sale of their books by the narration of portents.

If this is so,—and doubtless it is—then no doctrine can be more foolish than that which claims to conceive a morality and civilisation without religion. Just as no well-established physical science is possible without the guidance of abstract mathematical truth, so no knowledge of morality can arise except together with abstract metaphysical truths, without, that is, the idea of God. When the religious consciousness is extinguished or obscured the conception of society and the state is extinguished or obscured with it.   Jews, Christians, Gentiles and Mahommedans possess this conception because all alike believe in some deity, whether as an infinite free spirit, or as several gods consisting of mind and body, or as one single God, an infinite free spirit in an infinite body.   The Epicureans did not possess such a conception, attributing to God as they did body alone, and chance together with body : nor did the Stoics, who made him subject to fate. And Cicero made the admirable remark to the Epicurean Atticus, that he could not discuss laws with him unless he first granted the existence of the divine providence. Hobbes, who revived Epicureanism, and Spinoza, who revived Stoicism, as we have seen entirely failed to understand the nature of society and the state.   One must consort with primitive man, stupid, hirsute, unclean and dishevelled, to refute those learned authors of " desiccated literature," with Peter Bayle at their head, who maintain that human society can and indeed does live without religion.

The absence of the idea of God supplied the chief argument in Vico's criticism of Grotius and Puffendorf, two of these authors whom he held in great honour as " princes " of the school of natural rights.   Neither of these writers, he says, lays down the principle of divine providence as primary and essential.   Grotius does not expressly deny it : but on account of his very attachment to truth, he endeavours to exclude it, and asserts that his system will stand even if all knowledge of God be removed. Hence Vico accuses him of Socinianism, since he makes human innocence consist in the simplicity of human nature.   Puffendorf is still worse : he seems to ignore providential direction, and begins with the scandalously Epicurean supposition that man is thrown into this world with no help or attention from God, without even that spark within his heart which is destined to grow into the flame of morality : and having been reproved for this, he tries to justify himself in a special essay, but does not succeed in discovering the true principle on which alone society can be explained.

Now why, in face of all these energetic declarations and arguments of Vico's on the necessity of religion to morality, did we say above that the only point of real resemblance between him and Grotius, Puffendorf and the natural-right school generally was his purely immanental conception of ethics ? Because, if we examine the point closely, Vico is not in opposition to the method of that school. Like them, in constructing his science of human society he excludes with Grotius all idea of God, and with Puffendorf considers man as without help or attention from God, excluding him, that is, from revealed religion and its God. As for these two writers, so for Vico the subject under consideration is natural rights, not supernatural : the law of the Gentiles, not of the chosen people : the law which arises of itself among the caves, not that which comes down from Sinai. Vico's opposition, which he expresses with his accustomed confusion and obscurity, turns not upon assertions like these, but upon the actual conception of religion. In one word, the religion of which he speaks is not the same as that of which Grotius and Puffendorf spoke, or rather did not speak.

Religion, as we have already seen, means for Vico not necessarily revelation, but conception of reality : either that which expresses itself as it does in the period of fully developed mind in the form of intelligible metaphysic, which passes from the thought of God to explain logic by its reasoning and to condescend to purify the human heart by morality : or that which takes concrete shape, as it does in the earliest stage of humanity, in the form of poetical metaphysics. One may easily ignore revealed religion when inquiring into the foundations of morality : but how can one ever ignore this natural religion, identical as it is with knowledge of the truth ? Plutarch, discussing the primitive religions of terror, asks the question whether it would not have been better, instead of worshipping the gods in so impious a manner, that there should be no religion at all : but he forgot that from these cruel superstitions brilliant civilisations developed, and no civilisation could ever have grown from atheism. Without a religion, whether gentle or fierce, rational or fantastic, to give the idea, more or less clearly defined, more or less elevated, of something superior to the individual and uniting all individuals, the moral will would have no object for its volition.

At this point we see the meaning of what we have described as the second, practical or ethical, signification of the word " religion " in Vico. In this signification, Vico justifies and vindicates the impious saying that " fear creates the gods " : he even places the source of religion in the longing for eternal life which man feels when stirred by a universal sense of immortality hidden in the depths of the mind. In this second signification, religion is a practical fact, indeed it is morality itself, as in the first meaning it was truth itself.

If the meaning of religion for Vico, either as the condition of morality, in the first sense of the word, or as synonymous with it, in the second, is once understood, it is clear that when he condemned Grotius and Puffendorf for their omission of this most important concept, he was substantially doing nothing but clenching his criticism of the insipid moralising and the concealed utilitarianism of these two thinkers. On other occasions also he resorted to the valuable weapon of the concept of religion, with the same end in view. Because if he sometimes credited philosophy with the task of assisting mankind by raising and directing fallen human nature, at other times he decided that philosophy is rather adapted to reasoning, and that the moral philosophers with the greatest powers of reasoning are of value only to stimulate the senses by their eloquence to perform the duties of virtue, while religion alone has the power of making men act virtuously. Then in the empirical science corresponding to this part of the philosophy of mind, Vico turns religion (or poetical metaphysic) and philosophy into two historical epochs, making the former characteristic of the barbaric period and the latter of the civilised. He maintains, as he is clearly bound to do, that religion is the sole foundation of all civilisation and of philosophy itself, and rejects Polybius's saying that if there had been philosophers in the world religion would have been unnecessary. How could philosophy have arisen, he objects, had not states, that is, civilisation, arisen first ? and how could states have arisen without the aid of religion ? Thus the saying ought to be reversed : without religion there is no philosophy. It was religion, it was the divine providence that tamed the sons of Polyphemus and reduced them to the humanity of Aristides and Socrates, of Laelius and Scipio Africanus.

The conception again of the " state of nature," which served in the treatises of the school of natural rights as an hypothesis and a means of exposition with a view either to developing the argument independently of mystical theology without evoking too many protests, or to conveying implicitly their utilitarian theories, acquired in Vico's hands a new function and a new content. A perfectly honest Catholic, having satisfied his conscience by separating revealed from human religion, he was in a position to assume the state of nature as a literal and actual reality. It is an ideal reality, in so far as it represents in the dialectic of the practical consciousness a moment necessary for the genesis of reality, the pre-moral moment : a historical and empirical reality, as the approximately actual condition of those periods of anarchy and disturbance which precede the rise of civilisations or follow upon their fall. The natural-right school acquiesced more or less in the traditional doctrine of the church, namely that the Gentiles, in the dispersion following on the confusion of Babel, had taken away with them a residuum of revealed religion, a vague memory of the true God, and that hence arose the possibility of social life and of false gods, shadows of the true God : and thus the " state of nature " had been put forward in their system as something abstract and unreal. Vico worked out strictly the distinction between Jews and Gentiles, and conceived the state of nature as devoid of any help coming from previous revelation : as a state in which man stood alone, so to speak, face to face with his own chaotic and turbulent passions. It was a state actually without morality, but — in contradistinction to the utilitarian hypothesis—pregnant with moral requirements, and was transcended by this implicit character becoming explicit. But this transcendence was brought about naturally, not by means of divine grace : the true divine grace is human nature itself, shared by Gentiles no less than Jews, all equally illuminated by a divine light.

Man's will is free, weak though it is, to make his passions into virtues ; and in his struggle towards virtue he is helped in a natural manner by God through providence. Certainly Vico did not intend to deny the efficacy of direct and personal divine grace as well : but following his usual method he separates the latter from the natural operation of providence, which is the only question of importance for him and the only one he considers. So far as concerns the controversies on grace, he always likes to maintain a middle position between two extremes represented typically, according to him, by Pelagianism and Calvinism : and ever since as a young man he studied the works of Richard, the theologian of the Sorbonne, he had accepted his demonstration of the superiority of the Augustinian doctrine, just because it was intermediate

between these extremes. A moderate doctrine of this
kind seemed to him, as he says, to provide a suitable
foundation for a principle of the natural rights of nations
which should explain the origin of Roman and other
Gentile law, while at the same time remaining in agreement
with the Catholic religion. He was inclined to admit
that there was a privileged nation, namely the Jewish ;
and that in the struggle against the passions the Christian
had an advantage over the non-Christian, because in cases
where natural grace failed he might be helped by supernatural. But, in a word, miracles are miracles, and the
New Science is not a science of the miraculous.

That it is not, is proved by Vico's criticism on the
third of the " principles " of natural rights, against John
Selden, a famous man in his day though forgotten later,
and author of *De iure naturali et gentium iuxta disciplinam
Hebraeorum* (1640). Selden disagreed with Grotius, in
this as in certain other questions, in not denying, and
even in exalting, the value of religion : he conceived moral
and civil life impossible for mankind except through
revelation. This revelation, made by God to the Jewish
people, passed from them according to Selden by several
channels to the Gentiles : Pythagoras for instance had
learnt from Ezekiel; Aristotle, at the time of the campaigns
of Alexander in Asia, formed a friendship with Simon the
Just ; Numa Pompilius acquired some knowledge of the
Bible and the prophets. This was enough to reassure
any believer who had been frightened away from the
works of the natural-right school by their heterodox
tendencies. But Vico will have none of this ultra-religious
system. If Grotius ignored providence and Puffendorf
denied it, Selden was wrong, said Vico, in supplying it,
making it a *deus ex machina*, without explaining it by
the essential character of the human mind. It was a
system not only unphilosophical but incompatible with
sacred history, which admits to a certain extent even in

the case of the Jews a natural, not revealed, law : and it was only because, during the captivity in Egypt, they lost sight of this that the direct intervention of God with the laws given to Moses took place. Nor did the theory agree, as to the alleged dissemination of Jewish knowledge and laws among the Gentiles, with the words of the Jew Josephus and of Lactantius ; and in general, it was unsupported by even the smallest documentary evidence. Vico's conclusion therefore remains unaltered. The Jews enjoyed in addition the extraordinary aid of the true God : but the other nations attained civilisation solely through the ordinary light of providence.

Whether or no Vico quoted and interpreted Grotius and Puffendorf accurately is for us a question of small importance. His exposition and estimate of other philosophers matter less than his own doctrines, whatever their historical relations, which, to tell the truth, are many in number. Nevertheless it will be as well to indicate briefly, as regards the difficulties which may arise upon this point, the answer which we think plausible. Any one who after reading Vico's censures opened the *De iure belli et pacis* and found that Grotius explicitly includes among his three fundamental principles, with reason and the social nature, the divine will, and that this ignoring of God amounts to little more than a mere phrase laying emphasis on the power of the social nature and reason, which would take effect " even if we were to grant that God does not exist " (*etiamsi daremus non esse Deum*) or that he does not care for human affairs, " which cannot be granted without the grossest impiety " (*quod sine summo scelere dari nequit*) : any one who opened Puffendorf and read a most solemn denunciation of the Grotian hypothesis as impious and absurd, and a declaration that natural laws would remain hanging in the air devoid of force apart from the will of God as legislator ; any one who read these words might be led to accuse Vico of negligence or even of insincerity in his criticisms of his predecessors. But in truth Vico did not know what to make of a God set side by side with other sources of morality, or set above them as a superfluous source for the sources : he, searching for God as he did in the heart of man, saw and felt the gulf fixed between him and those who no longer had him in their hearts and barely kept him on their lips through habit or prudence. A more subtle question would be to ask why,—if Vico agreed with the natural-right school in ignoring revelation, and if he instead of rejecting it deepened their superficial immanental doctrine,—why he put himself forward as their implacable enemy and persisted in boasting loudly before prelates and pontiffs of having formulated a system of natural rights different from that of the three Protestant authors and adapted to the Roman church. The supposition that he acted thus through politic caution might be advanced if instead of Vico we were dealing with, for instance, a passionate and powerful but deceitful friar like Tommaso Campanella : but the spotless character of Vico entirely precludes it, and we can only suppose that, lacking as his ideas always were in clarity, on this occasion he indulged his tendency to confusion and nourished his illusions, to the extent of conferring upon himself the flattering style and title of *Defensor Ecclesiae* at the very moment when he was destroying the religion of the church by means of the religion of humanity.

CHAPTER VIII

MORALITY AND LAW

WITH the dazzling light of his originality still shining before our eyes, it is impossible to fix our attention upon those doctrines and classifications which Vico drew from the traditional philosophy and placed especially in the first book of the *Diritto universale* : though it is precisely these that have become favourites with many readers, and are now almost common property through the frequent quotation of them. That God is " infinite power knowledge and will " (*posse nosse velle infinitum*) and man " finite power knowledge and will struggling towards the infinite " (*posse nosse velle finitum quod tendit ad infinitum*) : that the state is the image of God, and because " it has all things beneath it, nothing above " (*omnia infra se, nil superius habet*), therefore " it renders account to God alone and to no one else " (*uni Deo, praeterea reddat rationem nemini*), and that just as in God freedom is inherent in his eternal reason, so the state freely obeys the laws it has itself established : that justice " directs and equates utilities " (*utilitates dirigit et exaequat*), directing, like an architect, in the building-up of the state, the two particular kinds of justice, commutative and distributive, the two divine artisans that measure utility with the two divine measures, arithmetic and geometry, so that " what is equal when you measure is also just when you choose " (*quod est aequum cum metiris, idem est iustum quum eligis*), these and similar assertions seem not merely lacking in originality but even false or meaningless, adorned though they may be with the name either of Aristotle or of Campanella or of other philosophers of the ancient world or the Renaissance. If, to take one, justice consisted in measuring, a philosophy of justice would be unnecessary, for the science of calculation and measurement would be enough. Vico himself at one point involuntarily and ingenuously discloses the vicious circle of this metaphor substituted for a concept, by saying that men ought " to share utility equally among themselves, only preserving a *just* difference where it is a question of desert, and that to preserve the equality."

More profitable than collecting these second-hand formulae would be to collect the many acute observations of moral psychology found here and there in his writings, expressed in his gem-like style ; or to recall his little-known theory of laughter, which he derives from disappointed expectation and from the weakness of the mind, and therefore denies the faculty both to animals and to the perfect man, considering a man who laughs to be a satyr or faun, intermediate between a brute and a man. But abstaining from such a collection, which forms no part of our plan, we would rather observe that even in the commonplace distinctions and classifications mentioned above Vico shows a certain merit : he recognises, even while he propounds them, the necessary confusion and identification of all or many of these distinctions. Thus after distinguishing the two kinds of justice, the three kinds of virtue and the three kinds of law, he ends by declaring that these dualities, triplicities and multiplicities each form a unity.

Justice and virtue also, for Vico, form a unity, since that power of truth, or human reason, which is virtue in so far as it struggles with selfishness, is also justice in so far as it directs or equates utilities. This implies that Vico does not distinguish, at least in the systematic exposition of the *Diritto universale,* between law and morality : a distinction which indeed received little emphasis in the doctrine of natural rights, and is barely indicated in Grotius, for instance, as one between a greater and less degree of morality. Vico's doctrine of punishment is also purely moral, and deduced from the ethical concept of remorse. It is inflicted, he says, by the law, and is nothing but a social reinforcement of the individual conscience, in the case where the offender does not himself expiate his crime by means of remorse and internal punishment.

But the more the problem of the relation between law and morality is absent in Vico's theoretical formulation and systematic treatment, the more present it is in his particular observations ; indeed it may be said to pervade the whole of the New Science. Nor could it be otherwise, seeing that this relation refers to the distinction between the moral will and the inferior or earlier forms of will ; and we know that all Vico's tendencies were towards exploring the lower and obscure region of the mind, both cognitive and practical, in the sphere alike of imagination, will and passion.

He always realised the supreme importance of the passions ; and if he could not approve of giving them the upper hand, if he always considered the Epicurean morality a morality " of idlers shut up in their pleasure-gardens," he did not at all approve of excessively severe moralities such as that of the Stoics, which was no less than the other a morality of " solitaries," not one for men living in a state. Stoicism certainly preaches an eternal and immutable justice, and makes honour the criterion of human action ; but it does violence to human nature, dehumanises it, annuls it and drives it to despair by pretending that it is quite insensible to the passions, by ignoring the utility and necessity of the bodily nature, by inculcating that rule — a rule " harder than iron "—that sins are all equal and that he who strikes a slave is as guilty as he who kills his father. The same doubts must have been aroused in Vico's mind by Jansenism, as he complains that " out of hatred of probability, Christian morality in France is becoming rigidified." We ought to follow not these solitary philosophers but rather those political ones, especially the Platonic type, which recognises that the passions should be not eradicated but moderated and " converted into human virtues." Thus out of cruelty, avarice and ambition, the three universal faults of mankind, Providence elicits the warrior, the merchant and the judge ; the bravery, wealth and wisdom of states. From these three failings, which would destroy mankind on the earth, civil prosperity is formed.

Concerning matters of utility, Vico observes that " in themselves," *ex se*, they are neither good nor bad (*neque turpes neque honestae*) but become so merely through their relation to the moral consciousness (" but their unfairness is baseness, their fairness, honour: *sed earum inaequalitas est turpitudo, aequalitas autem honestas* "). In the empirical science of utility, he defends against Grotius a " prior natural law," *ius naturale prius*, to which belong self-defence and the procreation and upbringing of children : and this right he connects with the Stoic ἀδιάφορον. That it has no moral authority is proved by the fact that the law which follows it in the historical order, the "posterior natural law," *ius naturale posterius*, defined by Justinian as " that which is established among all men by natural reason and is preserved by all nations alike " (*quod naturalis ratio inter omnes homines constituit et apud omnes gentes peraeque custoditur*), is prior in the order of right, *prius iure*, overcomes the former when they conflict and sets upon it the seal of immutability. Now, although this first natural law is defined and exemplified in a merely empirical manner, it is surely at bottom nothing but pure law, law not yet moralised.

But it is upon the concept of " certitude " that law as distinct from morality properly, according to Vico, rests. The word certitude is used by him in many senses, neither clearly distinguished nor harmonised nor deduced one from another : though they all as we have seen unite, rather confusedly, in the general idea of the spontaneous as distinguished from the reflective form of the mind. Certitude in its practical signification implies among other things an opposition to the " truth " of volition, and is, in a word, force as against equity and justice, authority as against reason, mere will as against the moral will. These are distinctions occurring to our own thoughts, rather than stated by Vico, who both distinguishes and fails to distinguish. For instance, he affirms that " certitude proceeds from authority, truth from reason " (*certum ab auctoritate est, verum a ratione*) and immediately afterwards adds that " it is quite impossible for authority to conflict with reason, for in that case there would be not laws but abortive laws " (*auctoritas cum ratione omnino pugnare non potest, nam ita non leges essent, sed monstra legum*). At any rate, the New Science seems to him, by reason of this treatment of certitude, to contain a philosophy of authority, which, he adds, " is the source of what theological moralists call external justice." That is to say, he connected the concept of certitude with the distinction and terminology of external and internal, already employed by the scholastic morality, which, used about this time by Christianus Thomasius, were destined without any great philosophical merit on his part to give an impetus to the investigation of the philosophical relations between law and morality.

Another and kindred meaning of practical certitude in Vico is the so-called letter of the law, *formula legum* ; which may stand in opposition to reason and the moral consciousness, but none the less has its own peculiar value : " *dura lex, sed certa : durum sed scriptum est*—the law is harsh, but it is certain; it is harsh, but so it is written." It is in a word the value of law simply as law, which though devoid of any real ethical content yet has always the value that comes from a command over the will. " The certitude of law " (writes Vico) " is a darkening of the reason supported merely by authority, and makes the law harsh in practical experience by laying down their certitude, which in good Latin (*certum*) means particularised, or in the scholastic terminology individualised." To a certain extent Vico grasped the individual character which lies at the root of every law. That one must " judge according to law, not according to example " (*legibus non exemplis iudicandum*) is a comparatively late principle : the first laws were strictly "*exempla,*" exemplary punishments. From real examples were derived the ideal examples employed by logic and rhetoric : and when the intelligible universal was understood, it was recognised that law had a certain universal character.

The primitive society sketched by Vico is, in its juristic aspect, the myth so to speak of pure law or practical force. Once upon a time men lived possessed of immense bodily strength, and proportionately feeble in understanding, who thought all strength greater than their own divine, and this belief constituted their law. They thought of the gods simply as beings stronger than themselves, whom they were compelled to obey, though with a bad grace : like Polyphemus, who if he had been strong enough would have fought Zeus himself, or Achilles, who told Apollo that if only they were equally matched he would not hesitate to try his strength against him. The wisdom of providence decreed that these fierce men, not tamed as yet by the rule of reason, should at least fear the divine nature of force and measure reason by its standard. This is the foundation of the principle of the " external justice of war." But the myth of the period of force cannot have the strictness of a philosophical concept, and consequently these strong men are considered by Vico from another point of view as ethically the best : " strongest " and " best," *fortissimi* and *optimi*, are regarded as synonymous terms : and their law, though not truth or rational law, is not pure certitude, but truth " mixed with certitude," *ex certo mixtum*. But the very mixture of certitude with, and its preponderance over, truth, which is here asserted, postulates the concept of pure certitude as presupposed by Vico.

When Vico accused Grotius and the school of natural rights of commencing their history half-way, with the civilised ages, and overlooking the earlier periods, the accusation, in its bearing upon the philosophy of practice, may be translated into a charge of ignoring the ideal moment of force and confining the attention to justice, equity and morality. The moment of force, constituting the other and earlier " half," was the field chosen by Hobbes, before him by Machiavelli, and still earlier by Epicurus, all of whom treated of this moment alone, " with impiety towards God, infamy to rulers and injustice towards nations." Hence the conclusion is easy, that in refuting the utilitarians and the theorists of force, Vico was at the same time recognising and absorbing the need which they represented, their only mistake having been that they developed this need in an abstract and one-sided way. His " state of nature " is in some respects like that of Hobbes, with the difference that mankind transcends the latter owing to the recognition of utility, the former owing to the religious and moral consciousness. But Vico does not on this account express any gratitude to Hobbes or Spinoza, Machiavelli or Epicurus, since he believed himself to have found in a classical author all the materials and the stimulus he required, all the counterpoise necessary to the Platonic philosophy. This was one of his " four authors," the one of whom we said earlier that we had still to see the use which Vico made, namely Tacitus. This writer for his part contemplates with his unequalled metaphysical powers man as he is, while Plato contemplates him as he ought to be. Just as Plato in his universal science explores every corner of nobility, so Tacitus " descends into every scheme of utility," in order that among the infinite chaotic chances of malice and fortune the man of practical wisdom may act well. To the union in his mind of Greek philosopher and Roman historian, which he interprets, as is easily seen, in the manner usual among the " Tacitean " politicians of the seventeenth century, Vico attributes his own success in sketching a real idea of eternal history, " which the wise man would construct both of esoteric wisdom such as Plato's, and of common wisdom such as that of Tacitus." To Tacitus, finally, he owed the impulse towards the supreme task of making concrete his ideal, and realising the republic of Plato in the " dregs of Romulus."

CHAPTER IX

THE HISTORICAL ASPECT OF LAW

As the cognitive mind passes from feeling without noticing to noticing with disturbed and confused faculties, and thence to the reflection of the clear mind, so analogously the volitional mind passes from the state of nature to practical certitude and thence to practical truth. In the correlative empirical science, the transition is more or less that from the savage to the heroic or barbaric condition and from the latter to the civilised. In these three types of society, all the manifestations of life correspond: thus there are three kinds of character, three kinds of manners and customs, three kinds of law and therefore of states, three kinds of language and writing, three kinds of authority, reason and justice, and three divisions of history. Confused and sometimes self-contradictory though Vico may be in fixing the particulars of these various correspondences, his general idea is plain. Where reflection is at a low ebb and imagination flourishes, the passions also flourish, habits are violent, governments aristocratic or feudal, families subjected to strict paternal rule, laws severe, legal procedure symbolical, language couched in metaphor and writing in hieroglyphics. Where on the other hand reflection predominates, poetry becomes either separate from or charged with philosophy, manners and customs lose their violence, the passions are brought into subjection, the people take the government into their own hands, all members of the family are alike citizens of the state, law is mitigated by equity and its procedure simplified, language loses its metaphorical clothing and writing becomes alphabetical. Mixed forms, which some politicians aim at producing artificially, would be abortions : and though we do find natural hybrid forms which retain a tinge of the earlier, each one, by reason of its own unity, always tries so far as possible to divest its subject of every property belonging to other forms.

Which of the various social types forms the foundation of the others and supplies the criterion for judging them ? or what is the criterion and standard by which they must all alike be judged ? For Vico, such a question is meaningless. Governments, he says, must adapt themselves to the nature of the people governed : the school of princes is the morality of nations. We may shudder at war, at the law of the stronger, at the reduction of the conquered to slavery, that is, to chattels : but the society which expressed itself in these customs was necessary and therefore good. The worship of strength, as we have said, occupied the position and discharged the function of the as yet impossible rule of reason. Later came the period of fully developed human reason, when men no longer valued each other by the standard of force, but by virtue of their rational nature, which is the true and eternal human nature, recognised one another as equals. The change of time brought change of customs : and the new were no less good, but no more so, than the old.

It would be as useless to seek the common measure of these various social types, as to ask what is the real age of the individual life, the common measure of childhood, youth, maturity and old age. The comparison is one presented by Vico himself. As children shape all their ideas according to their whims and carry them out with violence, as youths animate everything by their imagination, as grown men guide their affairs rather by pure reason and old men by sound prudence ; so it is with the human race, which after its feeble, isolated and poverty-stricken origins, grows at first in unrestrained liberty, then rediscovers the necessaries, utilities and comforts of life by genius and imagination (the age of poetry), and finally cultivates wisdom by means of reason (the age of philosophy). Similarly, natural right arose first in laws so to speak of just passion and just violence : then it was clothed in various myths of just reason : and finally it was openly proclaimed in its pure rationality and noble truth.

By such a method of handling and passing judgment upon governments, laws and customs, Vico escaped another of the leading doctrines or suppositions of the school of natural rights, the abstraction and anti-historicism we mentioned in its own place, which resulted in the conception of a natural law standing above positive law and therefore constituting a kind of eternal code, a perfect scheme of legislation, not yet fully actual but to be actualised, whose outlines show up clearly in the works of the school through their veil of doctrine and philosophy. But this eternal code was in its most important part a contingent and transitory code ; or at least it advocated a code in agreement with the reformatory and revolutionary tendencies of these writers, publicists as they were rather than philosophers.

Vico rids himself of the ideal eternal code without seeming to do so : though he is quite ready to recognise that the "philosophers' natural right," *ius naturale philosophorum*, is in idea eternal, and inexorably laid down "in accordance with eternal reason," *ad rationis aeternae libellam*. But from this verbal concession of eternity made out of respect for the old traditional scholastic philosophy, whose influence he felt now and then, he goes on to deny its real eternity and supra-historical character ; since instead of placing it above

and outside history he puts it in the place which belongs
to it, within history.   The law of violence or heroic law,
after passing into the law of uncivilised society, gradually
attains a certain limit of clarity, in which state the only
thing wanting to its perfection is that some school of
philosophers should complete it by establishing it with
reasoned principles, upon the idea of eternal justice :
and this reasoning and systematisation is the "*ius naturale philosophorum,*" the extreme form of the historical
development of law, not its unchanging rule ; a product,
not a standard.   Hence Vico's charge against Grotius
of confusing the "*ius naturale philosophorum,*" the law
composed of reasoned principles derived from moralists,
theologians and, in part, jurists, with the natural law of
nations, *ius naturale gentium* (in Grotius's language, confusing natural law with an arbitrary or positive form of law):
of misunderstanding the Roman jurists, who intended
to speak solely of the latter : and of offering to correct and
venturing to criticise writers whose faults on inspection
vanish.

The eternal code, considered in its essentials, is a
Utopia : and since the first and greatest of Utopias is
Plato's Republic, it is important, in order better to decide
the point at issue, to examine Vico's attitude towards the
political scheme of Plato.   If we may listen to his own
words, the *Republic* was another of his many incentives
and examples when he conceived the New Science.   With
the study of Plato began the unconscious awakening in
him of " the thought of conceiving an ideal eternal law,
to be expressed in a universal state built on the idea or
plan of providence, on which idea, indeed, are founded
all the states of every period and race : an ideal Republic
like that which Plato ought, as a consequence of his
divine metaphysic, to have conceived."   He ought, but
could not, owing to his " ignorance of the first man's
fall " ; ignorance, that is, of the original state of nature

and of the exclusively poetic or " common " wisdom
which followed it : an ignorance maintained by the error,
common to the minds of all men, of measuring by oneself
the almost unknown nature of other people, as Plato
exalted the rude and barbaric beginnings of Gentile man
to the perfect state of his loftiest esoteric knowledge of the
divine, and fancied these earliest men to possess a high
degree of this esoteric wisdom, whereas on the contrary
they were really " brutes, all stupidity and ferocity."
In consequence of this learned error Plato, instead of
conceiving an eternal Republic and the laws of an eternal
justice by which Providence governs the nations of the
world and directs it by means of the common needs of
mankind, by which it is led to the common consciousness
of the whole human race, " conceived an ideal Republic
and a merely ideal justice, by which nations are not
guided at all." In fact, they ought not to be guided by
it : since among the determinations of the perfect state
there are some which are dishonourable and detestable,
such as the community of wives. Thus Vico took from
Plato the idea of an eternal state, but entirely inverted
it by the reservation which he added to it, that the true
eternal republic is not the abstract state of Plato, but the
course of history in all its phases, including the brutes at
one end and Plato at the other. This is the " republic of
mankind," the " great state of mankind," the " universal
republic" (*generis humani respublica, magna generis humani
civitas, respublica universa*) of which he means to investigate
the " form, ranks, societies, occupations, laws, crimes,
punishments, and science of jurisprudence " (*formam
ordines societates negotia leges peccata poenas et scientiam
in ea tractandi iuris*) and to follow the development of all
these " from their origin, the beginnings of humanity,
under the control of divine Providence, national custom
and authority " (*a suis usque primis humanitatis originibus,
divina providentia moderante, moribus gentium ac proinde*

auctoritate), that is to say, " by means of the various elements of human utility and necessity, or even by means of opportunities arising by the spontaneous action of circumstances " (*per varia utilitatum et necessitatum humanarum rudimenta, sive adeo per ipsarum sponte rerum oblatas occasiones*). The " great state of the nations founded and governed by God " is thus nothing else than History.

While refusing a fixed code and the draft of a model society, we do not mean to deny the possibility of a practical aspect of the science conceived by Vico, the New Science in its triple form of ideal history, typical history and historical history. Every truth has its practical side, that is to say, its practical consequences : and thinking in this or that way of the nature and develop-ment of mankind involves this or that practical line of conduct. A man who believes for instance in the docile innocence of savage races will approach them with a smile on his face, kindly words on his lips and the alphabet and catechism of rights and duties in his hand : one who believes in Vico's " brutes " will adopt somewhat sterner methods, perhaps even fire and the sword. One who, like Vico, believes that " custom is more potent than law " and that " custom changes not at a blow, but gradually and slowly " will not be inclined to hasty legislation, and will not delude himself into thinking he can remodel human nature after an ideal of his own devising. Such conduct in any case is not theory, but practice : and when the attempt is made to reduce it to theory, either a chaotic confusion of necessary and contingent determinations results, or else if we avoid these errors and strive to attain a strictly doctrinal form of conduct, we get neither more nor less than the scientific theory itself, from which our conduct derived.

The thought of following up the New Science with a practical theory appropriate to it evidently occurred to

Vico. Even in the first Italian edition of the work he stated two " practical " corollaries : first, a new art of criticism, to serve as a light to distinguish the truth in obscure and legendary history ; and secondly an art of diagnosis, so to speak, for determining the degrees of necessity or utility in human affairs, and as its ultimate consequence, the chief end of this science, consisting in the recognition of indubitable symptoms of the conditions of nations. Properly considered, these arts of criticism and diagnosis unite into one, namely the better knowledge which it was possible, owing to the principles laid down by Vico, to obtain concerning the past and present life of nations.

This idea is repeated and explained in other parts of the same work. The sciences, studies and arts developed up to now, says Vico, deal with particular objects : the New Science, on the other hand, investigating as it does the principles themselves which lie at the source of all studies, is able to establish the ἀκμή or state of perfection of the entire system, and the degrees and extremes by which and within which human nature like all other mortal things must run its course and come to an end : so that through this science we can answer the practical questions how a nation in its rise may come to its state of perfection, and how in its decadence it may be stimu- lated to new life. The state of perfection would consist in a nation's resting upon fixed principles both demon- strated by unchanging reason and put into practice by human habits ; principles in which the esoteric wisdom of the philosopher would extend a helping hand to the common wisdom of nations, thus uniting men of the greatest academic reputation with all those of wisdom in the state, the philosophers with the statesmen ; and the science of civil matters divine and human, religion and law, a theology and morality imposed by command and acquired by habituation, would be supplemented by the science of natural laws divine and human, a theology and morality imposed by reason and acquired by ratiocination : so that to transgress such principles would be true error, the wandering not of men but of wild animals.

The practical aspect of the New Science, then, was simply a summary or duplicate of the science itself, emphasising the two leading elements of spontaneous and reflective wisdom, certitude and truth, and the necessity of bearing both in mind.

Years later, in one of the elaborations of the second *Scienza Nuova* made by Vico, we again meet with the idea and the phrase of a practical aspect of this science, in the title of a special concluding paragraph which he proposed to add to his work. It begins thus : " The whole of this work has now been thought out as a mere contemplative science dealing with the common character of nations : for this reason it may seem to offer no assistance to human prudence in order either to prevent or to delay the entire ruin of nations on the path of decadence, and thus to lack the practical side which every science must have whose subject-matter is dependent upon the human will, all such sciences being called practical." Now in what could such a practical side consist ? " This practical application can easily be found from the contemplation itself of the course of the history of nations : which the wise men (statesmen) and princes of states observing, could by means of good ordinances, laws and examples recall peoples to their ἀκμή or state of perfection." In other words : a man warned is half saved. Contemplation is the only principle of conduct which the New Science can supply. The other half of salvation depends not on the person warning, namely thought, but upon the person warned, upon action. It does not occur to Vico to try to determine the " ordinances, laws and examples " whose adoption would be of value in this or that crisis or situation. This would not be a philosopher's task, as in fact he himself clearly recognises next moment, when he says : " The only practical principles we philosophers can supply are ones which can be confined to the academic sphere."

It would certainly be rash to claim precise knowledge of Vico's reasons for omitting this note on practical principles in the final manuscript of the last edition of the *Scienza Nuova*, just as he had omitted in the second work of that title the assertions on the subject which had appeared in the first. But we may at least venture to guess that the principal reason was the obvious emptiness of this passage, promising as it did a practical application which it failed to provide, and finally confessing that such a practical application was either impossible or already included in the theory itself.

CHAPTER X

THE true and only reality then, in the world of nations, is the course of their history : and the principle which regulates this course is Providence. From this point of view the New Science may be defined as a " rational civil theology of the divine providence." Bacon, among his historical sciences, had named a *Historia Nemeseos* (history of Divine Retribution). What for Bacon was little more than a mere name was for Vico a clearly stated problem and a developed theory. Philosophers, according to him, when they did not ignore Providence entirely, as materialists and determinists, considered it solely in the sphere of natural law, calling metaphysic by the name of " natural theology," and supporting the identification of God with the natural order observed in the motions of bodies, such as the spheres and the elements, and with the final cause which was seen to exist over and above the other natural causes. As against all this it was important to work out the doctrine of Providence " in the economy of matters civil."

It was observed by some of his earliest commentators, and the observation has been frequently repeated since, that Vico used the word " providence " indifferently in a subjective and an objective sense : sometimes to indicate the human belief in a provident deity controlling their doctrine, sometimes to denote the actual operation of this providence. The double or triple meaning of a single word in Vico's terminology is a thing which by now need cause no astonishment. We have often already been obliged to take pains to distinguish his homonyms and unite his synonyms. Hence we may at once recognise that one meaning of " Providence " for Vico might be and indeed is the belief in Providence, man's idea of God, first in the form of myth and later in the pure and rational form of philosophy. The Gentile nations of antiquity, he says, " began their metaphysical poetic wisdom by contemplating God in the attribute of his providence," upon which rested augury and divination. Without this idea, then, wisdom, the consciousness of the infinite, cannot take shape within man, nor can morality, the fear of and respect for the higher power which governs the affairs of men, arise. But in this sense of the word a further discussion of providence is unnecessary, after what we have said on the subjects of mythology and of the relation between morality and religion.

We therefore pass at once to Providence in its second sense, the real and strict conception of it ; and here it seems advisable to leave Vico for a moment and to clear up certain points of doctrine.

It is a common observation that to create a given fact is one thing, to know it when created quite another. The knowledge of what a fact really is often comes in the life of the individual years later, in the life of mankind centuries later, than the fact itself. The very persons who are directly responsible for a given fact as a rule do not know it, or know it in a very imperfect and fallacious manner ; so much so that the illusions which are said to accompany human activity have passed into a proverb. The poet thinks he is singing of purity when he is really singing of sensuality, and of strength while he is really singing of weakness ; he believes himself to be a dreadful pessimist and is really childishly optimistic : imagines himself a devil, when he is a good fellow without an ounce of vice in him. Philosophers deceive themselves no less. We need not go far to find examples. The philosopher we are studying supplies a whole series of them ; few have been more in the dark as to the real tendencies of their own thought. The politician also deceives himself ; very often he believes and declares himself to be fighting for liberty while he is a mere reactionary, or while believing himself to be serving the cause of reaction is really inciting to revolt and aiding the cause of freedom : and so on. Such illusions are easy to understand. Individuals and nations in the heat of creation, or scarcely yet passing out of such a state, can perhaps express their state of mind, but cannot treat it in the critical spirit of historical narration : and accordingly, when they cannot reconcile themselves to waiting in silence, they compose imaginary histories of themselves, *Wahrheiten und Dichtungen* at once. In fact this proved difficulty of understanding one's actions while acting is one motive of the wise advice to speak of oneself as little as possible and of the suspicion with which autobiographies and memoirs are regarded. Such works are interesting and possibly even valuable ; but they never present the strict historical truth of the facts they narrate.

Human labours are thus veiled in the mists of illusion which arise from individuals. The superficial historian clings to the veil, and in his attempt to describe the course of events, uses these illusions to make his voice carry. In this way the history of poetry takes the form of a narration of the intentions, opinions and aims of poets, or of those attributed to them by their contemporaries ; the history of philosophy becomes a series of anecdotes concerning the sentiments, whims and practical aims of philosophers : the history of politics, a tissue of intrigue, base interests, gossip and greed. But a more careful historian, or one of a different type, will have nothing to

do with history of this kind. His first act is to dispel
the mists, to sweep away the individual and his illusions,
and to look facts in the face as they appeared in their
objective succession and their supra-individual origin.
Real, true history arises independently of individuals,
as a product growing to completion behind their backs,
the product of a force apart from individual agents,
which may be called Fate, Chance, Fortune or God.
The individual, who at first was everything, and filled
the whole stage with his posturing and declamation, is
now, in this second aspect of history, less than nothing ;
his actions and cries, stripped of all serious potency,
provoke laughter or pity. We look in terror at the Fate
that dominates him, we stand aghast at the strange
coincidence of chance or the caprices of Fortune, we bow
before the inscrutable designs of the divine providence.
The individual appears in turn as the inert material, the
powerless plaything and the blind instrument of these
forces. But deeper thought leads us beyond even this
second view of history. The pity which the individual
seems to arouse and the amusement he evokes are in
reality deserved not by him but by his fancies, or rather,
by those individuals who mistake fancy for truth. Real
history is composed of actions, not of fancies and illusions :
but actions are the work of individuals, not indeed in so
far as they dream, but in the inspiration of genius, the
divine madness of truth, the holy enthusiasm of the hero.
Fate, Chance, Fortune, God—all these explanations have
the same defect : they separate the individual from his
product, and instead of eliminating the capricious element,
the individual will in history, as they claim to do, they immensely reinforce and increase it. Blind Fate, irresponsible
chance, and tyrannical God are all alike capricious : and
hence Fate passes into Chance and God, Chance into Fate
and God, and God into both the others, all three being
equivalent and identical.

The idea which transcends and corrects alike the individualistic and supra-individualistic views of history is the idea of history as rational. History is made by individuals : but individuality is nothing but the concreteness of the universal, and every individual action, simply because it is individual, is supra-individual. Neither the individual nor the universal exists as a distinct thing : the real thing is the one single course of history, whose abstract aspects are individuality without universality and universality without individuality. This one course of history is coherent in all its many determinations, like a work of art which is at the same time manifold and single, in which every word is inseparable from the rest, every shade of colour related to all the others, every line connected with every other line. On this understanding alone history can be understood. Otherwise it must remain unintelligible, like a string of words without meaning or the incoherent actions of a madman.

History then is the work neither of Fate nor of Chance but of the necessity which is not determination and the liberty which is not chance. And since the religious view, that history is the work of God, has this advantage and superiority over the others, that it introduces a cause for history other than fate or chance, and therefore not properly speaking a cause at all, but a creative activity, a free and intelligent mind, it is natural that out of gratitude to this higher view no less than by the suitability of the language we should be led to give to the rationality of history the name of God who rules and governs all things, and to call it the Divine Providence. In so naming it, we at the same time purge the title of its mythical dross which debased God and his providence afresh into a fate or a chance. Thus providence in history, in this final logical form, has double value as a criticism of individual illusions, when they come forward as the entire and only reality of history, and as a criticism of divine transcendence. And we may say that this is the point of view which always has been and always is adopted, as if instinctively, without the profession of an explicit theory, by all minds naturally gifted with that particular faculty which we call the historic sense.

If now, to return to Vico, we ask how he solved the problem of the motive force of history, and what was the precise content for him of the concept of providence in the objective sense, it is perfectly easy to exclude the supposition that his was the transcendent or miraculous Providence which had formed the subject of Bossuet's eloquent *Discours*. It is easy both because in all his philosophy he invariably reduces the transcendent to the immanent, and repeats over and over again here that his providence operates by natural means or (using scholastic phraseology) by secondary causes : and because upon this point his interpreters are practically unanimous.

No less insistent is his criticism of fate and chance, or according to his threefold division fortune, fate and chance. He observes that the doctrine of fate moves in a vicious circle, because the eternal series of causes in which it holds the world bound and chained, depends upon the will of Jupiter, and at the same time Jupiter is subject to fate ; whence it results that the Stoics are themselves entangled in that " chain of Jupiter " with which they would imprison all things human. These three concepts, corresponding to that of opportunity when an object of desire is in question, to that of good luck in the case of unhoped-for events, and to that of accident in the case of the unexpected, are distinctions of the subjective understanding rather than anything else : objectively they come under one single law which may also be called fortune, if with Plato we recognise opportunity as the mistress of human affairs : and all three are manifestations and paths of the divine Providence which is intelligence, liberty and necessity. The creator of the world of nations " was indeed Mind, since men made it by their intelligence : it was not Fate, because they made it by free choice, nor yet Chance, since to all eternity on doing thus the same results follow."

Vico lights up in the most fanciful ways the comedy of errors formed by man's illusions as to the end of his own actions. Men thought they were escaping the threats of the thundering sky by carrying their women into caves to satisfy their animal passions out of God's sight : and by thus keeping them safely secluded they founded the first chaste unions and the first societies ; marriage and the family. They fortified themselves in suitable places with the intention of defending themselves and their families : and in reality, by thus fortifying themselves in fixed places they put an end to their nomadic life and primitive wanderings, and began to learn agriculture. The weak and disorderly, reduced to the extremity of hunger and mutual slaughter, to save their lives took refuge in these fortified places, and became servants to the heroes : and thus without knowing it they raised the family to an aristocratic or feudal status. The aristocrats, feudal chiefs or patricians, their rule once established, hoped to defend and secure it by the strictest treatment of their servants the plebeians : but in this way they awoke in the servants a consciousness of their own power and made the plebeians into men, and the more the patricians prided themselves on their patriciate and struggled to preserve it, the more effectively they worked to destroy the patrician state and to create democracy. Thus, says Vico, the world of nations issues " from a mind widely different from, sometimes quite opposed, always superior, to the particular ends set before themselves by men : which restricted ends have been made means to wider ends, and employed to preserve the human race upon this earth."

It may be gathered from some of our quotations from Vico that he sometimes tended to conceive men as conscious of their own utilitarian ends but unconscious of moral ends. This would logically lead to explaining social life on exclusively utilitarian principles, and to considering morality as an accident relatively to the human will and therefore not really moral : an external accretion more or less capable of holding mankind together, or the obscure work of a supramundane providence. This utilitarianism especially creeps into a passage where he says that man, on account of his corrupt nature, being under the tyranny of self-love which compels him to make private utility his chief guide and to want every useful thing for himself and nothing for his fellow, unable to hold his passions in check so as to direct them by justice, in the state of nature desires only his own safety; after taking a wife and begetting children, desires his safety and the safety of his family ; after attaining civil life, desires his own safety together with the safety of his city ; after extending his rule over other peoples, he desires the safety of the nation ; after joining with other nations in wars, treaties, alliances and commerce, he desires his safety and that of all mankind : and " in all these circumstances he principally desires his own interest." For this reason " it can be nothing else than divine providence that binds him down within such ordinances as to maintain by justice the society of the family, the state and ultimately of mankind ; by which ordinances since man cannot attain what he wants, at least he wants to attain as much utility as is permitted : and this is what is called justice." The public virtue of Rome, he writes elsewhere, " was nothing but a good use made by providence of grave, unsightly and cruel private faults, that states might be preserved at a time when human minds, being in a state of extreme particularity, could not naturally understand a common good."

Utilitarianism was however, as we know, strongly repugnant to Vico's observed ethics, founded as the latter is upon the moral consciousness or shame ; and hence these statements, which unconsciously tend in that direction, can only be explained as resulting from the disturbance sometimes produced in his mind by the lingering remains of the transcendent or theological conception of providence, and also from the confused character of his thought, which prevented him from keeping the idea of individual illusions clearly distinguished from that of individual aims ; so that he sometimes substituted the second when he ought to have been dealing solely with the first. If the provident deity is "the unity of the spirit which informs and animates the world of nations," these do not fail to obtain their particular ends in order that it may move on to its universal ones, but both alike are realised in them : and man is at every moment both utilitarian and moral, or at least supposes himself to be moral when he is utilitarian or utilitarian when he is really moral.

In any case, and in spite of these vacillations or rather confusions, the conception of particular ends as the vehicle of universal and of illusion as accompanying and co-operating with action implies a dialectical conception of the movement of history, and the transcending of the problem of evil. This problem is in fact very little emphasised by Vico, owing to the strength of his belief in the universal government of providence and of his persuasion that so-called evil is not only willed by man under the appearance of good, but is itself essentially a good. In a few rare passages in his earliest writings, where he encounters the problem of evil, Vico solves it simply in the sense that we men because of our iniquity which leads us to "regard ourselves, not this universe of things " (*nosmetipsos, non hanc rerum universitatem spectamus*) consider as evil those things which run counter to us, " which yet, since they contribute to the common nature of the world, are good " (*quae tamen, quia in mundi commune conferunt, bona sunt*).

Vico's conception of history thus became truly object-ive, freed from divine arbitrament, but freed equally from the rule of trifling causes and gossiping explanations, and acquiring a knowledge of its own essential end, which is to understand the nexus of facts, the logic of events ; to be the rational reconstruction of a rational fact. Historical study at this time suffered less from the first of these errors (the theological conception had been ever since the beginning of the Italian Renaissance falling into universal decay) than from that form of history which was just then acquiring the name of " pragmatic," which restricted itself to the personal aspect of events, and failing by these means to reach full historical truth tried to gain warmth and life by means of political and moral instruction. A monument of pragmatic history arose in Vico's own country and contemporaneously with the *Scienza Nuova* : Pietro Giannone's *Civil History of the Kingdom of Naples*. The author was a man of his own district and age, and wrote a great work in the sphere of polemic, and even in certain respects of history : but such that all its greatness only serves to emphasise the greatness of Vico's book. If Vico had had to describe the origins of ecclesiastical property and power in the Middle Ages, he would have been able to write of some-thing very different from the guile of popes, bishops and abbots, and the simplicity of dukes and emperors. And as we shall see, whenever he undertook to investigate any part of history he actually did discover in it something very different from these things.

CHAPTER XI

THE LAW OF REFLUX

THE mind, after traversing its course of progress, after rising from sensation successively to the imaginative and the rational universal and from violence to equity, is bound in conformity with its eternal nature to re-traverse the course, to relapse into violence and sensation, and thence to renew its upward movement, to commence a reflux.

This is the philosophical meaning of Vico's " reflux," but not the exact manner in which we find it expressed in his writings, where the eternal circle is considered almost exclusively as exemplified in the history of nations, as a reflux in the civil affairs of man. Civilisation comes to an end in the " barbarism of reflection," which is worse than the primitive barbarism of sensation ; for while the latter was not without a wild nobility, the former is contemptible, untrustworthy and treacherous ; and thus it is necessary that this evil subtlety of malicious intellect should rust away through the long centuries of a new barbarism of sensation. We must however withdraw and purge the conception of " reflux " from historical facts and the sociological scheme, not only to explain the absolute and eternal character which Vico attributes to it, but also to justify the historical representation and sociological law founded upon it, and drawing their cogency primarily from it.

The laws of flux and reflux, laid down by the philosophers and politicians of Greece and of the Italian
Renaissance, were founded no less than Vico's upon a
philosophy, but upon a very superficial one ; they assumed
their object to possess external and empty political forms,
and endeavoured to fix the succession of these forms
upon data of experience or by vague reasonings. But
Vico's object is the forms of culture, including in themselves all the activities of life, economy and law, religion
and art, science and language, and referring them back
to their inmost source, the human mind, he establishes
their succession " according to the rhythm of the elementary forms of the mind." Thus all the learning which has
been expended in comparing the Vician reflux with the
theories of Plato or Polybius, Machiavelli or Campanella,
is practically wasted : the more so that Vico (who, as we
know, though often misunderstanding his predecessors
cannot be accused of wishing to pass them over : in fact,
where he thought he found parallel or identical ideas in
them, he was apt to boast of the fact) felt no need of
mentioning this point, or thought it unimportant. The
" circular movement " (ἀνακύκλωσις) of Polybius, the
economy of nature by which states alter, change and
return to the same point, has been thought almost an
anticipation of the eternal ideal history ; but Vico sets
Polybius with the others, when he asks the reader to
consider " how (little) philosophers have thought with
knowledge upon their principles of civil government, and
with what (little) truth Polybius has reasoned upon its
changes." Campanella connected his historical cycles
with astrological laws ; and Machiavelli conceives the
catastrophe which opens the reflux thus : " When human
craft and malignity have gone as far as they can go, it
happens of necessity that the world purifies itself by one
of the three methods (pestilence, famine and deluge,
beside the human methods of new religions and languages)

in order that men, having become few and chastened, may live more conveniently and become better." The one precedent to which Vico refers, but only to interpret it in a way altogether his own and in fact to give it a totally new content, is the ancient Egyptian tradition of the three successive ages of gods, heroes and men.

If the philosophy lying at its root gives strength to Vico's sociological theory of reflux, the historical element with which it is leavened to some degree weakens it. Vico was especially versed in and attached to Roman history, which had been the first of his historical studies and the object of many years' devotion. The history of Rome accordingly, whether because of his deeper study of it or because of its complexity, impressiveness and long duration, came to stand in Vico's mind as the typical or normal history, to serve as a standard for all others, and be confused with the law of flux and reflux itself. Rome showed him the asylum of Romulus, that is, the transition from the state of nature to the political organism : aristocracies, monarchical at first in appearance only, later not even in appearance : democracy, issuing from its struggle with aristocracy and ending in real monarchy, the perfect form of civil life ; thence by a process of degeneration, the barbarism of reflection or civilisation, incomparably worse than the primitive noble barbarism, and following in its train a second condition of wandering in a state of nature and a new barbarism, a new youth, the Middle Ages. It is the history of Rome hardly generalised at all and supplemented here and there by that of Greece, that appears in the Vician aphorisms formulating the laws of social dynamics. Men first feel the prick of necessity, then the attraction of utility : next they become aware of convenience, and after that take delight in pleasure ; then dissipate themselves in luxury and finally fall victims to the madness of abusing their resources. There must at first be men of brute strength like Polyphemus, that man may obey man in the state of family life, and to induce him to obey the law in the future state of civil life. There must be noble and proud men like Achilles, not inclined by nature to yield to their equals, in order to establish over the family the aristocratic type of republic. Then valiant and just men like Aristides and Scipio Africanus are necessary, to open the path to popular liberty. After this arise men of great apparent virtues accompanied by faults no less great, like Alexander or Caesar, acquiring immense popular reputations and introducing monarchy. Later still there must be serious reflective natures like Tiberius to consolidate the monarchy; and lastly wild, dissolute and shameless characters like Caligula, Nero and Domitian to overthrow it.

Owing to this rarefaction of Roman history into typical history, and the simultaneous consolidation of typical history into the history of Rome, Vico's law of reflux is riddled with exceptions, much more common and serious than those of the corresponding empirical laws; so that if as he believes his empirical science is identical with the ideal laws of the mind, its alleged permanency throughout all eternity and the whole universe seems the merest irony. He says that Carthage, Capua and Numantia, the three cities which threatened to dispute with Rome the empire of the world, failed to accomplish the ordained course of human affairs: since the Carthaginians were thwarted by the acuteness of the native African temperament, which by maritime commerce they increased still further: the Capuans by the soft climate and fertility of rich Campania: and the Numantines by their suppression in the first burst of heroism at the hands of Rome, led by Scipio Africanus the conqueror of Carthage, and aided by the forces of the world. And passing from ancient to modern times, America would now be traversing the path of human affairs but for its discovery by Europeans:

Poland and England are still aristocratic, but would have arrived at perfect monarchy had not the natural course of civil affairs been hindered by extraordinary causes. As for the Middle Ages, they cannot be considered as in Vico's estimation a true return to the state of nature, if they open with the establishment of Christianity, the religion of the true God ; nor in any case does the return to the state of nature and to barbarism seem the only path open to a nation that has attained its ἀκμή, its culmination. The alternative is that a decadent nation should lose its independence and fall under the rule of a better. Nor, lastly, is decadence inevitable if statesmen and philosophers working in harmony can preserve the perfection that has been reached and check the threatened destruction, and if in point of fact, as he observes, the aristocratic republics which survived his own day as remnants of the Middle Ages succeeded in preserving themselves by arts of " superfine wisdom." His own time Vico thought to be one of high civilisation. A complete humanity, he says, seems to be scattered to-day over all nations. A few great monarchs rule the world of nations, and those barbarian monarchs who still exist do so either owing to the persistence of the " common wisdom " of imaginative and cruel religions, or because of the natural temperaments of their respective peoples. The nations which form the empire of the Czar of Russia are of a sluggish disposition ; those of the Khan of Tartary are an effeminate race ; the subjects of the Negus of Ethiopia and the King of Fez and of Morocco are few and weak. In the temperate zone Japan maintains a heroic character not unlike that of Rome in the period of the Punic wars ; her people are warlike, her language resembling Latin, her religion a fierce one of terrible gods all loaded with formidable weapons. The Chinese on the other hand, whose religion is mild, cultivate literature and are humane in the highest degree : the peoples of the Indies are also

humane and practise the arts of peace ; the Persians and
Turks mingle the rude doctrine of their religion with an
Asiatic softness, the Turks especially tempering their arrogance with pomp, magnificence, liberality and gratitude.
Europe is above all humane, composed as it is of great
monarchies and universally professing the Christian faith
which inculcates an infinitely pure and perfect idea of
God and commands charity to the whole human race.
Vico fixed his attention upon the confederacy of the
Swiss cantons and the united provinces of Holland, which
reminded him of the Aetolian and Achaean leagues, and
on the composition of the German Empire, a system of
free states and sovereign princes, which seemed to him a
kind of attempt in the direction of a great aristocratic
state ; the most perfect of all, and the ultimate form of
civil life, since no other can be conceived superior to it,
reproducing as it does the earliest form, the aristocracy
of patricians each supreme in his own family and all united
in the ruling class of the first state ; but reproducing
it in a form not of barbarism but of the highest civilisation.   Such is the humanity by which Europe is on every
hand distinguished, that it abounds with every element
contributory to human happiness, mental pleasures no
less than bodily comforts, and all this in virtue of the
Christian religion, teaching as it does sublime truths,
supported by the most learned philosophers of the Gentile
races and of the three greatest languages of the world,
Hebrew, Greek and Latin, and thus uniting the wisdom of
authority with that of reason, the choicest philosophical
doctrine with the most highly developed philological
learning.   Can this lofty civilisation, safeguarded as it
is by Christianity, be moving, or ever likely to move
towards a new state of nature ?   It is difficult to discover
Vico's real opinion on this point.   Among his verses
there is a poem of a profoundly pessimistic tone, but this
is a youthful effusion, and in any case refers to the end of

the world as imminent, rather than to a future social decadence. In his letters there is a melancholy picture of the condition of learning in his time : but it applies to this restricted field only, not to the sphere of social and political life. On the other hand, in his last philosophical work, the *De mente heroica*, referring to those who declared that all things were now perfect and that no new tasks could arise, he says that the tide of progress is flowing at its strongest. " The world is still young : for only in the last seven hundred years, four hundred of which were spent in barbarism, how many new discoveries have been made ! How many new arts have arisen ! How many new sciences have been developed ! " (*Mundus iuvenescit adhuc ; nam septingentis non ultra abhinc annis, quorum tamen quadringentos barbaries percurrit, quot nova inventa ! quot novae artes ! quot novae scientiae excogitatae !*) But we may observe that the *De mente heroica* is an official oration, and that Vico may on that account have suppressed for the occasion his doubts or his deepest convictions. In any case, how can we reconcile the prophecy of an imminent collapse with the rise of that creation of providence, the New Science, shedding upon the life of nations a light which rendered possible the diagnosis and cure of their ailments ? On the whole it is probable that the difficulty of determining Vico's opinion as to the fate of contemporary society is due to the fact that he had really no settled conviction on the subject, and was led hither and thither in various and contrary directions by the influence of hopes and fears.

If it had not been disturbed by the scheme of Roman history, the empirical theory of the reflux would never have been forced to admit so many and serious exceptions; nor would it have fallen into such painful confusions. It would have accommodated its author's historical observations with greater ease, and its general characteristics would have been much simpler and more general. It would have consisted primarily in the determination and illustration of the connexion between predominantly imaginative and predominantly intellectual, spontaneous and reflective, periods, the latter periods issuing out of the former by an increase of energy, and returning to them by degeneration and decomposition. Political history shows over and over again the spectacle of aristocracies declining from their first strength to a debased and contemptible state and yielding before the onset of classes less refined or even absolutely uncultured, but of stouter moral fibre ; while these again, after becoming civilised in their turn and attaining the highest development of the historical idea whose germ they bear within themselves, enter upon a new period of decay and fermentation, from which issues a new ruling class in the vigour of a youthful barbarism. The history of philosophy again shows positive and speculative periods ; philosophical solutions congeal into scholastic theory and dogma, the mind reverts to the mere unthinking observation of particular fact, and the speculative process arises once more. Literary history, too, speaks of periods of realism and idealism, romantic and classical periods : of a corrupt classicism, Alexandrian or decadent art, and of a romantic barbarism which arises from it. These are true cases of Vico's reflux. But since the nature of the mind which underlies these cycles is outside time and therefore exists in every moment of time, we must not exaggerate the difference of the periods : and if on the one hand the outline of the law must be distinct, it must on the other hand not lose a certain elasticity. We must never forget that at every period, aristocratic or democratic, romantic or classical, positive or speculative, and even in every individual and every fact, moments both aristocratic and democratic, romantic and classical, positive and speculative can be observed ; and that these distinctions are to a great extent quantitative and made for the sake of convenience. These facts should lead us to avoid alike maintaining the law at all costs and so falling into artificiality, and rejecting it entirely and so refusing the help which may be derived from general and approximative views.

Thus understood and amended, not only is the theory free from the great and striking exceptions which are necessary when it is modelled upon the history and final catastrophe of Rome, but the accusations of undue uniformity lodged against Vico disappear. Vincenzo Cuoco, one of the first, if not the first intelligent student of Vico's works, remarks concerning and in criticism of the law of reflux, that "nature never resembles itself; it is man who by compounding his observations forms classes and names." This is perfectly true; but if applied to this case it would be an argument not against the Vician reflux but against every sort of empirical human science. Others accused Vico of overlooking groups of causes of great historical weight, such as climate, racial and national character, and exceptional occurrences. But, omitting the fact that he often mentions these things, for he connects national character and climate with the forms and changes of states, and mentions events and circumstances which upset the natural and ordinary course of national history, for example in his discussion of Greek history, the truth is that he was bound to ignore them and could not waste time over such things, since his concern was with uniformities and not with divergences, or rather with certain uniformities and not with certain others which compared with the former were negligible divergences. Similarly— the parallel is an obvious one, and indeed is more than a parallel—any one who attempts to trace the general characteristics of the different periods of life, infancy, childhood, adolescence and so forth, will ignore the comparative rapidity and slowness of development due to differences of climate, race or accidental circumstances.

Another of these true but irrelevant charges is that Vico denied the communication and interpenetration of civilisations, and insisted that they arise separately in different nations without any mutual knowledge and therefore without reciprocal imitation. This charge has been met by the observation that Vico does not fail to record cases of the influence of one people upon another and of the transmission of civilisations and their products; the transmission for example of alphabetic writing from the Chaldaeans to the Phoenicians and from them to the Egyptians; and that in any case his law is not empirical but philosophical and refers to the spontaneous creative activity of the human mind. The point at issue is however precisely the empirical aspect of this law, not the philosophical: and the true reply seems to us to be, as we have already suggested, that Vico could not take and ought not to have taken other circumstances into account, just as—to recall one instance—any one who in studying the various phases of life describes the first manifestations of the sexual craving in the vague imaginations and similar phenomena of puberty, does not take into account the ways in which the less experienced may be initiated into love by the more experienced, since he is setting out to deal not with the social laws of imitation but with the physiological laws of organic development. If it is said that even without imitation or sophistication the sexual craving arises no less and demands satisfaction, such a statement doubtless merely asserts the incontrovertible truth of a certain very ancient Eastern tale included by Boccaccio in the *Decameron*: but at the same time it supplies the most complete parallel to the famous and much controverted aphorism of Vico.

Nor is the Vician law of reflux necessarily opposed, as has often been thought, to the conception of social progress. It would be so opposed if instead of being a law of mere uniformity it were one of identity, in agreement with the idea of an unending cyclical repetition of single individual facts which has been adopted by certain extravagant minds of both ancient and modern times.   The reflux of history, the eternal cycle of the mind, can and must be conceived, even if Vico does not so express it, as not merely diverse in its uniform movements, but as perpetually increasing in richness and outgrowing itself, so that the new period of sense is in reality enriched by all the intellect and all the development that preceded it, and the same is true of the new period of the imagination or of the developed mind.   The return of barbarism in the Middle Ages was in some respects uniform with ancient barbarism ; but it must not for that reason be considered as identical with it, since it contains in itself Christianity, which summarises and transcends ancient thought.

Whether the conception of progress is formulated and thrown into relief by Vico is quite another question. Vico does not deny progress ; he even refers to it in speaking of the conditions of his own time as an actual fact : but he has no conception of it and still less does he throw such a conception into relief.   His philosophy, while it attains the lofty vision of the process of mind in obedience to its own laws, nevertheless retains by reason of this failure to apprehend the progressive enrichment of reality an element of sadness and desolation.   The individual character of men and events is obliterated in Vico ; individuals and events are represented merely as particular cases of one aspect of the mind or of one phase of civilisation.   Hence we always find Aristides alongside of Scipio and Alexander alongside of Caesar : never Aristides simply as Aristides, Scipio as Scipio, and Alexander and Caesar as Alexander and as Caesar.   Progress implies that each fact and each individual has its own unique function ; each makes its own contribution, for which no other can be substituted, to the poem of history ;

and each responds with a deeper voice to the one that went before.

But the reason why Vico was bound to miss the idea of progress and why his studies in history were inevitably one-sided can be clearly perceived only after a review of his metaphysics.

CHAPTER XII

METAPHYSICS

BY " metaphysics " we understand Vico's conception of reality as a whole, not of the world of man by itself ; and we also include in the meaning of the word his ultimate negative conclusion asserting the unknowability or the imperfect knowability of one or more spheres of reality, or of that highest sphere in which the others reunite.

In point of fact, as we observed in considering the second and latest form of his theory of knowledge, Vico drew a sharp line between the world of man and the world of nature : the former transparent to man because created by him, the latter opaque, because only God its Creator has knowledge of it. And his conception of the total and ultimate reality, the metaphysic which he expounds together with his earlier theory of knowledge, retains the value granted to it by that theory and no other : it is a probable conjecture, but one incapable of verification, and reaches completion in the certitude of revealed theology. Hence this metaphysic remains out of all possible connexion with the New Science, which proceeds by the certain method of truth and cuts itself off from revelation. Vico never rejected it. He discusses it in his autobiography of 1725, the year of the first *Scienza Nuova* ; he refers to it with satisfaction in 1737, seven years after the second *Scienza Nuova*, when his scientific life was, as he himself considered, at an end. But though he never rejected it he always kept it aside, so to speak, in a corner of his mind.

This point established, it might seem that there can be nothing more to be said of any philosophical importance about Vico's metaphysics. But this is not the case. Since every department of philosophy implies in itself every other, and since we can therefore always deduce from the treatment of one of the so-called particular philosophical sciences the character of the whole, it is legitimate to examine the New Science and to consider what metaphysic is implicit therein ; to determine what philosophical complement is logically supported and demanded by this science.

The New Science, which asserted the full knowability of human affairs, not merely on the surface, like a psychological treatment, but in the depths of their nature : the New Science, which transcended the individual to attain the conception of the mind which informs all things and is Providence : the Science which with divine pleasure contemplated the eternal cycle of the mind, elevated as it was to such a height, necessarily tended to interpret the whole of reality, both Nature and God, as Mind. That this tendency was objective to the New Science, and not subjective to Vico, in whose mind the science so to speak thought itself out, need hardly be repeated. Vico personally not only did not encourage it but actually curtailed and repressed it so energetically as to leave no trace of it in his works. There was no philosophical doctrine of which he had such terror and against which he so frequently waged war as that of pantheism ; and perhaps this polemical preoccupation is the only trace, though quite an involuntary trace, visible in his writings of the tendency which he must have observed in himself. He was, and wished to remain, a Christian and a Catholic ; transcendence, the personality of God, the substantiality of the soul, though his science did not lead him towards

them, were uncontrollable necessities to his consciousness.
But just as this fact allowed Vico to repress but not to
eradicate the essential logical tendency of his thought,
so it enables us to recognise that tendency in the facts
themselves. An Italian critic, Spaventa, is right when
he says that in Vico the necessity of a new metaphysic
makes itself felt ; another, a German Catholic, is equally
right in defining his system as " semi-pantheistic." It
would perhaps be more dangerous to go on to say, with
the Italian above mentioned, that Vico makes an advance
on the Cartesian idea of two substances and the Spinozistic
of two attributes, and even on the Leibnitian doctrine of
the monad, and that he transcends parallelism and pre-
established harmony by distinguishing the two providences, the two attributes, nature and mind, in such
a way that the one is a step to the other, and by conceiving the point of union and the origin of the opposition
as an unfolding or development, so that nature is regarded
as the phenomenon and proper basis of mind, the pre-
supposition which mind creates to itself in order to be
really mind, to be a true unity. For while we may doubt
whether the distinction of the two attributes or two
providences, the natural and the human, is a well-grounded
and inevitable consequence of conceiving substance as
mind and thought, it is impossible to deduce the evolutionary transition from one to the other as a tendency
implicit in Vico's conception of thought. There is
certainly particular documentary evidence for this latter
particular tendency : but it is scanty and unconvincing,
and occurs not in the system of the New Science but rather
in the chronologically earlier system.

For the metaphysic laid down by Vico in the earlier
phase of his thought is not, as it has seemed to some,
and as it may at first sight appear, entirely devoid of
significance and value. It shows the same aversion to
materialism and the same love of idealism which inspire

the meditations of the New Science. The philosophy of Epicurus, which takes as its starting-point matter already formed and divided into ultimate particles of various shapes, composed of other parts which are supposed to be indivisible owing to the absence of void between them, seemed to him a philosophy such as to satisfy the naïve mind of a child or the uncritical mind of a woman ; and the delight with which he followed the explanation of the forms of material nature according to this philosopher, in the poem of Lucretius, was equalled by the amusement and pity with which he watched him forced by stern necessity to lose himself in countless ineptitudes and follies in trying to explain the phenomena of thought. Vico accused the Cartesian physics no less than the Epicurean of a " false position," since it also takes ready-formed matter as its starting-point, differing from the Epicurean matter in that, while the latter limits the divisibility of matter at the atoms, the former makes its elements infinitely divisible ; that the one places motion in the void, the other in the solid ; the one initiates the shaping of its infinite worlds by a casual declination of atoms from the downward path of their own weight and gravitation, the other generates its indefinite vortices from an impetus imparted to a section of inert and therefore not yet divided matter, which on receiving this motion divides into fragments, and, hampered by its mass, necessarily makes an effort to move in a straight line, and being unable to do so through its solidity begins, divided as it is into fragments, to move about the centre of each fragment. In this way while Epicurus entrusted the world to chance, Descartes subjected it to fate ; and it was in vain that to save himself from materialism he superimposed upon his physics a quasi-Platonic metaphysic, by which he attempted to establish two substances, the one extended and the other intelligent, and to make room for an immaterial agent ; for these two parts were not reconciled in his system, since his mechanical physics included in itself a metaphysic like the Epicurean, establishing one kind and one only of active material substance. For similar or analogous reasons Vico rejected the philosophies of Gassendi, Spinoza and Locke ; and the physical science of other authors such as Robert Boyle seemed to him valuable for purposes of medicine and the "spargiric art," but useless for philosophy. Galileo he considered to have looked at physical science with the eye of a great geometrician, but without the aid of the full light of metaphysics. He had sympathy with philosophers who were also geometricians, and therefore with the Pythagorean or Timaean physics, according to which the world consists of numbers; with the Platonic metaphysics, which from the form of our minds without any other hypothesis establishes, upon our knowledge and consciousness of certain eternal truths which are in our mind and cannot be ignored or denied, the eternal idea as the principle of all things ; with the doctrine of metaphysical points, attributed by him to Zeno the Stoic ; and finally with the philosophy of the Italian Renaissance, the period adorned by Ficino, Pico della Mirandola, Steuco, Nifo, Mazzoni, Piccolomini, Acquaviva and Patrizio.

The fundamental concept of his cosmology was supplied by the metaphysical point, in which the employment of mathematics in metaphysics, a process admitted by Vico as analogous to that of construction, found expression. Just as from the geometrical point proceed the line and the surface, and the point which is defined as having no parts supplies the proof that lines otherwise incommensurable can be divided equally into their component points, so it is legitimate to postulate points not geometrical but metaphysical, which though not extended generate extension. Between God, who is rest, and matter, which is motion, the intermediate place is taken by the metaphysical point, whose attribute is conation, the indefinite energy and attempt on the part of the universe to bring into being and sustain each particular thing. The existence of matter is nothing but an indefinite power of keeping the universe extended, which underlies all extended objects equally however unequal they may be, and also an indefinite power of motion underlying all particular motions, however unequal. Behind a grain of sand lies something which when this particle is divided gives to it and preserves in it an infinite extension and magnitude; so that the whole mass of the universe is included in the grain of sand, if not actually, yet potentially and in capacity. This effort of the universe, underlying each smallest particle of matter, is neither the extension of the particle nor the extension of the universe : it is the thought of God, which, free from all materiality, gives motion and impulse to the whole. Every particular determination of reality agrees with this fundamental truth. Time is divisible, eternity indivisible ; disturbances of the mind wax and wane, its quiescence has no degrees; extended things are corruptible, unextended things permanent in their indivisibility ; body can be divided, mind cannot ; possibilities are at a single point, accidents are everywhere ; science is one, while opinion produces differences ; virtue is neither in one place nor another, vice walks up and down in every direction ; the good is one, the bad is innumerable ; in every kind of thing in a word the best occurs in the category of the indivisible.

Substance in general, which underlies and sustains things, is divided into two species, extended substance or that which equally supports unequal extensions, and thinking substance which equally supports unequal thoughts. And just as one part of extension is divided from another but indivisible in the substance of the body, so one part of thought, that is to say a determinate thought, is divided from another but indivisible in the

substance of the soul. Activity or freedom is peculiar
to the soul, and entirely denied to body : and Descartes,
in making a conation of body the beginning of his physics,
was strictly adopting the methods of a poet and falling
into the anthropormorphic conceptions of primitive
races. The phenomena which students of mechanics
call activities, forms, or powers, are insensible movements
by which bodies move either, as the ancients said, towards
their centres of gravity, or, as the modern theory of
mechanics asserts, away from their centre of motion.
The communication of motion, moreover, is just as inconceivable in body as is activity. To grant it would be
equivalent to granting the interpenetration of bodies,
since motion is nothing but matter in motion ; the blow
given to a ball is only the occasion for the energy of the
universe, which was so weak in the ball as to make it
seem at rest, to expand and thus to give it an appearance
of more sensible motion. On the other hand, Vico
agreed with the Cartesians, especially Malebranche, as
to the origin of ideas, which he inclined to believe that
God creates in us from time to time. He also held with
the Cartesians that the lower animals are automata ;
and he agreed with all contemporary thought as to the
subjectivity of secondary qualities.

Setting aside these last doctrines, which are not Vico's
own, indeed he scarcely refers to them, the fundamental
doctrine of metaphysical points is all his own. His
attribution of it to an imaginary Zeno, in whose person
were combined and confused the Eleatic and the Stoic
(a mistake common in the philosophical literature of the
time), can deceive nobody, and did not even deceive Vico
himself, who when pressed explained how he had been
led to that interpretation of Aristotle's statements about
Zeno, and finally says that if the doctrine cannot be
accepted as that of Zeno, he will adopt it as his own,
without the patronage of any great names. Nor on the

other hand can it be traced to the Leibnitian monadology. We cannot be sure that Vico was acquainted with this doctrine. In any case he does not mention it, while Leibniz he does mention in terms of deep respect : and the resemblance is very vague, for the metaphysical points are not monads. The discovery by Leibniz and Newton of the differential calculus may however be said to have influenced him. It was then for the first time becoming known in Italy ; and its terminology of maximum infinities, greater and less infinities, and so on would, says Vico, completely baffle the human understanding, since the infinite admits neither of degrees nor of multiplication, but for the help of a metaphysic which shows that all actual extension and actual movement is a power or capacity for extension and motion always equal to itself and infinite. The contributions of Platonic lines of thought (the Platonism of the Renaissance) and those of Galileo, especially the latter, to Vico's conception have been worked out with even more justice : his originality however is in no degree impaired by these facts.

The idea in which his originality found expression was, no doubt, fantastic and arbitrary, and in consequence bound to remain undeveloped and without influence on Vico's other conceptions. To the reviewer in the *Giornale dei letterati*, who called this metaphysic a mere sketch, the author replied that it was quite complete : an abortion in fact, rather than a sketch, and, as such, complete. And in the *Scienza Nuova*, beside a few references to the refusal to attribute activity to matter, there is one fugitive but interesting attempt at a connexion with a geometrical or arithmetical metaphysic on the model of that described above. In this passage it is stated that upon the order of material and complex civil affairs the order of numbers, which are abstract and absolutely simple, is imposed : and the fact is noted that governments begin with the

one, in domestic monarchy, pass to the few in aristocracy, advance to the many and the all in popular republics, and finally return to the one in civil monarchies, so that humanity moves perpetually from the one to the one, from domestic monarchy to civil monarchy.

But if we can and must deny all value to Vico's cosmology, if the contradictions and obscurities in which he involves himself are manifest, and were observed by critics of his own time, still we cannot deny its dynamic nature as opposed to the mechanicism of contemporary philosophy. The theory of metaphysical points, in which God appears as the great geometrician who creates by knowing and knows by creating the realities of the universe, is as it were a symbol of the necessity of interpreting nature in idealistic language. We find here and there a theologian Vico, an agnostic Vico, or even a fanciful Vico composing cosmological and physical romances: but look where we will among his works, we shall never find a materialistic Vico.

Even this by no means overbold metaphysic aroused suspicions of pantheism, though the author insisted upon the theological doctrine that God's activity is convertible *ab intra* with the thing created and *ab extra* with the fact, and that therefore the world was created in time ; that the human soul, which as a mirror of the divine thinks infinity and eternity, is not bounded by the body and therefore not by time, and is therefore immortal ; and that man, even if God were to reveal it to him, cannot understand how the infinite enters into finite objects. However, he thought it necessary to conclude his replies to his critics by collecting statements demonstrating his orthodoxy, and clinching the matter with the remark that " since God is in one sense substance and in another His creatures, and since the *ratio essendi* or essence is proper to substance, the created substances even as regards their essence are diverse and distinct from the substance of God."

Vico's thought was limited by the idea of transcendence, which prevented him from attaining not only the unity of reality, but also a truly complete knowledge of that world of man which he had so powerfully explained by means of the opposite principle. We now see why Vico, though he did not deny the fact of progress, could have no real conception of it. It has been observed that the conception of progress is foreign to Catholicism and dates from the Protestant Reformation, and that therefore the Catholic Vico was bound to deny himself the use of it. But the conception of an immanent providence is no less irreconcilable with Catholicism, and yet Vico is saturated with this idea. This means that he did not lack the impulse : rather he was unable to pass a certain point beyond which his faith would have been too obviously defeated. Progress, deduced from the immanent providence and introduced into the New Science, would have accentuated the difference within the uniformity, the origin at every moment of something new, the perpetual enrichment of the flux at every reflux : it would have changed history from an orderly traversing and retraversing of the line drawn by God under the eye of God to a drama whose *ratio essendi* is contained within itself : it would have enmeshed and drawn with it the whole universe and realised the thought of infinite worlds. In face of this vision Vico paused in apprehension and stubbornly refused to proceed : the philosopher in him had yielded to the Catholic.

CHAPTER XIII

TRANSITION TO HISTORY : GENERAL CHARACTER
OF VICO'S TREATMENT OF HISTORY

IT is clear from the facts above discussed that the historical portion of the New Science could not take the shape of a history of the human race in which peoples and individuals were recognised as playing each its own unique part in the whole course of events. To enable it to fulfil such a function Vico would have had to close up his system of thought, which was still at one point incomplete and not impervious to the religious idea, and to elevate his provident deity into a progressive deity, determining flux and reflux as the eternal rhythm of the process. Or on the other hand in order to attain the vision of individuality, in the diametrically opposite sense, in history, he would have had to abandon his rudimentary idealistic philosophy, break down the distinction between ordinary and extraordinary providence, and trace the history of man on the plan which God had revealed or permitted him to discover. Vico's orthodoxy rebelled against the former alternative, while his philosophy kept him from the second : and the result of his dilemma was that the history he reconstructed was not and could not be a universal history.

In consequence, it was not what is called a philosophy of history, if that phrase is taken in its original sense of a " universal history "—one which concentrates its attention upon the broadest and least obvious connexions of facts—"philosophically narrated," more philosophically, that is, than is usual with annalists, anecdotists and compilers dealing with courts, politics and nations. The controversy as to whether Vico or Herder can claim to be the founder of the philosophy of history must be frankly decided in favour of Herder, whose work shows just that procedure of universal history which is lacking in the New Science. On the other hand it would be easy to find numerous predecessors for Herder, beginning with the Hebrew prophets and the scheme of the Four Monarchies, which remained not only in the Middle Ages but well into modern times the constructive scheme of universal history. Nor would it be out of place to add that the so-called philosophy of history, in so far as it is a universal history, constitutes neither a special philosophical science nor a form of history capable of sharp distinction from the rest, except when the passion for making it self-subsistent gives it the appearance of an abstract history or a historicised philosophy. Thus when Vico or Herder is credited with the foundation of a new science in the philosophy of history, the compliment is a doubtful one : a fact which especially in the case of Vico has gone far to obscure the value of their work. In fact, the "New Science of the common character of nations," understood as the equivocal science of the philosophy of history, has eclipsed the New Science as a new philosophy of mind and a rudimentary metaphysic of thought.

The conflict which for the general consciousness existed between science and faith reappears in Vico's treatment of history as a distinction and opposition between Jewish and Gentile history, sacred history and profane. Jewish history was not subjected, he believed, to the laws of history in general. Its course was unique, and its development proceeded on principles peculiar to itself, namely, the direct action of God. The New Science, which in its philosophical part did not give the explanatory principles of this process, was in consequence not compelled to deal with it in its historical part. This is perhaps what Vico would have wished. But the wish was met, setting aside the necessity of guarding against the charge of impiety, which was certainly a danger, by his scruples as a believer, and a conscientious believer; which urged him to look for some kind of harmony between the two histories, since however sharply distinguished (he recalled how even a Gentile writer, Tacitus, had described the Jews as " unsociable "), both alike developed under terrestrial conditions and had points of mutual contact, at least in the origin of mankind and its regeneration by means of Christianity. Following the inherent tendencies of his thought, Vico ought to and would willingly have avoided the narration of universal history and confined himself exclusively to questions of philosophy and philology. But as it happened, he was compelled now and then to depart from his programme and to attempt at once a unification of the two histories and a defence of sacred history based on arguments supplied by science and profane history.

This is the least successful, but a profoundly significant part of his work. He was forced to admit, though the admission was opposed by all his discoveries and outraged his whole system of thought, that the Hebrews had enjoyed the privilege of always keeping intact their memories of the beginning of the world, a memory which other nations claimed in vain ; and hence sacred history must supply the true origin and succession of universal history. The necessity of connecting his views on primitive civilisation with Biblical chronology, with the date usually assigned to the creation of the world, with the traditions of a universal deluge and of a race of giants —the necessity of finding, as he says, the " continuity of sacred with profane history "—led him to the most extravagant flights of fancy. After the flood, in the year 1656 from the creation, at the separation of the sons of Noah, while the Hebrews began or continued their sacred history with Abraham and the other patriarchs and then with the laws given to Moses by God, all the other descendants of Shem, Ham, and Japhet, the first race more slowly and for a shorter period, the second and third with greater rapidity and for a longer time, lapsed into the state of nature and wandered over the earth as insensible and savage brutes. And while the Hebrews, subjected to their theocratic government, strictly educated and practising ablution, remained of normal stature, the members of the other races, living without either physical or moral discipline, wallowing in dirt and excrement and absorbing nitrogenous salts (just as the earth is enriched and made fertile by excrement), grew to monstrous and gigantic size. The state of nature lasted a hundred years for the Semites and two hundred for the other two races ; at the end of which the earth which had long been sodden with the moisture of the universal deluge began to dry up and emit dry exhalations or fiery matter into the air so as to generate lightning. With lightning, as we already know, and with the mythology of the thundering sky, which is Jupiter, arose in these brutes the consciousness of God and of themselves, by which they became human. Thus begins the " age of the gods," which, socially, is that of domestic monarchy where the father is king and priest. In the course of this age the system of greater deities was gradually established, and the giants, by means of their religions of terror and their domestic education taming the flesh and developing the spiritual element in them, and by the practice of washing, shrank by degrees to the normal size of the men whom we find at the beginning of the next or heroic age.

Such are the chief points in Vico's quaint reconstruc-

tion of the earliest history of man upon the earth, harmonised with the account in sacred history. We shall be less
inclined to amusement or ridicule if we reflect upon the
tragedy underlying the comedy: the tormented conscience of the believer which in its struggle with the
philosopher seeks refuge in these extravagant ideas.
At any rate, they gave Vico a series of insecure stepping-
stones—the flood, the giants, the dry exhalations—which
enabled him to cross the torrent of religious tradition
and reach the dry land of critical history, where he found
the primary starting-point of his philosophy of mind,
the state of nature. It may further be suggested that the
contact with Hebrew history—the only one which presented itself to him as a history in the strict sense,
a *unicum*, something absolutely individualised even if
in a miraculous manner—suggested to him the few
attempts met with in his works to assign to various
peoples a special function or mission ; thus it sometimes
appeared to him that the Hebrews represented *mens*,
the Chaldeans *ratio*, and the Japhetic races *phantasia*.

Parallel to this imaginary history of the origin of the
human race on the earth is Vico's attempt at Biblical
apologetics. He lost no opportunity of adducing proofs
from profane sources to confirm the statements of sacred
history. For instance, a confirmation of the flood and
the giants is supplied by the similar traditions of Greek
and other nations. The theocratic government, which
is not definitely mentioned by any profane history but
merely alluded to obscurely by poets in their tales, is
met with in the government of the Hebrews before and
after the flood. The Hebrews again knew notning of
divination because they lived in direct contact with the
true God, while the Chaldees had a system of magic or
divination according to the movements of the stars, and
the European peoples a system of augury. One certainly
feels in all this something of an effort, a will to see or not

to see : a kind of self-interruption and stimulation to belief. It is not infrequent among cultured and scientifically educated believers. Again, in his exposition of the historical genesis of grammatical forms, where he says that verbs began with the imperative, the monosyllabic command given by the father to wife, child or slave (*es, sta, i, da, fac,* etc.), Vico draws from this an indirect demonstration of the truth of Christianity, because the roots of Hebrew verbs are always found in the third person singular of the past tense ; a clear proof that the patriarchs must have given their commands to their families in the name of a single God (*Deus dixit*). This, in Vico's opinion, is " a lightning to confound all those writers who have believed the Hebrews to be a colony proceeding from Egypt ; since from the beginning of its foundation the Hebrew tongue had its origin in a single God." But in truth these lightnings instead of descending upon the head of the unbeliever serve only to illuminate the poverty of the arguments upon which apologetics rest, even with a man like Vico ; and, objectively considered, the division introduced by religious scruple between sacred and profane history, and the consequent dogmatic treatment of the one, with its strange hypotheses and defences, and critical treatment of the other, produced and still produces an irresistible impression that the seclusion of sacred history from human science is due to the impotence not of the human science but of the sacred history ; its impotence, that is, to preserve itself intact within the limits of science. Seldom has a religious scruple so endangered the cause of religion.

But Vico had far too genuine and exacting a scientific sense added to his natural antipathies to permit him ever to become a Selden or a Bossuet ; and hence this apologetic for and harmonisation of sacred history remains in him a mere episode, which it is possible to ignore. And since on the other hand he was not permitted to treat philosophy and history as entirely profane and to represent the complex movement of history according to the fundamental criterion of progress, his only course was to look at the facts from the point of view which his philosophy left open to him, that of flux and reflux, the eternal process and the eternal phases of the mind. Here lay his strength. Here he could recognise the specific, if not strictly the individual, character of laws, customs, poetry and myth, of whole social and cultural formations which history down to his own time had entirely misunderstood. For this reason, in narrating history he was bound to confine himself to emphasising the common aspects of certain groups of facts belonging to various nations and periods. In the New Science, he says, " the whole history of the laws and deeds of Rome and Greece is set forth, not in its particularity and in time, but following the substantial identity of intention and diversity of the modes of expression." Elsewhere he says, " the facts are adduced after the fashion of examples, because they are understood by means of principles," for " to see the principles confirmed by the innumerable host of their consequences is a thing which must await certain other works of ours, which are either as yet unpublished or now in process of publication." In other words, as we know, this science contains on the one hand a philosophical side, and on the other a descriptive or empirical, exemplified in history, in which the Romans figure not as Romans but in virtue of the common nature which they share with Greeks and possibly with Japanese ; the history of Rome under the kings or in the early Republican period demonstrates its affinity with that of the earlier centuries of the Middle Ages ; and Homer stands not as Homer but as an example of primitive poetry, and across the centuries finds and greets his brother in Dante. It is at once a strength and a limitation, because history emphatically does not fundamentally consist of these resemblances; but without the perception of the resemblances how could we ever determine the differences ? Dante is not Homer, the barons are not the " patres," the Athenian Solon is not the Roman Publilius Philo; but certainly Dante is in some respects more closely related to Homer than to Petrarch, the early barons are nearer to the "patres" than to the later courtier-nobles, and Solon is more akin to a Roman tribune or dictator than to any other of the seven sages among whom he is usually placed. To observe these resemblances means denying or rejecting other more superficial ones, and preparing the way for knowledge of individuality by indicating the approximate place where the truth is to be found. Vico classifies, rather than narrates and represents; but there is classification and classification; it may be pressed into the service of a superficial thought or of a profound one. And the historical side of the New Science is one great substitution of profound for superficial classifications.

In this process, which constitutes the strength of Vico's treatment of history, the deficiencies and errors come not from outside the limits of the process but from causes at work within these limits themselves. It has been alleged in defence of Vico that a great part of his errors is due to the scantiness and inadequacy of the materials at his disposal. But the materials for any study are always scanty and inadequate compared to our thirst for knowledge; and in judging a historian the question is not this, but the method, cautious or incautious, on which he employs the materials that are at his disposal. Again, it has been said that Vico has the faults of his age; but this is to forget that he was born in the century which saw the development of the highly critical philology of Joseph Scaliger and the whole Dutch school, and that Zeno, Maffei and Muratori were his contemporaries in Italy. The truth is that just as the attitude of thought already described in Vico confused pure philosophical method with the determinations of empirical science and historical data, so it confused historical research with the mixture of philosophy and empirical science. Vico was in a state similar to that of drunkenness ; confusing categories with facts, he felt absolutely certain *a priori* of what the facts would say : instead of letting them speak for themselves he put his own words into their mouth. A common illusion with him was to seem to see connexions between things where there was really none. This made him turn every hypothetical conjunction into a certainty, and read in other writers instead of their actual words things that they had never written, but which were internally spoken by himself unawares and projected into the writings of others. Exactitude was for him an impossibility, and in his mental excitement and exaltation he almost despised it : what harm can ten, twenty, a hundred errors do to what is substantially true ? Exactitude, " diligence," as he says, " must lose itself in arguments of any size, because it is a minute, and because minute also a slow-footed virtue." Fanciful etymologies, daring and groundless mythological interpretations, changes of name and date, exaggerations of fact, false quotations are met with throughout his pages, and many may be found noted in the fine edition of the second *Scienza Nuova* by Nicolini. Thus, as we observed in speaking of his philosophy that Vico's was not an acute mind, so now in speaking of his historical work we must say that it was not critical. But as while we denied him acuteness on a small scale we acknowledged his profundity or acuteness on a large scale, so here also we ought to add that if Vico lacked the critical sense in small matters, in great matters he had abundance of it. Careless, headstrong and confused in detail ; cautious, logical and penetrative in essentials ; he exposes his flank or rather his whole body to the attacks of the most miserable and mechanical pedant, and over-awes and inspires respect in every critic and historian however great. And, *totus mens* though he is and all absorbed by his own discoveries, often he does not give his power of investigation and observation time and room to develop, and instead of history he invents myths and investigates romances; but when he allows the power free play, it does wonders in the field of history too, as we shall try to show in the following chapters.

But to judge the historical views of Vico by confronting them, as many have done, with those of modern historical research and praising or depreciating them accordingly would hardly be conclusive. Where the two terms of the comparison agreed the agreement might be fortuitous : where they diverged, the later doctrine might be but a development or consequence of the earlier attempt, and in any case the modern state of historical knowledge by no means provides an absolute standard. On the other hand it would be out of place, as well as beyond our power, to rehandle all the problems dealt with by Vico to see what there is of truth and falsehood in his conclusions. That would mean no less than writing a third *Scienza Nuova* more adapted to our own times. Our task is merely to indicate the principal historical problems which Vico set before himself, to state the solutions he gave, and always to keep in mind the state of knowledge not in our own day but in Vico's, so as to determine what progress in historical study may be set down to his influence.

CHAPTER XIV

NEW PRINCIPLES FOR THE HISTORY OF OBSCURE AND LEGENDARY PERIODS

THE period of historical research which preceded the life of Vico was, as we have said, by no means credulous or uncritical. The day was past when "chronicles of the world" were compiled, when any fable and any falsification however gross was accepted as history : and the seed sown by a few humanists had borne fruit in the Italian men of learning, the French juridical school, the school of Scaliger mentioned above, and all the great chronologists, epigraphists, archaeologists, topographers and geographers who in the seventeenth century formed the first immense critical collections of sources for ancient history. While the philologists were thus improving and perfecting their methods, detecting impostures and bridging lacunae, Bayle, Fontenelle, Saint-Évremond and many others were engaged in spreading a scepticism or historical Pyrrhonism as it was also called, due to the intellectualistic philosophy ; and thus anticipating the polemic against the truth and utility of history which was to arise with immense vigour in the following century.

This latter tendency was hypercritical rather than critical, its end being the destruction of history in general : and since historical scepticism was very apt to assume the character of a paradox adapted to the needs of elegant society and the wits, its influence on the progress of

research was very small, or at most it succeeded in producing strong reactions, one of which is represented by Vico, in
favour of tradition and authority. It is on the other hand
only proper to observe the failings of the first seriously
scientific efforts of philologists and antiquaries. They re-
habilitated witnesses, laid bare falsifications, reconstructed
lists of rulers and magistrates, connected chronology and
contradicted certain legends : but, whether owing to the
tendencies of thought usual among pure scholars and
philologists or because of the general atmosphere of their
century's culture, they neither had nor conveyed a feeling for the antique and the primitive. Strong in detail,
they were weak in essentials. When one of the most
brilliant grasped, for instance, the importance of ballad-
literature as a means of transmitting history at a period
when the use of writing was unknown or uncommon, he
did not receive from this observation and others like it
such a shock as might stimulate him to recast from top
to bottom his intuition and conception of primitive life,
as was the case with Vico, who almost in a flash grasped
the philosophical form of certitude and the two periods
of mental and social life corresponding to it in actual
history : the periods of obscurity and of legend.

Vico himself started from a kind of scepticism, a
scepticism as regards the prejudices of scholars and
nations generally about the character and facts of
antiquity : and in combating these prejudices he drew
up a series of principles or " aphorisms," inspired apparently by Bacon's " idola," to which they present an
analogy in the field of historical research. Vico puts the
student on his guard first against the " magnificent
opinions " which have been held up to his own day
" concerning the most remote and least known antiquity":
a naïve illusion whose origin he traces to the fact that
man when in a state of entire ignorance erects himself
into a rule for the universe. Here is the closest analogy

with Bacon : for this statement is precisely like the class of "*idola tribus*," in which thought makes itself the rule of things " on the analogy of man, not of the universe " (*ex analogia hominis, non ex analogia universi*). On the same observation is founded the remark that " rumour grows in its course," *fama crescit eundo*, and Tacitus's *omne ignotum pro magnifico est*, everything unknown is taken for something great. Hence arises the habit of interpreting ancient customs in the expectation of finding them similar or superior to those of modern civilised life. Thus Cicero admired the humanity of the early Romans in calling enemies in war " guests " : not realising that the fact was precisely the opposite of this, and that guests were *hostes*, strangers and enemies. In the same way Seneca, by way of proving the duty of kindness to slaves, recalled that masters were anciently called " fathers of the family " ; as if "*patres familias*" might not have been the very reverse of kind not only to slaves and servants but to their own children, regarded as on the level of slaves. The same prejudice led Grotius, in his desire to show the gentleness of the ancient Germans, to collect a great number of barbaric laws in which homicide was punished by a fine of a few pence : which is on the contrary really a proof of the cheapness of the blood of poor rustic vassals, who are precisely the " *homines* " mentioned by these laws.

In the second place, he warns us not to trust to the " conceit of nations," all of which, Greek or barbarian, Chaldean, Scythian, Egyptian, or Chinese, claimed, as Diodorus Siculus observes, to have founded humanity, discovered the amenities of life, and preserved their memory intact from the beginning of the world. Each of them, having for several thousand years had no communication with the others which might have led to the sharing of ideas, resembled in the obscurity of its chronology a man who sleeping in a very small chamber is misled by the darkness into believing it much too large ever to touch it with his hand. He who accepts these dreamer's boasts for certain knowledge finds himself in the difficulty of having to choose between the various memories of various nations, all of which with equal justification claim to be original.

By the side of national conceit Vico placed the " conceit of the learned," who desire their own knowledge to be as old as the world, and consequently delight in fancying an inaccessible esoteric wisdom among the ancients, coinciding miraculously with the opinions professed by each one of themselves, which they dress in the garb of antiquity in order to enforce their acceptance. Such was the mistake not only of Plato, especially in the researches of the *Cratylus*, but of all historians, ancient and modern : Vico himself had fallen into it, and was therefore able to study it closely in his own case, when in the *De antiquissima* he believed himself to have found in the etymologies of Latin words the proof of an Italian metaphysic exactly agreeing with his own doctrines of the conversion of the *verum* with the *factum* and of metaphysical points.

From these three prejudices, especially from the conceit of the learned, follows the fourth, here called that of the " sources " or " channels of culture," ironically called by Vico the theory of " scholastic succession among nations." Upon this theory Zoroaster for instance instructed Berosus for Chaldaea, Berosus in his turn Mercurius Trimegistus for Egypt, Mercurius taught Atlas the Ethiopian lawgiver, Atlas Orpheus the Thracian missionary, and finally Orpheus established his school in Greece. Long journeys these, and easy forsooth to those primitive nations which, scarcely out of the state of savagery, lived perched on mountains in almost inaccessible situations, unknown even to their neighbours ! And these long journeys were undertaken with the object of spreading discoveries, which any nation could make for itself. If, when nations came to know each other through wars and treaties, they were found to agree, that was because they all contained some motive of truth and sprang from the same needs of man. Was it necessary to suppose the Athenian or Mosaic law to have affected that of the Romans, as did these " comparers " or derivers of laws, in order to explain the origin of the right recognised in Palestine, Athens and Rome to kill the thief by night ? Was it necessary for Pythagoras to travel spreading the doctrine of the transmigration of souls, which we find as far afield as India ?

There remained the prejudice of considering the ancient historians as best informed about primitive times : whereas in the history of origins they knew as little as, or less than, ourselves. As for Greek history, Vico found, or rather imagined that he found, in Thucydides, a confession that the Greeks up to the generation preceding that historian knew nothing of their own antiquity : and he also observed that it was only in the time of Xenophon that Greek historians began to have any precise information upon Persian affairs. Roman historians commonly began with the foundation of Rome : but the beginning of Rome was certainly not the beginning of the world. Rome was a new city founded in the midst of a large number of small and more ancient peoples in Latium : and even in the case of Rome Livy refuses to guarantee the truth of the facts of the earlier centuries of its history up to the Punic wars, which he is in a position to describe more accurately. He even confesses frankly that he does not know at what point Hannibal made his great and memorable entry into Italy, whether by the Cottian Alps or the Apennines. So well informed were the ancient historians !

Owing to these and similar sceptical principles, the whole of Greek history to the time of Herodotus and of Roman down to the second Punic war seemed to Vico quite uncertain, an unclaimed territory, so to speak, where one might enter and take possession by squatter's right. He entered armed with positive principles directly issuing from the negative ones we have enumerated. For if Vico denied the credibility of historians distant in time from the facts they described, if he discounted national pride, if he laid bare the illusions and charlatanism of the learned, he nevertheless did not rest content with this work of destruction. In place of the old untrustworthy method he had banished, he endeavoured to supply a new, of better qualities and greater tenacity; a system of methods by which it was possible to acquire new historical documents and also to improve the study of those already known. No advance in historical knowledge is in fact ever made except by thus turning from the received narrative to the document underlying it, which alone has the power of confirming, correcting and enriching the narrative.

The first of Vico's contributions to historical method, the first source for the knowledge of the earliest civilisations which he exposed, is the etymology of language. The usual methods of this study in his time were purely arbitrary: it proceeded by considering the sound of each syllable or letter and looking for other superficial resemblances, and inferring from these facts the derivation of a word from this or that language, Latin, Greek or Hebrew. But etymology becomes a fruitful study only when it is remembered that language is the best evidence for the ancient life of a people, the life lived by them while the language was in the making: and when the student accordingly never ceases to explain language by customs and customs by language. Thus the etymology of abstract words leads us into the heart of a purely rustic society; for *intellegere*, to understand, for example, recalls *legere*, to collect the produce of the fields (hence *legumina*, vegetables); *disserere*, to discuss, refers to scattering seed; and the majority of words for inanimate things reveal relations with the human body and its members,

and the sensations and passions of man ; thus " mouth "
means any aperture, " lip " the edge of a pot, " forehead "
and " back " are used for before and behind ; and so on.
Vico aimed at one science of etymology common to all
native languages, composed of monosyllabic, and largely
onomatopoeic roots : another of foreign loan - words,
introduced after nations became mutually acquainted : a
third, of universal application, for the science of international law, from which it should appear how the same
men, facts or objects, looked at from the different points
of view of different nations, received different names ;
and finally a dictionary of mental words, common to all
nations, which should explain the uniform ideas of substances and the different modifications of them in national
thought concerning the human needs and utilities common
to all, according to the differences of their situation,
climate, character and customs, and should thus narrate
the origins of the various vocal languages, all converging
in an ideal common language.

The second source revealed by Vico is the interpretation of myths or fables, which agreeably to his doctrine
were not allegories, fictions or impostures, but the science
of primitive man.   In the *Diritto universale* Vico distinguished four different and successive characters of the
gods.   At first they represented natural facts, Jupiter
the sky, Diana the flowing water, Dis or Pluto the lower
earth, Neptune the sea, and so on ; secondly, natural
human affairs, for instance, Vulcan fire, Ceres corn,
Saturn the seed ; thirdly, social facts ; and finally they
rose to heaven and were translated to the stars, and
terrestrial and human things were distinguished from
divine.   But in the two *Scienze Nuove* he emphasised
almost exclusively the third or social meaning, which
became in his eyes the original ; since, he appears to have
thought, the earliest nations were too much intent upon
themselves, too much immersed in their hard and difficult

HISTORY OF OBSCURE PERIODS

life, to speculate in abstraction from social matters. Hence
he found reflected in mythology the institutions, inven-
tions, social cleavages, class-struggles, travels and warfare
of primitive nations. Even in considerably advanced
periods Vico was hostile to naturalistic or philosophical
explanations. The saying " know thyself " attributed
to the ancient sage seemed to him merely a piece of advice
to the Athenian democracy, to know its own strength,
later transferred to a metaphysical and moral sense.
Beside this principle of social interpretation he established
another of great importance : namely, that indecent
meanings were inserted in myths at a late and corrupt
period when men interpreted early customs in the light
of their own, or tried to justify their own lusts by fancying
that the gods had set them the example. Hence arose
the adulterous Jupiter, Juno as the implacable enemy of
Hercules' virtue, the chaste Diana soliciting the embraces
of the sleeping Endymion, Apollo persecuting modest
maidens even to their death, Mars, not content with
committing adultery with Venus by land, but pursuing her
even into the sea, and, worst of all, the love of Jupiter for
Ganymede and of Jupiter again, transformed into a swan,
for Leda. Such representations can only result in unrestrained vice, as happened in the case of the young
Chaereas in Terence's comedy. But in their original
shape and meaning all myths were serious and austere,
worthy of the founders of nations. The pursuit of Daphne
by Apollo for instance referred to the magicians or diviners
who arranged weddings and followed women through the
woods where they were still liable to promiscuous ravish-
ing ; Venus, covering her nakedness with the cestus,
was a modest symbol of solemn matrimony ; the heroes,
sons of Jupiter, were not the offspring of adultery, but
born of permanent and solemn marriages celebrated
according to the will of Jupiter as revealed by the diviners.
To the pure all things are pure, and impure to the impure :

the forests and mountain-tops could never beget the fancies of the closet and the brothel.

Beside these two rich sources, language and mythology, Vico names and employs a third, which he calls the " great fragments of the ancient world," that is to say, the memories preserved by historians and poets, such as the Egyptian tradition of the three ages of gods, heroes and men ; the language of the gods mentioned in Homer ; the thirty thousand names of the gods collected by Varro and referring to a like number of needs in the natural, moral, economic and civil life of the earliest times ; the grove of Romulus, which Livy calls " the ancient plan of founding cities," and a few other golden sayings of ancient historians. Till now these fragments had been useless for the purposes of science, lying as they did in dirt, confusion and incompleteness : but when cleaned, restored and fitted together they conveyed valuable information. Nor did he overlook the monuments of architecture and sculpture, though the use he made of them was slight, and he saw that they were in the long run of little practical value. He declared that as for the historic period the most certain documents are the public coins, so for the legendary and obscure period their place is taken by " certain traces remaining in marble," as proofs of ancient customs, like the Egyptian pyramids with their hierogly- phic inscriptions and other fragments of the ancient world found in every region and bearing similar pictographic characters. It is also worthy of remark that he gives examples of arguments founded on technical observations and leading to conclusions in the sphere of prehistoric archaeology : as for instance when he says that one early period of human life is distinguished by the eating of roasted flesh, the simplest and least elaborate kind of food, because it requires nothing except the fire : a later period by boiled flesh, which also requires water, caldron and tripod.

One powerful method of investigation in Vico's hands

is the comparative method, consisting in the comparison
of better-known processes of development with those
known imperfectly or in parts only, and the consequent
reconstruction of the latter on the basis of the former.
So for instance the principle of heroism, revealed by
evidence found in Roman history, helps to explain the
legendary history of the Greeks, to supply the deficiencies
of that of Egypt and to shed light on the unknown history
of all other nations of antiquity. Without denying the
fact of transmission from one nation to another, Vico
poured scorn upon the abuse of this conception, and
minimised its value in the case of primitive societies :
using in its place the idea of spontaneous development
and endeavouring to reconstruct the process by the comparative method. But he took this method in a very
broad sense, and made use in it of materials drawn from
the most widely varying countries and periods. To
explain for example how the thundering sky suggested
to primitive man the idea of a god, he mentions the
fact that the natives of America, when first they heard
the noise and recognised the deadly effects of firearms
in the hands of the Spaniards, believed them to be gods :
the rhapsodists of the Homeric poems reminded him of
the singers on the quay at Naples with their ballads of
Roland and the paladins : the transformations or meta-
morphoses described by the ancient poets resembled the
tales of goblins and fairies still told by mothers to amuse
little children, or the widely-scattered mediaeval legends
of the magician Merlin : he traces the mythology of the
hearth down to the custom of the log which in Boccaccio's
time at Florence the head of the family used to light upon
the hearth at the new year, sprinkling incense and wine
on it, and the Christmas-eve log among the lower classes
at Naples ; not to mention the custom in the Neapolitan
kingdom of counting families by " hearths." He brought
the serpent Python and all other mythical serpents into

relation with the viper of the Visconti " che i milanesi accampa " (" which calls to arms the Milanese ") and the hieroglyphic script with the " *rébus de Picardie* " used in the north of France.

It would be useless to look in earlier or contemporary philology for clear general precedents for these principles, negative and positive, established by Vico for the history of obscure and legendary periods.   They are too closely bound up with and essential to his whole philosophical thought ever to have originated apart from this thought itself.   The rude fragments of ancient Roman laws, customs and formulae, the Homeric poems, the words of the Latin language, when examined with unprejudiced eyes—the power which enables a man of genius to see things without distortion—and worked over by a mind ready to accept them in their true nature, were bound to excite in Vico, compared with the learned but colourless or falsely-coloured historical research of his day, a rebellion and upheaval like that which took place a century later in the mind of Augustin Thierry when he saw, depicted in the pages of Chateaubriand's poetical prose, Pharamond and his Franks, with their unrestrained movements, their rude and savage arms, their terrible war-cries and their barbaric songs.

CHAPTER XV

HEROIC SOCIETY

As the Franks, in the compilations of national history made by the Jesuit colleges and other French schools, appear stripped of all their characteristic features and reduced to wise monarchs, pious queens and devoted warriors of the Church, so ancient and primitive history, thanks to the rhetoric and the naïve ideas of scholars, has been painted in brilliant and untrue colours of the same kind as those with which Lebrun or Luca Giordano painted their pompous and theatrical pictures. Kings who devoted themselves to sage counsel in order to aid their subjects while at the same time not diminishing the splendour of their courts and the brilliancy of their happy nobles, philosopher kings such as made Plato sigh for the day when philosophers should rule or kings philosophise ; loyal and valiant knights, eager to sacrifice themselves for the common welfare ; statesmen who used to accomplish pilgrimages at speed in order to bring back from afar to their waiting citizens laws more wise than their own ; good fathers of families, admirable mothers, brave and obedient young men, loving and modest maidens, every one a personification of some virtue or even of all virtues at once, models of human perfection : such are the figures which sanctified by their venerable antiquity fill alike volumes and imaginations. These are the heroes of Greek and Roman history : and

all this splendid cloth-of-gold decoration must be torn
off and cleared away if we would attempt to discover
in the deepest recesses of the memory of mankind the
true heroes, the heroes of reality, not of literature, of
life, not of the stage : ignorant, superstitious, fierce, selfish,
harsh to their families, cruel to their inferiors, avaricious,
grasping, and yet, in spite of or even because of these same
characteristics of barbarism, heroes : virtuous with the one
kind of virtue possible and necessary in primitive times,
the virtue of strength, discipline, and a deep and uncom-
promising sense of religion.

The misrepresentation of the primitive hero as a wise
and virtuous member of a civilised society reaches its
height, so far as political history is concerned, in the
failure to understand the three chief words which sum up
the constitution of the state : king, people and freedom.
By a misunderstanding of the first, it is believed that the
original form of the state was monarchy, the absolute
monarchy which rests on the strength of the people and
keeps in check the nobles : which is really a late development in history, if not the latest. Into this error had
fallen Jean Bodin, whom Vico chose as the object of his
polemic. But Bodin, more acute than other political
writers, involved himself in a contradiction, because
though he accepted the common error he nevertheless,
observing the effects of an aristocratic republic in the
supposed freedom of ancient Rome, propped up his
system by distinguishing between state and government,
and asserting that Rome in the earliest period was popular
in state but aristocratically governed ; and since this
prop was too weak to bear the whole weight of the facts
he at last confessed that this republic was aristocratic
both in government and in state, thus contradicting
the whole of his own doctrine as to the necessary succession of states. The truth is that the kings of these earliest
periods were at Rome, as at Sparta and elsewhere, not

monarchs at all. The fathers, patricians or heroes
were monarchical kings only in the period of domestic
monarchy, when each family lived separately ; but they
were kings of a special kind, subject to no one but God,
armed with religions of terror and consecrated with the
most cruel penalties. On emerging from this first state,
when the fathers united into a patrician order, their king
was simply one or more of themselves, the mere magistrate of the order. Hence Rome, after expelling the
Tarquins by a purely aristocratic revolution, did not change
her state at all. She preserved her kings in the shape of
two consuls, " annual kings," two aristocratic kings who
were " deprived of no single detail of the royal power."
The two kings of Sparta had the same character ; they
were liable like the consuls to be held accountable for
their actions and could be condemned to death by the
ephors.

As these states had been falsely considered monarchical,
so, no less falsely, they had been taken as popular in
character. The people referred to in this way does
not coincide with, in fact it excludes, the plebs : the
" *populus* " was simply the patrician order, and freedom
meant simply the freedom of the patricians, the liberty
of the master : and the " *patria* " was appropriately
so called, because it really was *res patrum*, the property
of a few fathers. It is absurd to think that the plebs,
a horde of the most worthless labourers treated as slaves,
could possess the right of electing the king, and that the
fathers confined themselves to merely approving this
election in the senate. The relations between fathers
and plebeians were quite other than neighbourly peace,
mutual trust and hearty co-operation. The heroes,
according to a passage of Aristotle, took a solemn oath
to be eternal enemies of the plebs : that was the form
their democratic spirit took. And the " Roman virtue "
which sets before us so many and such glorious examples,

gives no example of kindliness to the common people. Brutus, who dedicated his house in the persons of his two sons to the cause of freedom : Scaevola, who terrified Porsena by punishing his own right hand in the fire : the stern Manlius, who executed his own son when he returned victorious through a successful breach of military discipline : Curtius, who leapt in full armour with his horse into the fatal chasm : Decius, who devoted himself for the safety of his army : Fabricius and Curius, who refused the Samnite gold and the kingdom of Pyrrhus : Attilius Regulus, who went to certain death to preserve the sanctity of a Roman's oath : what did these men ever do for the commons, except increase their miseries by war, plunge them deeper into the waters of usury, and immure them more closely in the private dungeons of the nobles where they were flogged bare-backed like the vilest slaves ? And woe to any aristocrat who allowed himself the slightest desire to alleviate these miseries ! He was promptly accused of sedition and treason and sent to his death ; the fate that in Rome befel Manlius Capitolinus, who saved the Capitol from the fires of the Gaul, and yet for his democratic sympathies was thrown from the Tarpeian rock ; the fate that came in Sparta, the hero-city of Greece as Rome was the hero-city of the world, to the great-souled king Agis, the Manlius Capitolinus of Lacedaemon, who, for trying to lighten the burden of the unhappy commons by a law abolishing debts and to aid them by another giving them testamentary rights, was strangled by the ephors. The famous " Roman virtue " amazes any one who is obsessed by the modern idea of a virtue consisting in justice and benevolence to all mankind. What virtue could live with such pride ? What moderation with such avarice ? What mercy with such cruelty ? What justice with such inequality ?

The heroes treated their own families no less harshly

than the plebs. The education of children was stern, rough and cruel. The Spartans, in order that their sons might not fear pain and death, beat them within an inch of their lives in the temple of Diana, so that they often fell dead in agonies of pain beneath their father's blows. In Greece as in Rome it was lawful to kill innocent newborn children, a custom the reverse of the modern, by which the delights which surround little children shape the softer side of human nature. Wives were bought by the dowries of the heroic period, a survival of which was the practice solemnly observed in Rome of marriage *"coemptione et farre"* (a similar custom is ascribed by Tacitus to the ancient Germans and must be considered universal among barbarous peoples), and were maintained simply as a necessity of nature for the procreation of children and in other respects treated like slaves ; as can still be seen in many parts of the old world and almost everywhere in the new. The acquisition of children and the thrift of the wife were simply reckoned as so much profit to the father and husband.

The counterpart of this political and domestic system is found in the ordinary life of the period, which was innocent of all luxury, refinement and ease. Pastimes were arduous, such as wrestling and hunting, to harden body and mind, or else dangerous, like jousting or hunting big game, to accustom men to think lightly of wounds and death. Wars were carried on under a religious aspect and were always therefore extremely bitter. From such wars resulted the system of heroic slavery, by which the conquered were held to be men without God, so that they lost civil and natural liberty at once. Foreigners were considered enemies : the earliest nations were intensely inhospitable. Brigandage and piracy were recognised ; and Plutarch says that the heroes considered it a great honour and prize of valour to be called " robbers."

It was, in fine, a society immediately proceeding out

of that of the gods, which as we know was the climax of the state of nature. In its passage from the prehistoric age as we should say in modern language into the dawn of history it still retained much of the earlier customs, those customs which Vico thinking of the lonely Polyphemus in his cave called " Cyclopean rules." The age of gold out of which it came, innocent, kindly, humane, tolerant and dutiful, as scholars and poets believed, was in reality one perpetual " superstitious fanaticism," tormented by a continual terror of the gods, to placate whom men used to offer human sacrifice, traces of which remain among the historic Phoenicians, Scyths and Germans, the tribes of America and even the Romans themselves, who afterwards substituted for it the ceremony of throwing straw puppets into the Tiber. Even the sacrifice of children was not unknown ; memories of it are preserved in Agamemnon's sacrifice of Iphigenia and elsewhere. But in this age of the gods, in spite of or by means of this cruel superstition, were founded the great institutions of humanity ; religious cults together with augurial divination, marriage and burial. Weddings, judgment-seats and altars, and the removal of the bodies of the dead from the reach of the malignant air and the wild beasts " taught the human brutes to be pious " as Foscolo says in his *Sepolcri*, merely versifying Vico's prose. These " cyclopes " who conjoined and confused in themselves the functions of king, wise man (that is divination) and priest, at first placed their dwellings on the heights of mountains, in places airy and therefore healthy, naturally fortified, and near the perennial springs, where were the nests of eagles and vultures, the birds with which augury dealt. Hence the importance of water and fire, which became symbols of the family ; the earliest marriages were solemnised " *aqua et igni*," between parties who shared a common spring and hearth, and therefore belonged to the same household ; so that they

must have been between brothers and sisters. The period
of the cyclopes was a strongly moral period. It was not
true of it that " pleasure and law were one " in the sense
fancied by later effeminate poets ; for these men, whose
minds like those which we may still find among the
peasants of to-day were insensible to the refinements of
vice, found that alone pleasant which was lawful and
that alone lawful which was useful. They were just
with the justice of a savage towards his god ; continent,
for they had made an end of promiscuous intercourse ;
brave, hard-working and high-spirited, as they were
bound to be, surrounded as they were by hardships and
perils. It was only later that these primeval groups of
humanity descended into the plains and began to till
them, and then, from living inland as they did at first,
travelled gradually to the sea, learnt the art of navigation
and founded colonies.

In this way families or *gentes* existed before states.
States were in fact formed of families grouped into an
order of *gentes maiores* or " ancient noble houses " as they
were afterwards called to distinguish them from others
added later to the order (for instance at the time of Junius
Brutus, to fill the vacancies in the Roman senate after
the expulsion of the kings) and called " *gentes minores.*"
But these *gentes* had within themselves an element of
differentiation and strife. Families were not composed,
as is generally believed owing to the common mistake of
giving modern meanings to ancient words, of wives and
children alone ; but also of slaves, *famuli*, those who,
being less strong and remaining longer in the nomadic
state of nature, finally " as sometimes wild animals,
driven either by extreme cold or by hunters, to save their
life betake themselves to inhabited places " had sought
refuge with the stronger, in the fortresses of the fathers.
In return for the protection thus granted they tilled the
father's land, and were bound and as it were tied to

them, and hence called *nexi* ; they followed them and served them, and therefore gained the name of *clientes*. The relation of slaves to fathers was the second form of human relation, the first being the natural one of matrimony ; it constituted the feudal status, which has wrongly been believed peculiar to a certain definite period of barbarism, the Middle Ages, whereas it existed in all heroic societies, and was the eternal feudal principle whence sprang all the republics of the world. As Tacitus says, speaking of the Germans, the chief oath of these slaves and clients was to guard and defend each his own master and to assign to his master's glory his own deeds of valour (*suum principem defendere et tueri, sua quoque fortia facta gloriae eius adsignare, praecipuum iuramentum erat*) ; which is one of the severest conditions of the feudal system. Moreover the father's children are rather confused with the slaves than distinguished from them. They are distinguished by their title of *liberi*, but are identified by their similar position of obedience and lack of separate personality.

The need felt by the fathers of securing themselves against the frequent mutinies of the slaves led to the mutual alliance of fathers, the patrician order and the heroic state. Of this state the slaves constituted the first plebs. They had no citizen's rights, since they were not citizens ; no solemnities of marriage, since the auspices were a monopoly of the fathers ; nor the right of making wills, since that right had and always kept the political character of a command. They were therefore excluded from the *comitia curiata* held by the patricians under arms, which survived later for dealing with sacred questions ; profane matters being everywhere in the earliest times, at Rome as in Greece and Egypt, considered as sacred. The king of the patricians, whom we have called the magistrate of the order, was thus especially their leader and general in their resistance to the slaves or plebeians.

But the heroes did not provide for the stability of their order by means of forcible resistance alone. Just as, when they abdicated their position of sovereignty in their respective families for one of subordination to the higher sovereignty of the order, they formed a kind of noble or armed feudal system, so to keep their slaves more or less reconciled to obedience they granted them, without admitting them to citizenship, a kind of rustic feudalism. The origin of property is thus explained in a way entirely different on the one hand from the charmingly poetical theory according to which men adorned with all the virtues of the golden age when justice dwelt on earth, foreseeing the disorder that might result from communism, themselves with kindly arbitration marked out the limits of fields, endeavouring not to assign to one nothing but fertile, to another nothing but barren ground ; to one a waterless portion, to another one abounding in perennial streams : and different on the other hand from the " philosophical " origin by a voluntary submission to the wise, or that invented by " politician kings " who derived property from violence. The granting of this rustic feudalism, which might be called the first agrarian law, distinguished three kinds of land-tenure : bonitary for the people, quiritary or noble, supported by arms, for the fathers, and eminent, belonging to the whole order. And since the strength of the order rested upon its wealth, it did all in its power to prevent the enrichment of the plebs ; and in war—here we see the social motive of the " Roman clemency "—deprived the conquered of their arms only, leaving them in bonitary possession of their lands and imposing upon them a suitable tribute. For the same reason the patricians were very reluctant to go to war, for then the plebeian multitude gained experience of warfare and became dangerous.

The detachment of law from force was slow, and traces of the latter remained in every part of the former. In the heroic republic there were at first no laws providing for the punishment of offences and the restitution of private injuries ; hence, failing judiciary laws, arose the need of duels and reprisals, which perpetuated the customs of the age of innocence or of the gods. Poetry and history describe some of these duels, which were armed judgments : for instance, that of Menelaus and Paris under the walls of Troy, and that of the Horatii and Curiatii, between Rome and Alba. It was a plan of divine providence, in order that between barbaric nations of scanty understanding and incapable of listening to reason war should not always beget war : that right and wrong might be to some degree determined by a belief in the favour or disfavour of the gods as the cause of victory or defeat.

These ordeals by battle were accompanied and superseded by ordeals by verbal formulae, used in their religious habit of mind with the most minute and scrupulous exactitude and with care not to alter a single letter (*religio verborum*). Horatius, who by killing his sister fell under the law " *horrendi carminis*," could never have been acquitted by the decemvirs, however free from blame they thought him ; and the people acquitted him, says Livy, " more through admiration of his valour than the justice of his cause " (*magis admiratione virtutis quam iure causae*). In later days Roman law still retained this character of verbal precision to such a degree that it forms the crux of several of Plautus's comedies, in which panders are at the mercy of enamoured young men who have led them to violate some legal formula.

The private law of this society corresponded closely with its economic constitution. It was an entirely natural society, confined to the necessaries of life, and did not use money ; hence the law knew nothing of contracts formed, according to the law of a later period, by mere consent. All obligations were ratified by giving the hand ; the first buying and selling was barter ; the rent of a house consisted in a mortgage on the soil for building it, the rent of land in planting it ; companies and credit were unknown.

The material character of the first contracts and the forcible character of early legal processes were gradually modified as time went on, and became symbolic. As the fiction of force in marriage-rites recalled the actual force with which the giants dragged the first women into caves, so no less the ceremonies of *mancipatio, usucapio* and vengeance had formerly been acts really performed. *Mancipatio* was performed as we said with the actual hand, that is with real force ; for instance, in occupation, the original source of all rights of possession ; *usucapio* by the permanent planting of the body upon the thing possessed ; vengeance was originally a duel or a " *condictio,*" private retaliation. Then they became ceremonies or fictions : *mancipatio* became a civil transference with solemn acts and phrases (*si quis nexum faciet mancipiumque uti lingua nuncupassit ita ius esto*—" If any one makes a thing bond to him and his possession, let the law be so that he publish it with his tongue ") ; *usucapio* a tenure which is supposed to last as long as life ; retaliation a series of personal actions accompanied by a solemn declaration of them to the debtor. There were worn in the forum as many masks as there were legal personalities, and under the " person " or mask of a paterfamilias were hidden all the children and all the slaves of the house. Instead of abstract forms, which were not yet thought of, living bodily forms were used. Heredity for instance was invented as mistress of hereditary property, and imagined to exist completely in every particular piece of inherited goods ; the idea of indivisible right again, was materialised in the glebe or clod of earth presented to the judge with the formula " *hunc fundum.*" This ancient jurisprudence was throughout poetical ; its fictions turned facts into falsehoods and falsehoods into facts, made the unborn live, the living dead, and the dead to survive in their posterity. It created numbers of empty legal personalities without subjects (*iura imaginaria*), rights invented by the imagination ; and the formulae in which the laws were expressed were called because of their strict rhythm of such and so many words " verses " —*carmina*. The fragments of the Twelve Tables, if carefully considered, end their sentences for the most part in an Adonian verse, which is ultimately a fragment of the hexameter metre ; and Cicero, realising this, begins his " Laws " with the sentence *Deos caste adeunto pietatem adhibento*. Cicero also tells us that the Roman boys used to sing the laws of the twelve tables " like a regular song " (*tanquam necessarium carmen*), and Aelian says the same of the Cretan children and the laws of Minos. The Egyptian laws according to one tradition were " poems of the goddess Isis," and those given by Lycurgus to the Spartans and by Draco to the Athenians were formulated in verse. The whole of the ancient Roman law was a " serious poem," or as Vico says elsewhere a " kind of Roman drama," *poema quoddam dramaticum Romanum*, performed by the Romans in the forum ; and ancient jurisprudence was a " severe poetry."

This poetic atmosphere in heroic society and this metrical tendency in its language are facts borne out by many witnesses and proofs, by the observations and conjectures of scholars and by the narrations of travellers and missionaries. Hebraists are divided upon the question whether Hebrew poetry is metrical or rhythmical; but Josephus, Origen and Eusebius are in favour of metre, and St. Jerome asserts that a great part of the book of Job is in hexameter verse. The Arabs, who had no knowledge of writing, preserved their language down to the time when they overran the eastern provinces of the Greek empire by handing on the memory of their national poems. The Egyptians wrote the lives of the dead in verse ; the Persians and Chinese committed to verse their earliest history, as also, according to Tacitus, the Germans and, according to Justus Lipsius, the Americans. And since of these two last nations the former was only known to the Romans late in their history and the latter to Europe at the end of the fifteenth century, there is good reason to suppose that the same is true of all other barbaric nations ancient and modern.

The earliest metre, found not only in Greece but in Assyria, Phoenicia and Egypt, was the heroic or hexameter. Owing to the slowness of thought and the difficulties of pronunciation it was bound at first to have a spondaic character (hence the final foot in the line was always a spondee) and only later when mind and tongue became more active did it admit the dactyl. Then, when this activity still further increased, arose the iambic (*pede praesto* as Horace calls it) which approximates most nearly to prose ; so much so, indeed, that the early prose writers before Gorgias practically used the iambic metre of poetry, and prose frequently passed over into iambic verse. Tragedy was composed in iambics, a metre which is naturally adapted to it, produced as it was to give expression to wrath, according to the story which makes Archilochus invent it to express his anger against Lycambus ; and if comedy afterwards adopted the same metre, it was only by the " meaningless following of example," not because the iambic metre was naturally suited to it as it was to tragedy.

The primitive language of these societies was poetical not only through its use of metre but also by being composed through and through of lively metaphors, vivid fancies, striking resemblances, apt comparisons, expressions by means of cause or effect, whole or part, elliptic or pleonastic figures of speech, onomatopoeisms or imitations of sounds by words, abbreviations, compound words, minute circumlocutions, characteristic epithets, contortions in syntax and episodes. All these are ways of making oneself understood devised by men ignorant of the precise words required, or of a word, if in conversation, understood by both parties. The episode is characteristic of women and peasants, who are unable to select what they need and omit what is alien to their subject ; contorted language is the result of inability to express oneself directly, or of being prevented from doing so, as may be seen in the case of irascible or contemptuous persons, who make use of the nominative and oblique cases but do not utter verbs. The very words of these languages taken one by one reveal in the frequency of their diphthongs a trace of the song out of which speech arose ; and this abundance of diphthongs still remains in the Greek and French languages, which passed rapidly and prematurely from the age of spontaneity to that of reflection. The German language would certainly offer a rich store of heroic forms, with its abundance of compound words which so happily translate those of Greek, and its syntax which exceeds Latin in complexity as Latin does Greek. If German scholars, says Vico several times with a wistful glance at a field of study closed to himself, would use the principles of the New Science in research upon the origins of their language, they would certainly make wonderful discoveries.

The conception of the universe prevalent among the men of this period, and the histories of themselves which they related, of their origins, warfare and fortunes, were also poetical, or rather mythical. It was even the case as we have seen that their conceptions in the sphere of social history preceded those of a cosmological, physical or psychological character. By a rigid application of this principle Vico developed his doctrine of " natural theogony," arising naturally in the imagination on the occasion of certain human needs and utilities : the genesis of the twelve greater Gods, *Di maiores*, that is to say, the gods invented by the *gentes maiores* and, to a great extent, brought by them to the foundation of the state. Jupiter or the sky, with his language of lightning, was the author of the first laws of the family ; Juno symbolised marriage, Diana matrimonial chastity, Apollo the light of civilisation ; Vulcan, Saturn and Cybele were respectively the fire with which the forests were burnt to make clearings, the sowing of seed and the tilling of land ; Mars symbolised the warfare of the heroes " *pro aris et focis*," and Venus civilised beauty. In addition to this celestial Venus arose a plebeian Venus to whom was given the attribute of doves ; not as typifying the passion of love, but because they were " *degeneres*," common birds in comparison with the eagle. A double signification, patrician and plebeian, was given in the same way to Vulcan and Mars. The stormy relations of the fathers with the slaves, the struggles and penalties referred to in the myths of Tantalus and Sisyphus, begin to be reflected in the twelve greater gods. Hercules, struggling with Antaeus, signifies the nobles of the heroic cities, and Antaeus the mutinied slaves led back into the primitive cities on the mountain-tops (Antaeus lifted up into the air) and overcome and bound down to the earth, that is to say forced back to their servile labour. The birth of the tenth divinity, Minerva, expresses the weakening and diminution of the heroic power, since the plebeian Vulcan (the mutinied slaves) strikes the head of Jupiter with an axe, the tool of a servile art. Mercury represents the granting of bonitary rights to the plebs and the maintenance of quiritary rights by the fathers. The last of the twelve deities, Neptune, arose wben the peoples descended to the sea-coast ; and the legends of Minos, the Argonauts, the Trojan war, the return of Ulysses, Europa and the bull, the Minotaur, Perseus and Theseus refer to colonisation and piracy.

The mythological interpretation of history does not

cease with the foundation of states. The founders of civilisation, Zoroaster and Mercurius Trimegistus, Orpheus and Confucius, even if they are not strictly gods, are at least poetical characters. Aesop is typical of the " *socii* " or slaves of the heroes and hence is represented as ugly, that is, devoid of civilised beauty (*honestas*) ; and his fable of the lions' society shows to perfection the real relation of the heroes to their slaves, in which the latter share the toils, but not the spoils. Draco, of whom Greek historians tell us nothing but that he imposed a stern code of laws, symbolises the cruelty of the heroes to their slaves. Solon was either a party-leader of the Athenian plebs, or else a simple personification of the plebs itself, considered from the point of view of its vengeance. In the history of Rome we find poetical figures in Romulus, to whom were ascribed all the laws of the orders ; in Numa, author of the laws dealing with sacred matters and religious ceremonies ; in Tullus Hostilius, who organised and legislated for the military system ; in Servius Tullius the author of the census (which has been imagined, contrary to all historical truth, the foundation of a popular republic, whereas it was really the foundation of an aristocratic) ; and in Tarquinius Priscus, who invented insignia of rank and military uniforms ; lastly, the Decemvirs and the Twelve Tables are turned into poetical figures, since to these events and persons were ascribed a great number of laws favourable to liberty and really dating from a later period.

Thus, before philosophers began to elaborate the system of myths by creating new ones when they believed they were interpreting the old (Plato for instance introduced into the myth of Jupiter the idea of the omnipresent and all-pervading ether, his own invention, and other philosophers saw in the birth of Minerva from the head of Jupiter a description of the divine wisdom, or in Chaos and Orcus the confused mass of the universal seeds of nature and the primitive matter of the world), poet-theologians had expressed their ideas in mythology, ideas in which the metaphysical and physical elements were very small, but containing a large nucleus of human and political fact. The Chaos of these theologian-poets was the confusion of human seed during the period of brutal community of women ; it was confused because devoid of human regulation, obscure because devoid of the light of civilisation. The misshapen monster Orcus devoured everything because men in this community had no human shape, and were absolved by the void, because through the impossibility of knowing their off-spring they left no trace of themselves behind. The four elements of the world corresponded to the four elements of social life : the air where Jupiter lightened, the water of the perennial springs, the fire that burnt the forests, and the earth, the scene of man's labours. Being and subsisting were conceived the former as the act of eating (peasants still say of a sick man, meaning that he is not dead yet, that he is " still eating ") and the latter as " standing upon one's feet." The composition of the body was analysed into solids and liquids, that of the soul into air : generation into the act of " *concipere* " or " *concapere*," that is, taking hold of neighbouring material bodies, overcoming their resistance and adapting and assimilating them to one's own nature : and all the internal functions of the soul were ascribed to the head, the breast or the heart.

Cosmographical ideas were narrow, confined as they were to the life of these societies. The first heaven was placed no farther off than the tops of the mountains, where the giants saw the lightning play : the lower world was no deeper than a ditch, and was only by degrees enlarged and sunk into the valleys as opposed to the sky, that is to say to the mountain-tops ; the earth was identified with the limits of the cultivated fields. In the course of

time the sky, the object of contemplation from which
auguries were drawn, was lifted to a greater height, and
with it the gods and heroes who were attached to the
planets and constellations; and thus arose poetical
astronomy. Geographical knowledge extended no farther
than the country inhabited by each nation; and this
is the reason why peoples travelling into foreign and
distant lands gave to the new cities and to the mountains,
hills, passes, islands and promontories the same names
which were borne by those of their native land. Asia or
India was at first for the Greeks the eastern part of Greece
itself, Europe or Hesperia its western, and Thrace or
Scythia its northern district.

But we will not enter into further details; indeed we
have omitted much already. It is not the detail that
gives its value to Vico's picture of the heroic age. His
etymologies, his mythical interpretations, the genesis
and chronological succession of his gods, the genesis and
succession of his phonetic, metrical and stylistic forms—
each, taken by itself, may be contested; but taken as
a whole they are rich with a truth which transcends the
single propositions. This truth is the mighty effort
to recall a form of humanity and society still doubtless
living in surviving records and monuments, still recognis-
able here and there in a fragmentary form in various
parts of the modern world; but for centuries, even in
Vico's days, buried beneath a mass of irrelevant fancies,
conventional types, and prejudices of every kind, which
prevented its true characteristics from appearing.

CHAPTER XVI

HOMER AND PRIMITIVE POETRY

THE poet of primitive society was Homer : and if such
was his character, he could not have enjoyed the profound
wisdom, the delicate and lofty sense of morality, and the
supreme knowledge of all the sublimest arts and sciences
which ancient philosophers and writers fancied him to
possess, and the common opinion of literary men and
critics still attributed to him in the seventeenth century.

What an extravagant philosopher Homer would have
been, if he had indeed been a philosopher : how miserably,
had he set out to do so, would he have organised Greek
civilisation ! His Jupiter indicates force, brute force, as
the standard of the respect due to him; his Minerva
despoils Venus, knocks Mars down with a stone, strikes
Diana and is in turn insulted by Mars ; and both Venus
and Mars are wounded by Diomed, a mere mortal. The
heroes Achilles and Agamemnon exchange insults such as
would hardly be used by servants in a comedy to-day :
they call each other " dogs " and quarrel in the most
uncivil manner for the possession of Briseis and Chryseis.
Ferocious in their customs, they leave the bodies of their
enemies to dogs and crows : intemperate in their pleasures,
they drink to excess. Lofty intelligence, kindness of
heart, balance of mind may be sought in vain in all their
actions and sentiments. The fact is, these heroes show
themselves men of the scantiest understanding, the wildest

imagination, the most violent passions ; boorish, barbarous, intractable, fierce, arrogant, defiant and obstinate in their resolves and at the same time flighty in the extreme, at the mercy of any new object that presents itself to their eyes. Here again, the most striking parallel may be found in the psychology of the peasant, who as may be seen every day embraces any reasonable motive proposed to him but owing to the weakness of his intellect soon abandons the idea he has been persuaded to adopt and slips naturally back to his first intention. In the same way the Homeric heroes sometimes acquiesce in the first word of opposition offered to them ; sometimes at a sudden mournful recollection they burst into bitter lamentation in the midst of their anger : or else, if while in the greatest misery they meet with something pleasant, like Ulysses at the feast of Alcinous, they lose all memory of their sorrows and become completely cheerful ; or else, when in a calm and peaceful state of mind, they take offence at a harmless word and flying into a blind passion threaten the speaker with a cruel death. Even the virtues which they possess in an eminent degree, their frankness, vigour, magnanimity and generosity, are tinged with this same character of unreflective passion.

The hero of heroes, Achilles, who bears on his shoulders the destinies of Troy, owing to a private wrong he had received from Agamemnon—a grave wrong, but an insufficient motive for the ruin of his country and his whole nation—condemned all the Greeks to defeat and destruction at the hands of Hector ; and he only determined to aid them in order to assuage the personal grief caused by Hector's slaying his friend Patroclus. If only this extreme aloofness had been due to passion and jealousy ! But though when Agamemnon deprived him of Briseis he made enough noise to fill heaven and earth and supply the plot of the entire *Iliad*, yet he never in the whole course of the poem shows a spark of real love : just as

Menelaus mustered the whole of Greece against Troy to avenge the rape of Helen but never suffers the least pang of jealousy against Paris who is enjoying her. So devoid is Achilles of common humanity, that when Hector wishes to arrange that the victor in the fight shall bury the vanquished, he forgets that they are equals in rank and that death levels all, and savagely answers: "When have men ever made a truce with lions, and when have wolves and lambs had the same wish?" and he adds, "If I slay thee, I will drag thee bound naked to my chariot round the walls of Troy three days" (as he actually did in the sequel) and finally, "I will give thee to my hounds to devour." And he would have carried out his threat, had not the unhappy father Priam come to him to ransom the corpse. But even in this deeply-moving interview, when he has received Priam in his tent after the latter has, escorted by Mercury, passed alone through the midst of the Greek camp, when he has welcomed him to his table, at a single involuntary word that falls from the lips of the unhappy old man as he bewails the loss of so valiant a son Achilles forgets the sacred law of hospitality; and, ignoring the full and complete trust which Priam had placed in him, untouched by the terrible misfortunes of such a king, by the respect due to a father and the veneration due to so old a man, without reflecting on the reversal of his fortunes, of all things the most apt to excite pity, flies into a bestial rage and shouts a threat that he "will cut off his head"! Death itself does not end his anger at the loss of Briseis, were it not that the beautiful and unhappy princess Polyxena, daughter of the once rich and powerful Priam and now a wretched slave, is sacrificed on his tomb, that the shade glutted with revenge may drink the last drop of her innocent blood; and in the lower world, when Ulysses asks him what state he prefers, Achilles answers that he "would rather be the commonest slave, but alive"! Such is the hero whom Homer adorns with the permanent epithet of " without reproach " (ἀμύμων) and celebrates in the hearing of Greece as a pattern of heroic virtue. Such a hero, whose reasoning powers are concentrated in his spear-point, can only be classed with those self-satisfied persons of whom we say nowadays that they are too fine to breathe the common air.

If Homer's greatest characters are so discordant with our civilised nature, the similes which he uses are drawn from savage beasts and wild nature generally. If the life which he represents—a life of children in its intellectual futility, of women in its imaginative vigour, and of head-strong youths in the violence of its passion—and the tales of which the *Odyssey* is full, tales worthy of an old woman engaged in amusing children, prevent our attributing any esoteric wisdom to Homer, the striking success of these wild similes is certainly not characteristic of a mind tamed and civilised by philosophy of any sort. Nor could that truculent and savage style in which he describes the various sanguinary battles, the diverse and extravagantly bloodthirsty species of butchery which especially go to make the sublimity of the *Iliad*, have originated in a mind humanised and softened by philosophy.

But who was Homer ? What opinions as to him can we find in ancient writers, and what facts can we draw from his poems ? An unprejudiced reader of the *Iliad* and *Odyssey* is at every step aware of and baffled by extravagant and inconsistent statements. The life portrayed is inconsistent : it takes us now here, now there, over a long period of time ; on the one hand we find Achilles the hero of force, on the other Ulysses the hero of wisdom : on the one hand, cruelty, barbarism, ferocity and brutality, on the other the luxury of Alcinous, the delights of Calypso, the pleasures of Circe, the songs of the Sirens and the pastimes of suitors who tempt and even win over the chaste Penelope. On the one hand we are shown boorish

and uncivilised manners, on the other jewels, magnificent
clothing, exquisite foods and the arts of sculpture in
bas-relief and metal-founding ; on the one hand a strictly
heroic society, on the other some signs of popular liberty.
This delicate life fits ill with the savage and cruel life
which especially in the *Iliad* is ascribed to the same
heroes at the same time. To regard them thus as contemporaneous is an impossibility. From the customs of
the Trojan period we have leapt abruptly into those of
the time of Numa, to such an extent that *" ne placidis
coeant inmitia "* we are compelled to suppose that the two
poems were the work of many hands extending over
many ages. The geographical allusions are equally
inconsistent. These, no less, bring us into varied and
distant physical surroundings. The scene of the *Iliad* lies
to the east of Greece, inclining to the northward : that
of the *Odyssey* in the west, inclining to the southward.
The language, again, is inconsistent. The confusion of
dialects persists in spite of the revision of Aristarchus,
and has been explained by the most extraordinary hypotheses, such as the theory that Homer drew the elements
of his vocabulary from all the various Greek nationalities.

Passing from the poems to the traditions of their
author, the lives of Homer by Herodotus (if Herodotus
really wrote it) and Plutarch are valueless. The
most elementary facts about Homer are unknown : it
is precisely concerning the man whom they considered
the greatest luminary of Greece that the ancients leave
us most completely in the dark. We know neither
Homer's date nor his birthplace : each one of the Greek
peoples claimed him as their citizen. It is said indeed that
he was poor and blind, but it is just these details which
excite our suspicion, as our laughter is aroused by the
argument of Longinus which makes the *Iliad* the work of
his youth and the *Odyssey* that of his old age. It would
be indeed remarkable if such knowledge were current

concerning a man in whose case the two trifling details of time and place were unknown ! Above all, criticism must ask how a single man could ever have composed two poems of such a length at a time when writing was not in existence : since the three inscriptions of heroic age, one of Amphitryon, another of Hippocoön and a third of Laomedon mentioned with an excess of good faith by Vossius are mere forgeries like those made by the strikers of false coins.

All these considerations led Vico to suspect that Homer himself was not a real person but one of those poetic characters to whom the ancient world ascribed long series of actions, works and events. If we try to conceive the Homeric poems not as the work of an individual but as two great storehouses of the manners and customs of earliest Greece, containing the history of its natural law and heroic period ; if instead of a single poet we imagine a whole nation of poets, and instead of a single act of creation, a national poetry developing in the course of centuries, everything falls into its place and finds an explanation. The extravagance of the legends is explained by the fact that the composition of the *Iliad* and *Odyssey* falls in the third period of their existence. In the hands of the theological poets they were true and severe, by the heroic poets they were altered and corrupted, and in this corrupt state they were incorporated in the two poems. The variety of customs is explained if we consider the various periods of composition, and so also the " young Homer " and " old Homer," which are symbolic of the earlier and later periods of primitive Greece. The diversity of sites assigned to his birth and death and the variety of his dialects are accounted for by the fact that different peoples produced the lays. Finally, it is explained why every Greek people claimed him as a citizen, just because these peoples were themselves Homer ; and why he was called blind and a beggar, because such were as a rule the singers who went about from fair to fair reciting their tales. Thus in order to be rightly understood Homer must lose himself in the crowd of Greek peoples and be considered an idea or heroic character ; a type of the Greeks in so far as they narrated tales in ballad form. Thus facts which had only caused confusion and lacked plausibility in Homer as then understood became natural and necessary elements of the Homer now rediscovered. Above all, this latter Homer deserves the high praise of being the first of all historians of Greece known to us. In Homer we have a proof of the original identity of history and poetry, and a confirmation of Strabo's assertion that before Herodotus, before even Hecataeus of Miletus, the history of the Greek peoples was written by their poets. In two golden passages of the *Odyssey* a man is praised for having told a story well and said to have " told it as a musician and a singer."

Vico did not undertake a detailed investigation into the way in which the Homeric poems were elaborated. He seems however to incline towards two chief poet-authors, one, a native of the east of Greece, towards the north, for the *Iliad*, the other for the *Odyssey*, a native of the west towards the south : and by the title " Homer " he understands a composer and compiler of legends. But on the other hand, owing to the purely ideal meaning which this name has for him, we must not rule out the interpretation that the two Homers in their turn may be two streams of poetry and two groups of peoples or of popular singers. The historic figures whom Vico finds before him are the rhapsodes, men of the people who wandered independently about the fairs and festivals of the Greek cities reciting the songs of Homer. From the time of their primitive composition long ages elapsed before the Pisistratidae had them divided and arranged into two groups, the *Iliad* and the *Odyssey*, a fact which shows clearly that in their time only a confused mass of material was to be found, and decreed that they should henceforth be sung by the rhapsodes at the Panathenaea.

It is however certainly not in the resolution, materially understood, of the individual Homer into a myth or poetic character that the importance of Vico's theory lies : and the same is perhaps the case with its truth. From the inconsistencies observed by him, and not always accurately observed (which are moreover unimportant, since the inaccuracies he notes might easily be balanced by the correct statements he omits), there was no strictly logical passage to the denial of the existence of an individual Homer, the principal author of one or both poems. These inconsistencies might serve to demonstrate that the poet or poets were working upon a rich fund of traditional material, of origin very various both as to time and place, and not regularly stratified according to origin, but having its strata confused and contorted. One or more poets, or even many poets and an able compiler of their lays, or a society of able compilers : these and similar hypotheses might equally well have been suggested, as happened later, and supported, as was later the case, by arguments neither more nor less cogent, because incapable of documentary proof. But underlying this resolution of Homer into a poetic character, as it underlay other resolutions made or attempted by Vico, lay the discovery of the long and laborious historical genesis through which the matter of these poems had passed, so that in this sense they might really be called a product of collaboration on the part of the whole Greek people. The substitution of a nation of Homers for a single Homer was only another case of mythology constructed according to the principles discovered by Vico himself : mythology which must be retranslated into scientific prose. In the same way Vico's analysis of the customs described in the Homeric poems may be, and is, not only here and there adulterated with a few inaccuracies, but is on the whole exaggerated and one-sided. Still, this analysis taken as a whole was a great advance and opened new paths to Homeric criticism. How could the stubborn illusion of the noble Homeric hero, a great lord and a good ruler, a shining example of all civil, military and domestic virtues, be dispelled except by setting against it the picture of a boorish Achilles, full of elemental passions, violent, stubborn, unreasoning, quick to a generous impulse but no less quick to outbursts of brutal wrath ?

Vico's progress in artistic appreciation of the Homeric poetry was no less marked. The recognition that a sound and rational philosophy was not to be found in the poet Homer would, in the mouth of any other critic of the time, have amounted to a slur on the poet : as expressed by Vico and as the consequence of his new aesthetic ideas it was a compliment. The errors which intellectualism and neo-classical criticism discovered in Homer led the critics to repeat freely the saying of Horace that " good Homer nods at times " : whereas Vico on the contrary exclaims " if he had not nodded so often he would never have been good ! " (*nisi ita saepe dormitasset, nunquam bonus fuisset Homerus*). Homer was a great poet precisely because he was not a philosopher. He had a retentive memory, a strong imagination and a sublime mind ; and neither the philosophies nor the arts of poetry and criticism which came after him could ever produce a poet at all like him. He was the only poet who could conceive heroic characters : his comparisons are incomparable, his speeches sublime, expressive of the individuality of the speaker, and created by the power of a vivid imagination : his diction is clear and splendid, his language composed entirely of similes, images and comparisons, and has none of those ideas of genus and species by which things are intellectually defined. He is not delicate but grand, for delicacy is a small virtue and grandeur naturally despises small things : or even, just as a great and rushing torrent cannot help the turbidness of its water, and must perforce sweep rocks and trees with it in the violence of its course, so too in Homer we may find things of no value.   But the torrent with all its impurities sweeps on its way superb and impetuous ; and Homer in spite of and partly because of his ruggedness is for ever the father and prince of all sublime poets.

This new departure in Homeric criticism brought with it implicitly a complete revolution in the history of ancient literature.   But on this subject Vico made only a few scattered remarks.   He was no specialist : he did not write from a specialist's point of view, and too often when documentary evidence and thought were unable to solve a difficulty he solved it by means of his fancy, a faculty which was however in his case radiant with gleams of insight.   Thus, the cyclic poets were not so called because of the circle of listeners in the centre of which they declaimed their poems, like the " Rinaldi " or ballad-singers whom Vico saw on the quay at Naples, and this circle had no connexion with the *vilem patulumque orbem* of Horace : but the observation that they differed little from these ballad-singers was sound.   In the same way, we need not linger on his guesses at the dates of Homer and Hesiod, nor need we take literally his division of lyric poetry into three periods, namely those respectively of religious hymns, funeral chants for dead heroes and melic lyrics or " musical airs," the last including Pindar, and admired, flourishing as it did at the epoch of the " pompous virtue " of Greece, at the Olympic games where these poets sang.   But still Vico has here put his finger on the difference between primitive and refined or cultured lyric poetry.   The origin of tragedy he ascribes to the dithyramb or dramatic satire, of which no example has come down to us, and in rural customs

compared by him to those which were still in evidence
during his own lifetime in Campania at vintage season ;
and he notes the relation between tragedy and the epic.
Tragedy had its rude beginnings at a time when the
heroic spirit was already dead : it perfected itself by
becoming subordinate to the Homeric poetry, deriving
its inspiration from Homeric characters and avoiding
original ones. The old comedy was closely related to
tragedy. Like the latter it was derived from a chorus,
and it preserved its archaic character in that it displayed
living persons and real actions. The new comedy on the
other hand was marked off by a profound change of spirit.
Here the effects of philosophy were directly felt. Imaginative genera were superseded by intelligible and rational
universals : and Menander and the other poets of the
new comedy, living in the most humane period of Greek
history, took their intelligible genera from human life
and depicted them in their comedies, over which one feels
that the breath of Socratic philosophy has passed. The
persons of the new comedy were cast in a mould, and
were not public but private characters : and as the chorus
represents the public and argues about public affairs only,
there is no room for it in the new comedy. About this
time began the practice of inserting idealised heroes of
perfect morals into poetry. Aristotle, remembering the
strongly individualised characters of Homer, still maintained as a principle of poetic composition that the heroes
of tragedy should be neither very good nor very bad, but
rather a mixture of great virtues and great faults. But
the poets of the late period, making use of the idea originated by philosophers, formed a " heroism of virtue " : a
heroism which may be called " gallant." Accordingly
they either invented entirely new legends or else used
old legends which had originally presented themselves to
the founders of the nation in an appropriately stern and
severe form, but softened them by adapting them to the

softening of manners.   Equally gallant is the " shepherd "
of the Greek Bucolic poets, Bion and Moschus, " wasting
away with the most delicate love." He makes the
general observation on Greek and Latin literature, that
the boundary between verse and prose was so strictly
guarded on both sides that no ancient writer ever composed both orations and poems—a rule to which perhaps
the only exception is the wretched verses (*ridenda poemata*)
of Cicero : and Vico tried to explain this fact by the
democratic habits which compelled orators studiously
to avoid the cultivation of lofty and fanciful modes of
expression, which would have puzzled the people and
hindered their full and clear comprehension of the point
at issue.

Vico does not treat Roman literature so fully as
Greek, which provided him with much more primitive
documents.   But he detected certain analogies between
the origins of Latin and Greek literature.   The first
poets and authors in the Latin language were the Salii,
sacred poets ; and this was natural in the beginning of a
nation's culture ; for in the primitive religious period the
gods are the only object of praise.   And just as the
earliest fragments of Latin known to us, the remains of
the hymns of the Salii, give an impression of hexameter
verse, so the same metre is felt in the records of Romans
who celebrated triumphs, such as the "*duello magno diri-
mendo, regibus subiugandis*" of Lucius Aemilius Regillus
and the "*fudit fugat prosternit maximas legiones*" of Acilius
Glabrio.   The first Roman poets, too, sang true stories :
this was the case with Livius Andronicus and his Romanid
containing the annals of early Rome, and with Naevius,
and later Ennius, who described the Punic wars.   Satire
also was levelled against real and for the most part
notorious persons.   The Romans however differed from
the Greeks in advancing with a more measured step and
not making the swift and abrupt transition from barbarism

to effeminacy : so that they entirely lost the history of
their gods (which Varro called the " obscure period "
of Rome) and preserved their heroic history, extending
down to the Publilian and Petelian laws, in common speech
only.   In its greatest manifestations the literature of
Rome is the work of cultivated poets like Virgil, whom
Vico admires for his profound knowledge of heroic antiquity, but says of him that so far as poetical power is
concerned he is not to be compared with Homer ;   a
verdict agreeing with that of Plutarch and Longinus,
but in opposition to the view of neo-classical criticism.
Another example of cultivated and reflective poetry is
to be found in Horace, who like Pindar in the pompous
period of Greece composed his odes at the most " ostentatious " epoch of Roman history, the Augustan age.

The Biblical literature would have given Vico materials
of great value for the study of primitive poetry ; and he
actually did move a few steps towards it when he observed
that poetry was the primitive language of all nations
" including the Hebrews " ;   and that Moses made no use
of the esoteric wisdom of the Egyptian priests and wrote
his history " in a style which has much in common with
that of Homer and often surpasses him in sublimity of
expression."   But Vico drops the subject at once, as if
he instinctively guessed what might come of treating the
Pentateuch as he had done the *Iliad*, and Moses like
Homer.   So he prefers to wax enthusiastic over the phrase
in which God describes himself to Moses " *Ego sum qui
sum*," to which he ascribes a metaphysical profundity
only attained by the Greeks when Plato conceived God
as τὸ ὄν, and unknown to the Latins down to the latest
period, for the word *ens* is not pure Latin but belongs to
debased Latin.   Or he contents himself with emphatically
pointing out that at a time when Greece was under the
sway of a superstitious and natural law, God gave to his
people a code " so full of weight as regards the dogmas of

divinity and so full of humanity as regards the practice
of justice, that not even in the humanest period of Greek
history could a Plato have conceived or an Aristides
executed it " ; a code " whose ten chief enactments contain
an eternal and universal justice founded upon the excellent
conception of a purified human nature, and are capable
of forming by habituation a character such as the maxims
of the greatest philosophers could only with great difficulty
form by ratiocination ; whence Theophrastus called the
Hebrews philosophers by nature." The success that
attended the " will to believe " was all the more striking
if as we suspect Vico had read the abhorred Spinoza's
Tractatus Theologico-politicus, where the Hebrew prophets,
while their " piety " is recognised, are said to be entirely
devoid of " sublime thoughts." Spinoza maintains that
they only taught " very simple things which any one
could easily discover, and adorned these with a style and
supported them by reasons most calculated to move the
mind of the multitude to devotion towards God " ; and
that the laws revealed by God to Moses were " nothing
but the laws of the particular government of the Jews " :
and he sets out to examine the text of the Bible and the
problem of the authenticity of the Pentateuch and the
respective authors of its various books.   We might almost
venture to say that it was Spinoza's Biblical criticism
that suggested to Vico his criticism of the composition
and spirit of the Homeric poems ; but that the latter,
after passing in this way from sacred to profane history,
from Moses to Homer, set his face stubbornly against the
opposite transition from Homer to Moses, from profane
history to sacred.

CHAPTER XVII

THE HISTORY OF ROME AND THE RISE OF DEMOCRACY

HEROIC society in the period of youthful vigour above described contains within itself, rigorously repressed, and in fact made into a support, the element of opposition; the slaves, clients or vassals, that is to say the plebs. But this element little by little succeeds in detaching itself from and opposing itself to the society, engaging it in a continual and undisguised conflict, so as by degrees to overthrow this old society and give life and form to a new society of which it is itself the material : a democratic society, the popular republic. Vico believes this process to be uniform in all peoples; but since references to histories other than that of Rome are either absent or very vague (he hardly mentions the origin of the Athenian democracy) the description of this process appears in the pages of the New Science as a fragment of Roman history, or as we should nowadays call it the social history of Rome.

Vico's guesses about the population and primitive culture of Italy are of no great importance. The subject belongs rather to archaeology and ethnography than to history, and Vico did not make a special study of it. In the *De antiquissima sapientia Italorum* he had provided the origins of Rome with a basis in an Italian civilisation of high antiquity, earlier than the Greek and derived

197

from Egypt, which the Romans absorbed in a manner
agreeing with their character ; by rejecting, that is to
say, its theoretical hypotheses while taking over their
practical results, just as they adopted from the Etruscans
their tragic religion and their art of tactics, and as they
later adopted laws from Athens and Sparta.   In this way
their ignorance and savagery remained unchanged, and
hence they spoke the language of philosophers without
being philosophical.   In his later writings Vico still for
a time maintained the priority and independence of the
earliest Italian civilisation as regards that of Greece,
and considered Pythagoras less as the founder than as
the student of Italian wisdom.   Finally, however, he
seems to have given up this view, just as he definitely
abandoned that which explained the origins of Roman
religion, language, customs and law by the imitation
of foreign peoples and " frankly confessed that he had
been in error here " owing to the example of Plato's
Cratylus.   What conditions brought about the rise
of Rome Vico does not precisely say.   He is certain that
if Rome and the world did not begin together, at least
the foundation of Rome was a new beginning.   The
point of departure which he assumes is the asylum of
Romulus, consisting of the " families " of fathers who gave
their hospitality to wanderers and made them into *famuli.*
There was no Trojan colonisation ; Vico knows Bochart's
treatise (1663) criticising the legend of Aeneas's arrival
in Italy and accepts its conclusions, which only confirm the doubts already entertained by certain ancient
historians.   For Vico, the Trojan origin of Rome is a
legend sprung from the union of two different examples
of national arrogance : that of the Greeks, who made such
a noise about the Trojan war and forced their Aeneas
into the history of Rome, and that of the Romans, who
accepted him in order to boast of a distinguished foreign
origin.   The legend moreover could not have arisen

much before the time of the war with Pyrrhus, when
Rome began to acquire a taste for things Greek. In
order to explain the infusion of Greek names and myths
into the story of primitive Rome and the similarity of
the Roman alphabet to the ancient Greek, Vico would
incline rather to the hypothesis that early in their history
the Romans conquered and destroyed some Greek colony
on the Latin coast, of which all trace has since been lost
in the mists of antiquity ; and that through receiving
its inhabitants in Rome as refugees and allies, they came
under the influence of several Hellenic traditions and
customs.

Vico does not spend much time over the historical
events of the royal period. Here in fact lay one of the
chief differences between his criticism and that which
had already been originated and was continued after
his time dealing with the first centuries of Roman history.
Vico aims not at substituting historical for legendary
anecdotes but at understanding the essence of institutions
and the ways in which they change. He uses two guiding
principles, as we have seen in considering the royal
period : first, that it was a period not of monarchy but
of aristocracy and that therefore the type of heroic
society or the patriarchal republic is applicable to it :
secondly, that the names of the kings are symbols or
" poetic characters " for the institutions of this society.
In Vico's judgment, as we have had occasion to observe,
the constitution of Servius Tullius should not be considered
the basis of popular liberty, as the later Romans considered it ; it was really the basis of the liberty of the
feudal lords, since by it the patricians granted to the
plebeians the bonitary tenure of their land together with
the duty of paying rent to and serving at their own
expense in war themselves, the patricians. And Junius
Brutus, in driving out the Tarquins and replacing them
by two consuls or annual aristocratic kings, restored to

the Roman republic its primitive form ; that is to say, he delivered the lords from the domination of their tyrants but left the people under the domination of their lords.

The patricians' oppression of the plebeians after the restoration of Junius Brutus and the struggles and resistance caused by it constitute the soul of the new development and contain the secret of the greatness of Rome, the " key to universal Roman history," *clavis historiae Romanae universae.* Polybius's explanation of this greatness is too vague. He describes it as due to the virtue or the religion of the patricians and relates the facts of this virtue rather than their cause. Vico also criticises Machiavelli, at one time because he adduces certain civil and military institutions as the cause of Rome's greatness without investigating the cause of those institutions, that is to say the character of Roman society : at another time for adducing what was only a partial cause, the high spirit of the plebeians. He thinks Plutarch worst of all, since envy of the virtue and wisdom of Rome leads him to ascribe her greatness to fortune. The fact was that Rome subjugated the other cities of Latium and then Italy and the world because her heroism was still young, while among the other Latin peoples it had begun to decay. Thanks to this youthful vigour the patricians were strong enough to preserve their order and the religion which formed its foundation and safe-guard (the nobles, Vico observes at this point, were always and everywhere religious, so that the first sign of contempt for religion among them is a symptom of national decadence) ; the plebeians were spirited enough to demand a share in religion, auspices and all civil rights ; the lawyers, lastly, were wise enough to interpret the old laws and apply them to any new case that might arise, and strove with all their might to alter the text of these laws as little and as slowly as possible. These were the chief causes of the growth and permanence of the Roman empire ; for in all its political changes it contrived to remain faithful to its principles. Prowess in war was another result of the rivalry of the orders ; since the nobles were naturally consecrated to the safety of their country, as the only means of preserving the civil privileges of their order, and the plebeians accomplished brilliant deeds in order to prove themselves worthy of patrician honours. And when the Romans extended their conquests and their victories over the whole world, they made use of four rules which they had already applied to the plebeians within Rome itself. They reduced barbarian provinces to the position of clients by planting colonies in them : they granted civilised provinces bonitary tenure of their land : to Italy they gave the quiritary tenure : and to the municipia, the towns which had earned better treatment, they accorded the same equality with themselves which the plebs had finally won.

The result of the first struggles, in which the point at issue was according to Vico the bonitary possession of land (a right already recognised in the constitution of Servius, but cancelled by the nobles in return for arrears of rent), is seen in the tribunate, and later, when the plebeians claimed the right of quiritary tenure, in the laws of the Twelve Tables, ratifying this plebeian victory. But the law of the Twelve Tables represented at the same time the victory of written law, the end of the secrecy with which the laws had been fenced round by the patricians, who alone knew, understood, interpreted and therefore applied them as they thought fit. This publication and codification of a written law cannot have been benevolently granted by the patricians out of that anxiety " not to despise the wishes of the plebs " of which Livy speaks ; rather they must have resisted it with all the stubbornness which Dionysius of Halicarnassus describes and expresses in the phrase " *mores patrios servandos, leges ferri non oportere*" (our fathers' customs must be preserved, and laws must not be passed).

Later historians decorated the origin of the Twelve Tables with various legends. They told, among other things, of the mission sent by the decemvirs to Athens to bring back new laws : a tale given by Livy and Dionysius, but unknown to Polybius and discredited by Cicero. How, in the savage aloofness of primitive nations, between whom oral communication could only have been instituted by the necessities of warfare, alliances and commerce, could the fame of Solon's wisdom have crossed the seas from distant Attica to Rome ? How could the Romans of that time have possessed such accurate knowledge of the quality of Athenian law as to believe it capable of setting at rest the strife between their plebeians and their nobles ? How could ambassadors have travelled between Greece and those Romans whom seventy-two years later the Greeks of Tarentum could still maltreat as strangers ? And what shall we say of ambassadors who returned carrying with them the Greek laws from Athens but without knowing what they meant ; so that but for the coincidence by which Hermodorus the pupil of Heraclitus, an exile from his country, happened to be in Rome, the Romans would have been unable to make any use of this unintelligible and inaccessible treasure ? Again, how could Hermodorus have translated the laws into Latin of such purity that Diodorus Siculus pronounced it devoid of the slightest taint of Hellenism, and with a perfection unattained by any subsequent writer of any period in a translation from the Greek ? How did he contrive to clothe Greek ideas in Latin words so appropriate (for instance, *auctoritas*) that Greeks, Dio Cassius among them, declare that their own language has no corresponding words by which to explain them ? Heraclitus's letter to Hermodorus must have been conveyed by the same mail that served Pythagoras in his distant voyages up and down the world : it is, in fact, an imposture of the first quality, and the whole story of the Athenian origin of these laws is due to the arrogance of scholars, who derived them first from the other Latin peoples (such as the Aequi), then from the Greek cities of Italy, then from Sparta and finally from Athens, with whose name, thanks to the renown of the Athenian philosophers, they were at last satisfied. No doubt, the laws of the Twelve Tables present resemblances not only to Athenian or Spartan laws but to those of various nations, the Mosaic code among others ; but this is due to the uniformity of national history. No doubt, the decemvirs were in antiquity supposed to have originated laws bearing clear traces of Greek influence, such as that prohibiting the Greek style of mourning at funerals : but this is because as we have seen the decemviral legislation, like the names of the various kings, became a " poetic character," and to it were referred all laws later recorded in the public archives which tended to the equalisation of liberty. But the original law of the Twelve Tables, with its primitive rudeness, inhumanity, cruelty and ferocity, which agrees so ill with the period of highly-developed civilisation at Athens, is a document of the greatest value for the ancient natural law of the Latin peoples, and the customs which had existed among them from the age of Saturn.

Quiritary tenure of land and a written code of law once gained, the struggle recommenced over the question of the right of marriage. The true meaning of this contest has been lost among the absurdities written on the subject by the ancient historians themselves, in the belief that its basis was the desire on the part of the plebeians' (who were little more than wretched and common slaves) to be allowed to form connexions with the nobles. This error has made Roman history even less credible than the legendary history of Greece ; for if we do not know the meaning of the latter, the former is in opposition to the true order of human desires. It shows us a plebs aspiring first to nobility, secondly to offices and magistracies, and finally to wealth : whereas men desire first of all wealth, then offices in the state, and lastly nobility. What the Roman plebs really claimed was not "*connubia cum patribus*" but "*connubia patrum*" : not the right of connexion by marriage with the nobles—a claim which they would not have wished to make, and was at bottom unimportant — but the right of contracting solemn marriages as the nobles did. For without such solemn marriages, without privilege of the auspices, the plebeians were in fact unable to enjoy the quiritary tenure of land and to transmit it to their families, deprived as they were of descent, kindred and relatives. The demand for *connubia* was, in a word, simply equivalent to a demand for the rights of citizens, and it was satisfied by the Canuleian law.

The next demand of the plebeians was for privileges depending on public rights. Of these they gained first the *imperium* together with the consulship, and lastly the offices of priest and pontifex, which carried with them knowledge of the law. In this way the system of seigneurial liberty planned by Servius Tullius grew into a system of popular liberty, and the census, which was originally paid to the patricians, was paid hereafter into the public treasury, out of which the expenses of the plebeians in war were paid. The tribunes now proceeded to demand the power of legislation ; for the previous laws, the Horatian and Hortensian, had not made plebiscites binding on the whole people, except upon the two special occasions which led to the secession of the plebs to the Aventine and Janiculum respectively. This new victory, which established the superiority of the plebs and transformed the aristocratic into a popular republic, was the Publilian law due to the Dictator Publilius Philo and decreeing that plebiscites should " be binding on all the Quirites " (*omnes quirites tenerent*). The authority of the senate came out of the struggle somewhat impaired, for while formerly the fathers had acted as " *auctores* " for the deliberations of the people, they were now the pro-posers of law to the people, which the latter then approved according to the formula submitted to them by the senate, or else " antiquated" the proposal (*antiquo*, to vote against a measure) and decided to make no innovation. Besides this, the plebs won the last office to be conceded to them, that of censor. The Petelian law, a few years later, abolished the last remnant of feudalism, the bond (*nexus*) which made the plebeians the bondmen of the nobles for debt and often compelled them to spend their lives working in their private prisons.

Some time later, when the division between patriciate and plebs with the corresponding *comitia curiata* and *tributa* was replaced by Fabius Maximus's division accord-ing to the property of citizens, who were now grouped into three classes of senators, knights and plebeians, the order of the nobles disappeared entirely : " senator" and " knight " were no longer synonymous with " patrician," nor " plebeian" with " base-born." The Senate however preserved sovereign dominion over the finances of the Roman Empire, though the Empire itself had passed to the plebeians ; and thanks to the so-called " *senatusconsultum ultimum* " it maintained this dominion by force of arms as long as Rome remained a popular republic. Whenever the people attempted to take it into their own hands, the Senate armed the Consuls, who forthwith declared traitors and put to death plebeian tribunes who had originated these attempts. This may be explained as a right of feudal sovereignty subject to a higher sovereign, a view con-firmed by the language of Scipio Nasica when he armed the people against Tiberius Gracchus : " whoever wishes

for the safety of the republic, let him follow the consul "
(*qui rempublicam salvam velit, consulem sequatur*).   And
indeed, once the road to office was opened by law to the
multitude which rules in a popular republic, there was
nothing left in time of peace but to contest its rule not
by laws but by force of arms, and for those in power to
pass laws for self-enrichment like the Gracchan agrarian
measures, resulting at once in civil wars at home and
unjust wars abroad.

With the triumph of the plebs and the change of constitution from aristocratic to popular, the whole face of
society changed.   In the first place, the aspect of the
family changed.   Here, during the rule of the patriciate,
testamentary succession was admitted only at a late
date and was easily cancelled, in order to keep wealth in
patrician hands : kindred even in the seventh degree
excluded the emancipated son from the paternal heritage :
emancipation had the effect of a penalty : legitimising
was not allowed : and it is doubtful whether a woman
could inherit.   But in the democratic society, since for the
plebs wealth, strength and power all depended on the
number of their children, family feeling began to grow up,
and the praetors began to consider its claims and to
satisfy them by means of the " *bonorum possessiones*,"
thus remedying the faults or shortcomings of wills and
facilitating the diffusion of wealth, the only thing desired
by the common people.

A change took place, again, in the meaning of the
institutions of property.   The civil tenure was no longer
a matter of public right, but was dispersed among the
various private tenures of the citizens now forming the
body of the popular state.   " Eminent " tenure no longer
signifies the strongest kind of tenure, unencumbered by
any actual charge, even a public charge, but applies
simply to an estate free from any private charge.
Quiritary tenure is no longer that of which the noble

was feudal lord and under the obligation to aid his client, the plebeian, if ousted from it : it has become a private civil tenure, capable of being defended by a civil suit as opposed to the bonitary which could be maintained by possession only.

The forms of legal process were pruned of the luxurious growth of fictions, solemn formulae and symbolic acts, simplified and rationalised : the intellect, the thought of the legislator was brought into play and the citizens conformed to an idea of a common rational utility, understood as spiritual in value. Causes, which were originally formulae safeguarded by accurate and precise language, became affairs or negotiations solemnised by agreement and, in the case of transference of tenure, by natural tradition ; and it was only in contracts said to be completed by word of mouth, that is to say in stipulations, that the safeguards remained " causes " in the strict ancient meaning of the word. Thus the certitude of the law, when the human reason was fully developed, passed into the truth of ideas determined by the circumstances of fact, a " formula devoid of any particular form " (*formula naturae*, as Varro calls it) which, like a light, informs in all the minutest details of their surface the details of fact over which it extends. In popular republics the ruling principle is the *aequum bonum*, natural equity.

The harsh punishments of the periods of domestic monarchy and heroic society (the laws of the Twelve Tables condemned those who set fire to another's crops to be burnt alive, perjurers to be thrown from the Tarpeian rock, and insolvent debtors to be cut in pieces while living) were replaced by milder penalties, since the multitude, whose members are weak, is naturally disposed to clemency.

Laws, which under the aristocracy were few, inflexible and religiously observed, multiplied under the democracy and became liable to change and modification. The

Spartans, who preserved their aristocracy, said that at Athens they had many laws and wrote them ; at Sparta few, but they obeyed them. The Roman plebs, like the Athenian, passed new laws every day, and the attempt by Sulla, the leader of the noble party, to reduce them by the institution of " *quaestiones perpetuae* " or permanent courts was in vain, for after his time laws were again multiplied.

War itself, which was under the aristocratic republics very cruel and resulted in the destruction of conquered towns and the reduction of the vanquished to the condition of labourers scattered over the country-side and cultivating it on behalf of the victors, was mitigated by the popular republics, which while they deprived the conquered of the rights of heroic society left them in possession of the natural rights of the human race. Empires grew, since a popular republic is much more adapted to conquest than an aristocratic, and a monarchy most of all.

But with all this humanisation of customs, the power of wise rule, political virtue, diminished. The ancient patricians enforced a rigid respect for law ; and each, possessing a large share of the public utility, set his own minor personal interests below this greater particular interest, guaranteed as it was by the state. Hence all courageously defended and wisely consulted for the good of the state. In a popular state on the other hand since the citizens controlled the state property by dividing it among themselves into as many small portions as there were citizens in the body of the people, and through the causes which produced that form of state, ease, paternal affection, conjugal love and desire of life, men were led to consider the smallest details favourable to their own private interest ; that is to regard nothing but the *aequum bonum*, the only interest of which a multitude is capable.

At this point arises spontaneously a new form of government, which has long been preparing and has now become inevitable, namely monarchy. The ordinary political writers make monarchy originate, without any of the numerous and complex causes which are necessary to produce it, at the very outset of human history, " as a frog," says Vico, " is born of a summer shower." Still less did it originate artificially by the royal law which Tribonian believes to have deprived the Roman people of its free and sovereign power and conferred it upon Octavius Augustus. The law which brought monarchy into being was a natural law whose formula of eternal validity is as follows : when in a popular republic every one seeks his private interest only and presses the public forces into its service at risk of destruction to the state, to preserve the latter from ruin a man must arise, as Augustus did at Rome (who as Tacitus says " received under his sovereign power the whole state, worn out with civil wars, taking the title of Princeps " : *qui cuncta bellis civilibus fessa nomine principis sub imperium accepit*) : a single man, who by force of arms takes in hand all the affairs of the state and leaves his subjects to look after their own affairs or after any public business he may entrust to them ; surrounding himself with a small number of statesmen as a cabinet to discuss public questions or principles of civil equity. Such a monarch is welcomed by nobles and plebeians alike : by the nobles, who after having been already humiliated by their subjection to plebeian rule abandon their ancient aristocratic claim to sovereignty and think only of securing a comfortable life ; and by the plebeians, who after an experiment in anarchy or unbridled demagogy (than which no tyranny is worse, since it produces as many tyrants as there are bold and dissolute men in the state) are led by their own misfortunes to welcome peace and protection.

Monarchy is then a new form of popular government. In order that a powerful man may become sovereign, it is necessary that the people shall take his side, and that he should rule in a popular manner ; making all his subjects equal, humiliating the great to protect the multitude against their oppression, keeping the people satisfied and content as regards the necessaries of life and the enjoyment of natural liberty, and employing a well-balanced system of concessions and privileges granted sometimes to whole classes (in which case they are called " privileges of liberty ") sometimes to particular persons, by promoting into a higher class men of unusual merit and exceptional virtues.

In monarchy, a " humane " government no less than democracy, the process of humanisation or softening of customs and laws, already begun under popular republics, still continues. The rigid bonds of the patriarchal family and kinship relax further. The Emperors, who tended to be overshadowed by the splendours of the nobility, made efforts to promote the rights of human nature common to nobles and plebeians. Augustus strove to safeguard the trusteeships by which formerly property had passed to persons incapable of inheritance thanks only to the conscientiousness of the injured heir ; he transformed such understandings from a right into a necessity, by obliging heirs to execute them. A number of senatusconsulta followed which placed *cognati* (relations generally) on a level with *agnati* (relations through the father). Finally, Justinian abolished the difference between property inherited and property in the hands of trustees, confused the Falcidian quarter with the Trebellian and put *cognati* and *agnati* on precisely the same footing as regards inheritance " *ab intestato.*" The latest Roman law was so entirely on the side of testaments that, while originally these could be broken for the slightest cause, they now had to be interpreted in the way most adapted to secure their validity. Once the "cyclopean" right of the father over the persons of his children had disappeared, his economic right over property acquired by them disappeared also ; and hence the emperors first introduced the *peculium castrense* (property obtained during military service) to attract young men to war, then the *peculium quasicastrense*, to attract them into the praetorian guard, and finally to satisfy those who were neither soldiers nor scholars the *peculium adventitium*. They deprived the *patria potestas* of its influence over adoptions, now no longer restricted to the small circle of relations ; they uniformly countenanced formal adoption (*arrogatio*) which was somewhat difficult owing to the difficulty of a father's becoming a subordinate member of another family; they considered emancipation as a benefit and gave to legitimization " by a subsequent marriage " all the efficacy of solemn wedlock. The *imperium paternum*, as an arrogant title seeming to detract from the imperial majesty, was altered into *patria potestas*. The humane tendencies of the monarchs extended moreover to that part of the ancient " family " which consisted of slaves : for the emperors restrained the cruelty of masters towards these, and benefited them by increasing the force and decreasing the solemnity of manumission ; and citizen rights, which were given originally only to distinguished foreigners who had deserved well of the Roman people, were granted to every one born in Rome, even of a slave father provided his mother were free or enfranchised. Punishments were also made milder, and the monarchs distinguished themselves by the gracious title of " clement." The letter of the law always tended to be more freely interpreted in the light of natural equity, and it may be said that Constantine absolutely cancelled the letter when he laid down the principle that any particular motive of equity should override the law. Thus was attained the precise opposite of the " *privilegia ne irroganto* " of the Twelve Tables (" that no exceptions be made ") : all privileges were exceptions to the law dictated by some particular merit in the facts which lifted them out of the sphere of legal generalisations. The restriction of rights to particular peoples was by degrees abolished : under Caracalla the whole Roman world was converted into a single Rome, since great monarchs desire the whole world to become one city, according to the thought of Alexander the Great, when he said that for him all the world was a single city of which his phalanx was the citadel. The praetor's edict gives place, under Hadrian, to the " perpetual edict " of Salvius Julianus, almost exclusively composed of provincial edicts.

With monarchy, the natural law of races gives place to the natural law of nations ; and hence this political, social and juridical form is the most suitable to human nature at its fullest rational development. Here too, as we have already had occasion to remark, we reach again after a long process the unity which existed in the person of the primitive father under domestic monarchy ; and the course of national history must be considered as absolutely complete. To go further is impossible : the only possibility, at this stage of the highest human civilisation and refinement, is corruption, the return of barbarism as a " barbarism of reflection " and a relapse into a kind of new state of nature, to return once more into a new and heroic barbarism.

CHAPTER XVIII

THE RETURN OF BARBARISM : THE MIDDLE AGES

OF this kind of " reflux " Vico mentions and examines only one instance : the period of European history which had in his own days for the first time been marked out definitely by historians and given the name (though Vico does not use it) of the " Middle Ages."

That this was a period of decadence and barbarism was certainly not a new thought for consciousness : for, especially in the humanistic period, a general feeling of estrangement and repulsion had been felt towards these centuries of " middle and low Latinity " in which the treasures of the classical literatures were neglected and scattered, and humane studies either lost their vigour or disappeared completely. This consciousness, general on the part of cultivated Europe, was especially full and vivid in Italy ; for that country could never forget that though for other peoples the Middle Ages had seen the rise of their fortunes, power and civilisation, for her they had meant the end of Rome's greatness, the humiliation of her name before the arrogant Vandal, Visigoth and Lombard, the devastation of rich cities, and the destruction of majestic monuments whose miserable wreckage could be seen on every hand. Machiavelli had opened his *Histories* with a famous and striking picture of the general change which followed the fall of the Western Empire. But to pass in review the ruins or to collect the antiquities of the Middle Ages was not the way to penetrate into the spirit of the period, any more than to note a man's faults and the marks which distinguish him from another is the same thing as understanding the soul of either. Vico was the first to understand the soul of the Middle Ages, that is to say, the mental, social and cultural constitution of the period.

Though living in a part of Italy rich not only in documents but in survivals of the Middle Age, Vico confesses that this second period of barbarism is much more obscure to him than the first, and that it is only the first that has enabled him to throw light upon the second. This he expressed by the mere fact that he named the period " the second barbarism," or the " return " or " reflux " of barbarism, and thus considered it as an instance of his ideal law of reflux. The Middle Ages seemed to him both a representation of the primitive conditions of life, and in consequence a reproduction of the social process developing out of them. It was a view as original as it was rich in truth : and it is no objection to it to say that Vico reveals the generic characters rather than the particular traits of the Middle Ages, because we know that the problem he set before himself was precisely the investigation of generic characters or uniformities, and that he avoided history properly so called in order to escape a dilemma between science and faith, between the purely immanental conception of history, excluding revelation and miracle, and the purely transcendent conception, miraculous and therefore difficult to treat in a scientific manner. Even in our own times, it is a fact worth noticing that we have seen a recrudescence of this attempt to harmonise religion and history by abstracting from the individual aspect of events and reducing history to a history of institutions and uniformities.[1] In this position

[1] See my preface to Sorel's *Reflections on Violence* (Italian tr., Bari, 1909), pp. xxii-xxvii.

assumed by the problem in Vico's mind we may see the reason for the fact, which some have thought very strange in a Catholic, that he lays no stress on Christianity, and when he encounters it at the outset of the Middle Ages dismisses it in a few words ; saying that God, having by superhuman ways shown clearly the truth of the Christian religion, when he opposed the virtue of the martyrs to the power of Rome, and the doctrine of the Fathers, together with the miracles, to the empty wisdom of Greece, and knowing that armed nations must arise on every hand ready to fight for the divinity of that religion's author, permitted the birth of a new order of civilisation among the nations, in order that the true religion might be established according to the natural course of human affairs.

We must be content then with the resemblances observed by Vico between mediaeval society and that of the early centuries of Greece and Rome, and not take offence if his exemplifications and proofs very often seem fallacious and fanciful. His main historical thought as we know already is robust enough to pass over the errors or to live in the midst of them unimpaired.

We see (to reconstruct his story or picture, with some rearrangement) in the Middle Ages groups of dwellings everywhere springing up on the mountains, each dominated by its fortress as in the divine age of the " cyclopes " ; for the unhappy people, ground down by the violence of barbarian invasions and intestine strife, had no other means of defence. The most ancient cities built in the Middle Ages and almost all capitals of states are as a matter of fact placed upon heights ; all new seigneuries formed at the time were called " castella " by the Italians ; and this perhaps is also the reason why nobles were called men " born in a high or conspicuous position " (*summo, illustri loco nati*) while the plebeians living in the plains below were " born in a low or obscure place " (*imo, obscuro loco nati*). We find asyla or sanctuaries again open especially with the ecclesiastical lords, who were in humanity in advance of their savage times ; here took refuge the oppressed and the terrified, to seek protection for person or property. Hence in Germany, a country which must have been wilder than the other parts of Europe, there remained almost more ecclesiastical than secular lords. A famous example of these political formations was the Abbey of St. Laurence at Aversa in the kingdom of Naples, with which was incorporated that of St. Laurence at Capua. This monastery governed either directly or by abbots or monks dependent upon it no less than a hundred and ten churches in Campania, Samnium, Apulia and the ancient Calabria, from the river Volturnus to the gulf of Tarentum ; the abbots of St. Laurence were lords or barons of almost the whole of this country. The small chapels which they built in mountainous and remote places for the celebration of the mass and other religious offices became natural sanctuaries for the population, and they built their houses round them : and this is the reason why in Europe so many cities, lands and castles bear the names of saints, and why the churches are the most ancient monuments of this period. Consequently we also find feudalism, not establishing itself in Europe for the first time, but appearing once more. It has been mistakenly believed to be a relic of Roman law after its destruction by the barbarians (such is the theory of Oldenorp and all other jurists) whereas really Roman law itself arose out of the ruins of the feudalism of early Latin barbarism, and mediaeval feudalism was not a new law of the European nations, but a very ancient law renewed by the last barbarism. This feudalism is far from being the " vile matter " which Cujas calls it : it is a heroic matter, one worthy to be celebrated by the most erudite and profound learning of Greece and Rome. And to what is it due, if not to this essential unity of nature, that the choicest expressions of

Roman law, which Cujas himself allows to mitigate the
barbarism of feudalistic learning, are so precisely adequate
to express the properties and attributes of the system
that no better terminology could be desired ?

With the Middle Ages, then, we return to the fundamental division between heroes and slaves, between
" *viri* " or " barons "(" *varones* " is the word still used
for men, " *viri*," in Spanish) and mere " *homines* " as the
vassals were called : between " *patres* " or " patrons "
and serfs.   The learned students of feudalism who translate "*feudum*" by "*clientela*" are really giving something
much more than a good linguistical equivalent ; they are
unawares giving a historical definition of the feoff.   The
first feoffs of the Middle Ages were necessarily personal,
like the first *clientelae* of Romulus : a form of vassalage
still extant in Vico's time in the north, especially in Poland,
where the " *kmet*" were a kind of slaves who were often used
as stakes in their lord's games, and passed with their
families into the hands of the winner.   Then came rustic
feoffs, real in character and consisting in uncultivated
land assigned by the victors to the conquered for their
sustenance, while they themselves kept the cultivated
land : these feoffs were called by the feudalists, with a
new elegance of Latinity and an equally sound historical
truth, " *beneficia*."   The ancient " *nexi* " were the new
"liege " or bound men, who were compelled to join in
all the friendships and quarrels of their lord, and supplied
what in Rome was called " *opera militaris*," and in the
Middle Ages " *militare servitium*."   The feudal bond
extended itself to larger political relations, and just as
conquered kings became allies or *socii* of Rome and
" upheld the majesty of the Roman people," so there
were sovereign feoffs subordinated to higher sovereignties
whose representatives, the great kings and lords of large
kingdoms and numerous provinces, took the title of
" majesty."

Republics became aristocratic once more in government if not in constitution : this is admitted by political writers, among others by Bodin, who even says that his own kingdom of France was purely aristocratic in constitution under the Merovingian and Capetian dynasties. Till the end of the sixteenth century living witnesses to the past remained in the aristocratic kingdoms of Sweden and Denmark ; and Poland, mentioned above, preserved the same constitution down to Vico's own time. The first state parliaments of Europe must have consisted like Romulus's senate of the elders of the nobility (*seniores*, hence *seigneurs*) ; and were armed courts of barons or peers like the *comitia curiata* of old. In these parliaments were decided feudal causes concerning rights or successions or the devolution of feoffs through felony or default of heirs : which causes, confirmed many times by these judgments, formed the customs of feudalism. Vico saw a relic of these parliaments in the Sacred Royal Council at Naples, the president of which assumed the title of " Sacred Royal Majesty," as the councillors did the title of " *milites*," and whose sentences admitted of no appeal to any other tribunal, but only a request for revision by the Council itself.

The governments, beside being aristocratic, were enveloped in an atmosphere of religion to such an extent that not only were bishops and abbots very often, as we saw, feudatories, but feudatories and sovereigns adorned themselves freely with religious insignia ; Catholic kings everywhere, in order to defend the Christian religion whose protectors they were, wore the dalmatic of the diaconate, consecrated their persons (whence the title " Sacred Royal Majesty "), and took rank in the church, as Hugh Capet took the title of Count and Abbot of Paris ; thus as we see from the earliest documents the French lords called themselves dukes and abbots or counts and abbots simultaneously. These early Christian kings

were the first to institute armed religious orders, by the
help of which they defended Catholicism against Arians,
Saracens and other infidels. "*Pura et pia bella*" returned
once more as in the heroic period ; the globe surmounted
by the cross worn by the Christian potentates on their
crowns recalls the cross upon the standards in the holy
wars or crusades. Heroic slavery returns, and lasts a
long time among Christian nations because, considering
war as the judgment of God, the victors believed the
vanquished to be abandoned by God and held them no
better than beasts (thus the Christians called the Turks
" dogs " and were in turn called " pigs " by them). The
ancients deprived the conquered of all things human
and divine. The new barbarians on occupying a city
endeavoured above everything to search out and carry
off the tombs or relics of saints, which the peoples of that
time buried and concealed with all possible care ; and
thus almost all translations of relics took place at this
time. A trace of this custom survives in the rule by
which a conquered nation must buy back from the victorious generals all the bells in the cities they have taken.

Analogous resemblances may be found in the juridical
regulation of property. The primary division of property
in feudal law is that into feudal goods and allodial goods.
Allodial tenure was in origin a highly secure right, unencumbered by any external charge, even a public one ;
and applied to property directly acquired or conquered
by the patricians or barons. Feudal tenure required the
approval of the lord by whom it had been granted.
Allodial tenure thus corresponded to quiritary *ex optimo
iure*, and feudal to bonitary ; and it was only when later
in modern Europe as previously in ancient Rome a new
census and treasury were formed, and when allodial
property was made subject to public charges, that it could
be contemptuously described as " goods of the spindle "
as opposed to feudal, " goods of the lance." Thus, to

take an example, the provinces which were later incorporated into the French kingdom had formerly been
sovereign principalities feudally dependent upon the
ruler of the said kingdom ; their sovereign princes being
free from all public charge in the tenure of their (allodial)
possessions.   Later, when through succession, rebellion
or failure of heirs these provinces became part of the
kingdom, the property was made liable to taxation and
tribute ; the tenure *ex optimo iure* was confused with
private non-feudal tenure subject to these charges, and
allodials in the noble sense of the word were identified
with allodials in the common sense.   The later students
of feudalism missed the point of the primitive distinction
just as the late Roman jurists forgot the meaning of
tenure *ex optimo iure*.   To the feudal tenure belonged
emphyteosis (so that the allodial right ultimately signified
both what the vassal paid to the sovereign and the planter
to his immediate lord) :   " commendations," identical
with the ancient *clientela* :   the " census " by which the
vassals were bound to serve their lords in war (the tribu-
taries, *angarii* or *perangarii*, being equivalent to the Roman
assidui) : the "*precaria*," which must originally have been
land granted by lords in response to the prayers of the
poor :   and " *libelli* " or transferences of non-movable
property which in this agricultural economy took the
place of commerce.   The exclusion of women from inheritance, which went back to the beginnings of Roman law,
was renewed in the form of the " salic law " in Germany
and among all the early barbarian nations of Europe,
though it preserved its force only in France and Savoy.

Punishments were cruel; death was called the "ordinary
penalty."   But there was in the Middle Ages no real
penal law and procedure dealing with private offences.
The murder of a plebeian was committed either by his
own lord, whom nobody could accuse, or by another
lord, who could indemnify the man's own lord for his loss

as if he had been a slave. This custom was still in force in Poland, Lithuania, Denmark, Sweden and Norway. Under the name of "canonical purgations" (though unrecognised by canon law) certain kinds of divine judgments or duels were practised throughout Europe ; and private vengeance flourished down to the time of Bartolo. In judgments concerned with allodial rights, the lords met in arms ; and in the kingdom of Naples even in Vico's own days barons avenged intrusions upon their own feoffs on the part of other barons not by civil suits but by duels. In a society ruled by force, what wonder that the robbers of the heroic age returned, and that "pirate" became a title of nobility ? Never has the fortune of kingdoms been so various or so inconstant.

The Roman law of Justinian, penetrated as it was by the idea of equity, was abandoned and fell into oblivion. In France and Spain any one who dared to appeal to it in a cause was severely punished ; in Italy it is certain that the nobles considered it dishonourable to regulate their affairs by Roman law, and professed to live according to that of the Lombards ; while the plebeians, slower in throwing off ancient customs, continued to practise certain parts of the Roman law by force of habit. In fact the law of the period consisted rather of habits than of statutes : rigid formulae and solemn ceremonial once more acquired importance, and a distinction was made between *pacta nuda*, naked agreements, and *pacta vestita*, agreements clothed and reinforced by these formulae and ceremonies. An example of the respect in which formulae were held is afforded by the action of the Emperor Conrad III. On taking Weinsberg, a town which had supported his rival for the empire, he condemned it to extermination, making an exception only in favour of the women and all they could bring out with them. The women came out of the doomed city carrying on their backs their sons, husbands and fathers : and the Emperor, standing before the gate at the head of his army with swords drawn and lances in rest to satisfy their leader's terrible wrath, watched them and allowed them to pass safe and sound out of respect for the letter of his own decree.

It was an illiterate period, a fact expressed by Vico in the statement that languages again became " mute " or hieroglyphic. The common tongues, Italian, French, Spanish and German, were not written down : only a few ecclesiastics wrote a barbarous Latin, and hence " cleric " and " scholar " became synonymous terms ; but among the very priests such ignorance prevailed that we find documents signed by bishops with the sign of the cross, as they were unable to write their own names. Owing to this paucity of learning an English law laid down that a man condemned to death should be reprieved if he could write, as a valuable craftsman ; and "man of letters" as well as " cleric " or " clerk " remained a name for a learned man. Hence the value and general employment of family arms to indicate the owners of a house, a tomb, land or livestock, and the frequency with which coats-of-arms are found on buildings of the time.

With barbarism returned the predominance of verse over prose. The prose of the Fathers of the Latin Church —and the same is true of those of the Greek—is full of poetic rhythms, so as to resemble a chant. The first modern lyric poetry was religious ; and if there was not strictly a Christian religious poetry, this was because the subjects of our theology transcend all intelligence and imagination and crush the poetic faculty. Poetry and history were once more confounded ; the romantic poets, the heroic poets of the return to barbarism, believed their own stories to be true, and thus Boiardo and Ariosto took as subject for their poems Turpin, Bishop of Paris. And just as the French language, when owing to the famous Parisian school and the highly subtle scholastic theology

it passed at a stroke from spontaneity to reflection, preserved pure diphthongs in great number while adopting
abstract terms, so the story of Turpin survived in France
like a Homeric poem. These authors of Latin poems
confined themselves entirely to history, for instance,
William of Apulia's *De gestis Normannorum in Italia* and
Gunther's *Carmen heroicum de rebus a Frederico Bar-
barossa gestis*. The first writers in the vernacular were in
Italy poets no less than in Provence and France. A
punctilious virtue like that of Achilles again appeared,
the complete morality of the duellist ; hence arose the
proud laws, the lofty duties and the vindictive satisfac-
tions of the knight-errants sung by the romantic poets.
Does not Cola di Rienzo seem to be a real Homeric character
in his swift outburst of emotion when, as we read in his
life, while speaking of the unhappy state of Rome he
excited both himself and his listeners to unrestrained
tears ? Hyperbole was a common type of thought, as
in children ; for " I often remember," writes Vico, " when
walking abroad that the gentle slopes which unfold
themselves before my eyes appeared when I was a child
to be steep and lofty mountains." Thus in the Middle
Ages Roland and the other paladins were represented as
gigantic in stature : and images of divine beings, the
eternal Father, Christ, or the Virgin, painted or sculptured,
were of colossal dimensions.

But the human mind is like land which, after lying
waste for long centuries, when first cultivated bears crops
of wonderful quality, size and abundance. Thus at the
close of barbarism in Italy after four savage and stormy
centuries, arose Dante, the Homer of the second barbarism,
just as somewhat later flourished the delicate verse of
Petrarch and the gallant and graceful prose of Boccaccio ;
all three incomparable in their way. And since barbarism
is, as we have already indicated, truthful, frank, faithful,
generous and magnanimous by nature, Dante puts on

the stage real persons and real actions of the dead ; and
his poem is called a " comedy " in allusion to the ancient
comedy which followed the same principle.   It is a poem
in which both the *Iliad* and the *Odyssey* find parallels ;
the former in the *Inferno*, where Dante employs his
choleric genius and all his vast imagination in describing
the effects of implacable wrath and recalling numbers of
merciless punishments, a worthy companion-picture to
the horrid slaughters of Homer (whose descriptions of
them inspire pity in us, but gave nothing but pleasure to
his own audience) ; the latter, the *Odyssey*, which celebrates the heroic endurance of Ulysses, is paralleled by
the *Purgatorio*, a spectacle of severe punishments borne
with immovable patience, and the *Paradiso* where infinite
joy is experienced with an infinite tranquillity of mind.
Another similarity between Dante and Homer lies in the
physiognomy of the former's language, which is so varied
that some suppose him to have collected it like Homer
from all the dialects of his nation ; an opinion of sixteenth-
century scholars which will not stand criticism, for it is
certain that when Dante used them these expressions
must have been current at Florence, and that a lifetime
would have been insufficient to collect them from this
side and from that when there were no writers in the
various dialects.   But the most important resemblance of
Dante to Homer is in poetic sublimity.   Dante is a divine
poet who to the delicate imaginations of to-day seems
rough and uncivilised, and often shocks by unwonted
harmonies an ear that has become morbidly sensitive
through effeminate music.   But he is received very
differently by men of severe tastes who refuse to be
satisfied with flowers, ornaments and graces.   Like Homer
too he is great not in esoteric wisdom but in the vigour of
his imagination.   Dante was undoubtedly a very learned
theologian, but that was his weakness rather than his
strength.   If he had known neither Scholasticism nor

Latin, he would have been a still greater poet, and perhaps the Tuscan language would have had what Latin never had, a poet who could in everything bear comparison with Homer.

The man who wrote this page of criticism on Dante and vindicated him once more after centuries of anti-Dantesque taste (or mere Dantesque grammar or Dantesque scholasticism) and vindicated him in the very height of the prosperity of the Arcadianism so hostile to him, deserved to have made the acquaintance of William Shakespear's genius, which he was perhaps the only man alive capable of understanding. But in Italy, as in most countries outside England, nothing was known of Shakespear at this time, and Vico has only the vague and belated remark about him that the English, untouched by the prevailing delicacy of the century, took no pleasure in tragedies which had not an element of atrocity in them, just as the earliest taste of Greek drama was for the abominable feast of Thyestes and Medea's impious slaughter of her brother and children. The tendency towards Teutonic poetry and literature remained in Vico as we know an aspiration only ; he was unable to get a clear view of it however closely he tried to examine it ; and when he does mention it upon the strength of second-hand information, it is only to say that in the German nation, especially in the purely agricultural province of Silesia, " poets arose naturally " ; in his search for an unsophisticated popular poetry he had in fact stumbled without realising his mistake upon the Silesian school of Hoffmanswaldau and Lohenstein, the German imitators of the Neapolitan Marino. But the only value of the anecdote is to illustrate anew the tricks played upon Vico by his lively fancy.

How the world emerged from the second barbarism and the feudal constitution, Vico does not say. He does not seem to have fixed his attention upon the communal movement which presents so many analogies with the struggles of the Roman plebs and the formation of ancient democracy. He makes game, here again, of those who traced the genesis of modern monarchies such as the French to a simple law like that of Tribonian by which, he explains ironically, the paladins of France deprived themselves of their power and conferred it upon the kings of the Capetian dynasty. He also observes that the baronial power, being dispersed and dissipated by reason of civil wars in which they were obliged to depend upon the people, was the more easily gathered up by sovereign monarchs ; and that thus the " *obsequium* " of vassals to their baron passed into the " *obsequium principis.*" But he gives quite a special importance to the rediscovery of Roman law (that " natural law of the European nations " as Grotius had called it) by the studies undertaken in the Italian universities. Men thus learnt anew the principles of natural equity ; the nobles and plebeians became equal in the eyes of civil law as they are already in human nature, the secrets of the laws passed out of the hands of the feudatories, whose power consequently diminished by degrees, and the humane government of free republics and perfect monarchies came into being. The reflux of heroic society had now undergone a contrary reflux ; it was no longer possible, under the conditions of modern civilisation, to recall it to life, just as it was impossible for the attempts of the Pythagoreans and Dion of Syracuse to restore the ancient aristocracies. The plebeians, once recognised as naturally equals of the nobles, no longer submitted to remaining inferior to them in civil life. And the few aristocratic republics which here and there survived in Europe were compelled to take infinite pains and all manner of wise measures in order to keep quiet and contented the multitudes whom they governed.

CHAPTER XIX

VICO AND THE TENDENCIES OF CONTEMPORARY CULTURE

HAVING reached, in his review of the course of history, his own time, a time of civilisation spread over all nations, Vico gives a rapid description of the contemporary world and then says no more : perhaps unsatisfied, at any rate uncertain or cautious. As he was not led to embark upon the New Science by the direct call of political problems, at least in the ordinary meaning of the phrase, he never descends from the contemplations of the New Science to the practical life, even in the form which it most usually takes with a philosopher, a work or short treatise criticising laws and institutions or suggesting improvements. Even when he does dimly conceive the idea of a " practical aspect " of his science, he never supposes that so far as he is concerned it could ever exist except " within the academies."

Practical philosophy " within the academies," that is to say, within the sphere of culture, is however still practical and political ; and it is assuredly not the least important branch of politics. And a historian or philosopher can never entirely avoid it, though he can emphasise it more or less and develop it more or less fully.

Vico does emphasise and develop it freely. The first expression of his scientific life was precisely an examination of modern methods of study and education as com-

pared with those of the ancients : an examination which
after various attempts and uncertainties in his first
discoveries, took form in his University inaugural lecture
of 1708, *De nostri temporis studiorum ratione.* In the
following years, engaged as he was upon the New Science,
he gave no further public demonstration of his discontent
with the prevailing tendency of studies ; but he expressed
his feelings on the subject all the more often and all the
more strongly in private letters, and did not wish to
pass over the question in his autobiography. We need
not then infer his polemical attitude from hints and
chance phrases of his chief work ; since he has himself more
than once converted these hints into explicit statements
and these chance phrases into leading propositions.

This polemic occupies two closely-related spheres
corresponding to the double aspect of the New Science as
a Philosophy of Mind and a Generalising Science. Under
the first aspect Vico had vindicated the claims of imagination, the imaginative universal, probability, certitude,
experience and authority, and therefore also of poetry,
religion, history, observation of nature, scholarship and
tradition. Under the second, he had traced a scheme
of the natural development of the mind both in the history
of mankind and in that of the individual, which he brings
into constant relation with the phases of history. Hence
his examination was bound to extend on the one hand
to the mental condition of his own time and on the other
to the way in which the education of children and young
people was conceived and undertaken. In both spheres
Vico saw the same defects ; he was met by the same arid
intellectualism which had made impossible the process
of thought and had mutilated and falsified the truth of
human history.

On emerging from grammar-schools, boys were immediately plunged into logic. The logic studied might be,
according to the teacher's taste, either the scholastic or

more often that composed by Arnauld and called the
Port-Royal Logic, itself in substance Aristotelian and
Scholastic, but full of dry judgments concerning abstruse
subjects in advanced sciences and far removed from
common knowledge ; overloaded in fact with examples
drawn from such sciences. Such a discipline was meant to
make boys critical and to eradicate from their minds not
only false, but even probable and plausible opinions. As
a matter of fact it eradicated nothing, since their minds
were still empty or scantily furnished, and unable to
make any use of criticism for lack of matter to criticise.
They were to be taught to judge before being taught to
apprehend, an order false to the natural course of ideas,
which are first apprehended, then judged, and finally
reasoned. The result was that minds educated in this
way became arid and unfruitful in development, and
believed themselves capable of judging everything, while
able to create nothing. They remained all their lives
intensely acute in formal thinking, but incapable of any
great labour ; critical, in fact, but sterile. This caused
not only unsoundness and arrogance of judgment but
incapacity in practical life, dealings with men, and civil
eloquence, which is founded less upon criticism than upon
plausibility, and attains its end by making opportune
remarks, understanding the psychology of one's inter-
locutor and acting in a manner adapted to it. Vico himself had suffered from the logico-critical method of education. One of his first teachers, the Jesuit Del Balzo, had
put into his hands the works of the epitomist Paulus
Venetus : and his mind, being too weak as yet to cope
with this kind of Chrysippean logic, almost broke down
under the strain ; so that having given up his studies in
despair it was eighteen months before he resumed them. He
preserved a happier memory of his youthful essays in poetry
in the wildest style of the Neapolitan school of Marino :
a form of diversion, he says, almost necessary to the mind

of the young when metaphysic has rendered it too subtle and too rigid in precisely those years when the ardour of youth ought to lead the mind into errors, so as to save it from becoming chilly and dry. This age, the " barbarism of intellect," vigorous in imagination and also, through the close connexion that exists between the two, in memory, requires to be nourished and exercised by the reading of poetry, history and rhetoric as well as by the study of languages. The art which it ought to learn is not criticism but " topic," the true art of the " *ingenium* " or faculty of invention. By means of this art children acquire materials which enable them to form sound judgments in later life ; for sound judgment depends upon a complete knowledge of its subject-matter, and " topic " is the art of discovering the whole content of any given thing. In this way young people simply by following the course of nature become at once philosophers and good speakers.

Some antidote is doubtless necessary to the exuberance of the imagination. But this must be sought in linear geometry rather than in logic : for geometry is to some extent pictorial in character, while it strengthens the memory by the great number of its elements, ennobles the imagination by the delicacy of its figures and stimulates the inventive faculty by forcing it to review all these figures in order to choose those suitable to the demonstration of the quantity required. But the whole value of geometry also was annulled by the method then in favour with the schools, the algebraic method, which like the scholastic logic numbs all the vigour of youthful faculties, obscures the imagination, enfeebles the memory, and renders the inventive power and the understanding sluggish ; thus damaging the liberal arts in four distinct ways, in the knowledge of languages and history, in invention and in prudence. More particularly algebra is fatal to the inventive faculty, because in using the algebraic method one is conscious only of the immediate field of vision ;

it weakens the memory because once the second sign is
found the first need no longer be remembered ; it blinds
the imagination, because that faculty is not used at all ;
it destroys the understanding, because it lays claim to
the power of divination. Young men who have devoted
their time to it on proceeding to deal with the affairs of
civil life find themselves, to their great grief and remorse,
unfitted for such a life. Hence, to make it useful in some
degree and to prevent these ill effects, it should be studied
for a short time only at the close of the mathematical
course, and employed only as a means of abbreviation.
The habit of reasoning is formed much better by metaphysical analysis, which in all questions begins by taking
truth in the infinity of being, and then descends by degrees
through the genera of the substance, eliminating in every
species that which the thing is not, till it arrives at the
ultimate differentia constituting the essence of the thing
we wish to know.

Education as a whole was suffering from an excess of
mathematics and a lack of concreteness. As if boys, on
emerging from academic life, were to enter a human
world composed of lines, numbers and algebraic symbols,
their heads were crammed with the magnificent phrases
"demonstration," "demonstrative truth," and "evidence,"
and the rule of probability was condemned ; though this
rule is the only guide of statesmen in their counsels,
generals in their campaigns, orators in their treatment
of a cause, judges in giving a decision, physicians in
treating bodily diseases, and moralistic theologians in
treating those of the conscience ; the rule which the
world accepts, and upon which it rests in all disputes and
controversies, in all measures, and in all elections; which
are universally determined by unanimity or the majority
of votes. Such an education bred up an empty and in-
flated generation, pedantry without wisdom and argument
without truth.

The educators themselves, that is to say, the general atmosphere of culture, resembled this scheme of education. Poetry was dead. The analytic methods had " numbed " (to repeat once more a word which Vico uses with great frequency and force) " all the generosity of the better poetry." And indeed Europe was never so entirely barren of all poetic growth as it was in the first half of the eighteenth century. Italy was reduced to the drama of Metastasio ; France had produced no one to succeed Corneille and Molière ; in Spain the national drama, that great outburst of the national spirit, was dead, and a rationalism imitating that of France was taking its place ; England seemed to have entirely forgotten that she once gave birth to Shakespear, and even Germany was wasting her time over neo-classical imitations. Not only did nobody create new poetry, but nobody wanted it. The philosophers, following Descartes and Malebranche, had declared a war of extermination against all the faculties of the mind which depend upon sense, and especially against the imagination, which they hated as the source of every error. They condemned the poets on the false pretext that they told " fables," as if the fables they told were not those eternal properties of the human mind which to the political philosophers, economists and moralists are the subject-matter of reasoning, and to the poets that of representation.

The Cartesians also used their authority to belittle the study of languages. Did not Descartes say that the knowledge of Latin was no greater knowledge than was possessed by Cicero's servant-girl ? Serious scholarship in Latin and Greek had come to an end with the writers of the sixteenth and seventeenth centuries ; the study of oriental languages was confined to the Protestants ; and Holland was the only country in which law was still a subject of research. The famous library of Valletta at Naples, rich in the finest editions of Greek and Latin works, was generously bought by the fathers of the Oratory, but for less than half its original value owing to the depreciation of books. In France the library of Cardinal Dubois found no purchaser and was sold in small lots. Princes no longer loved good Latin, and none of them thought of preserving to posterity by the pen of pure Latin scholarship even an event so weighty as the War of the Spanish Succession, comparable only to the second Punic war.

New methods were in great favour : but none of these could point to new facts discovered by their help. New formulae, old facts ; and instead of facts, a futile hope of attaining universal knowledge in the shortest time and with the smallest effort. Civil and political learning was neglected for physical science, and physical science for mathematical ; experience was almost ignored ; the inventive thought of the previous century all but entirely exhausted. Scepticism, the result of the Cartesian method, invaded the field of knowledge.

The whole of Europe was during this period still under the dominion of the French language, a language which differs from the Italian in its hostility to poetry and eloquence ; rich, says Vico, in terms of substance, and consequently, since substance is a brutal and immobile thing and does not admit of comparisons, incapable of giving colour, amplitude or weight to its statements ; it resists inversion and is barren of metaphor. The French have no periods but only members of periods : their prosody has no verse better than the so-called Alexandrine, a system of couplets more thin and lifeless than the elegiac : and their words admit of no accent except those on the last two syllables. French is a language incapable of the sublime, but well adapted to the petty: owing to its abundance of terms of substance or abstract terms it is adapted also to the didactic style, and instead of eloquence it offers *esprit.* It was not unfitting that criticism and analysis originated in France and made use of the French tongue.

The only possession of value which grew up day by day in all this poverty was the abstracts, the encyclopaedias, the dictionaries of science which bore the names of such men as Bayle, Hoffmann and Moreri : the idlest and most casual method of learning that could possibly be devised. The genius of the age was more drawn towards expounding second-hand knowledge in an abbreviated form than towards attempting to enlarge its bounds. That seemed impossible : so men went on compiling dictionaries of mathematics. Every one felt a thirst for cheap science. To be thought good, a book must be clear and simple, capable of being discussed with ladies as a pastime ; if it demanded wide and copious erudition of the reader, and forced upon him the unpleasant exercise of thought and synthesis, it was condemned as unintelligible.

These dictionaries and abstracts recalled to Vico's mind the similar products of the Greek decadence, the anthologies, lexicons and encyclopaedias of Suidas, Stobaeus and Photius. The whole culture of his time seemed to him to be repeating the downfall of Greek science, exhausting itself in a metaphysic either useless or harmful to civilisation and a mathematics engaged in investigating quantities intangible by rule and compass, and incapable of application. Like others among the best minds of his country he was persuaded that the republic of letters was approaching dissolution, if the divine providence failed by one of its innumerable secret paths to infuse new vigour into it. Where was now the wise man, the real " *sapiens* " whom Vico had found in history, first in the barbaric figure of the theologian-poet, then in the civilised and rational figure of Greek philosopher and Roman jurist, the man whom for to-day he hoped to find in the master of eloquence like himself, called to give unity, life and power to all knowledge ? Wisdom is indeed not this or that science, nor yet the sum total of science ; it is the faculty which rules over all studies and by which all the sciences and arts that go to make humanity are acquired. And since man is both thought and spirit, intellect and will, it must satisfy both these sides of man, the second as a result of the first : it must teach the knowledge of divine things, to bring to perfection things human. The wise man is man in his totality and entirety, the whole man.

The ideal is no doubt lofty, and the criticism upon the educational method and tendencies of thought current in his age are, no doubt, perfectly just. And yet among all these admirable truths, far in advance of the eighteenth century as they are, we feel in Vico the educationalist and critic something of the reactionary. We feel that, in his exclusive care for the fate of the highest and most austere science and his exclusive attention to the most complete form of human life, he failed to grasp the revolutionary importance of this scepticism or rationalism, this rebellion against the past, the necessary weapon of a warfare against kings, nobles and priests ; of these abstracts and dictionaries which were to develop into the Encyclopaedia; of this popular science, the forerunner of journalism, and these booklets for the use of ladies in fashionable conversation which were the nourishment of the eighteenth-century salons and prepared men's minds for the radicalism of the Jacobins. We feel in him here as in his philosophical system, the Catholic chained to the philosopher, the Christian pessimist weighing down the dialectic of immanence. Unable to realise his adversaries' progress, he does not comprehend their real nature as lower than himself, but yet constituting steps leading up to himself, steps which he ought to have traversed in order to attain a truer understanding and grasp of himself. His polemical attitude towards the culture of his time completes and confirms the analysis already given of the merits and defects of his philosophy.

CHAPTER XX

CONCLUSION : VICO AND THE LATER DEVELOPMENTS OF
PHILOSOPHICAL AND HISTORICAL THOUGHT

THE reader need not expect that having brought our
exposition to a close we shall add a verdict upon Vico's
work, or what is known as an " appreciation " of it. If
the verdict has not already emerged as a result of the
exposition itself, or as identical with it, if description and
criticism have been not one and same, the fault lies either
with ourselves or with the reader's lack of attention ;
and in either case it cannot now be repaired by ornamental
additions or redundant repetitions.

We confess also that we feel no sympathy with the
chapters commonly placed at the conclusion of critical
works upon philosophers and narrating the later history
of their ideas. For if these " ideas " are understood in
an extrinsic sense, in their influence upon society and
culture, such a review may indeed have a value of its
own,[1] but is foreign to the history of philosophy properly
so called : if on the other hand they are considered as
real and living philosophical ideas, their later history
amounts to neither more nor less than the history of
subsequent philosophy, and there is no reason for append-
ing it to a study of one philosopher rather than another.
Any other method implies the uncritical theory that ideas
are something solid and crystallised, like precious stones

[1] See Appendix II.

236

handed on from one generation to another, whose shape
and glitter can always be recognised unaltered in the new
diadems they compose and the new brows they adorn.
But in reality ideas are nothing but the unremitting
thought of man, and transmission for them is nothing
less than transformation.

It is nevertheless a fact that no one has written on
Vico without feeling a need of casting his eyes over later
years and noting the resemblances and analogies between
the Neapolitan philosopher's doctrines and those of fifty
or a hundred years after. And further, we ourselves, in
spite of the antipathy we admittedly feel, and the methodi-
cal criteria we professedly employ, yet recognise now the
same necessity. Why is this? Because Vico in his
own day passed for an eccentric and lived as a recluse;
because the later development of thought was almost
entirely untouched by his direct influence; because even
to-day, though well enough known in certain restricted
circles, he has not taken the place he deserves in the
general history of thought. How then can we show the
manner in which his doctrines, true or false, respond to
the deepest needs of the mind, more simply than by re-
cording the similarity of the ideas and attempts which
later appeared in such profusion and intensity as to stamp
their individuality upon the philosophical and historical
labours of a whole century? And even if after our
intrinsic examination of his thought this comparison
with the facts of later history seems unnecessary, it will
at least be granted that if our discourse like any other
must have its rhetorical conclusion, no peroration occurs
more naturally than one consisting in a rapid review of
subsequent philosophy and philology and emphasising
their points of contact with the thought of Vico.

We might even adopt the method by which he compares
the second barbarism with the first, and present the later
history of thought as a " reflux " of Vico's ideas. In the

first place his criticism of Descartes' immediate knowledge recurs, together with his conversion of the true with the created, in the speculative movement beginning with Kant and Hegel and culminating in the doctrine of the identity of truth and reality, thought and existence. His unity of philosophy and philology recurs in the vindication of history against the scepticism and intellectualism of the eighteenth century due to Cartesianism ; in the à priori synthesis of Kant which reconciles the real and the ideal, experience and the categories ; and in the historical philosophy of Hegel, the greatest exponent of nineteenth-century historical tendencies. This unity of philosophy and philology, a unity with Vico sometimes confused and impure in method, recurred in its faulty aspects also in the Hegelian school ; so that this mental tendency might with justice be entitled " Vicianism." The limitation which Vico tried to impose on the value of mathematics and exact science recurred, as did his criticism of the mathematical and naturalistic conception of philosophy, in Jacobi's critique of Spinozistic determinism and Hegel's of the abstract intellect ; and in the case of mathematics in particular Dugald Stewart and others recognised that its validity lay not in the postulates but in the definitions, and the " fictions " of which Vico speaks reappear in the modern terminology of the philosophy of these sciences. His poetical logic or science of the imagination passes into Aesthetic, so ardently studied by the philosophers, literary men and artists of Germany in the eighteenth century, brought by Kant into great prominence by his criticism of the Leibnitian doctrine of intuition as confused conception, and further advanced by Schelling and Hegel, who place art among the pure forms of the mind and so approach the position of Vico. Romanticism too, especially in Germany but also more or less in other countries, was Vician, emphasising as it did the original function of the imagination. His doctrines of language

recurred when Herder and Humboldt treated it not in-
tellectualistically as an artificial system of symbols, but
as a free and poetic creation of the mind. The theory of
religion and mythology abandoned the hypotheses of
allegory and deception, and with David Hume recognised that religion is a natural fact, corresponding to
the beginnings of human life in its passionate and
imaginative state ; with Heyne, that mythology is
" symbolic speech," a product not of arbitrary invention
but of necessity and poverty, of the " lack of words,"
which finds expression " in comparisons with things
already known " (*per rerum iam tum notarum similitudines*) ;
and with Ottfried Müller, that it is impossible to understand
mythology without entering into the very heart of the
human soul, where we may see its necessity and spontaneity.
Religion was regarded no longer as something extraneous
or hostile to philosophy, as a piece of stupidity or of
deception practised by the unscrupulous upon the simple,
but according to Vico's own doctrine as a rudimentary
philosophy ; so that the whole content of reasoned metaphysic was already to a certain extent implicit in poetical
or religious metaphysic. Similarly, poetry and history
were no longer kept distinct or set face to face to destroy
each other ; and as one of the great inspirers of the new
German literature, Hamann (who in many ways resembles
Vico in tendency, though unequal to him in mental power),
had already foreseen when he uttered the warning, " if
our poetry is worthless, our history will become leaner
than Pharaoh's kine," a breath of poetry revived the
historical study of the nineteenth century ; once colourless, it became picturesque : once frigid, it regained
warmth and life. The criticism of Hobbes' and Locke's
utilitarianism, and the affirmation of the moral consciousness as a spontaneous sense of shame and a judgment
entirely free from reflection reappeared in full panoply
with the Critique of the Practical Reason ; and that of

their social atomism and consequent contractualism in
Hegel's Philosophy of Right. The liberty of conscience
and religious indifferentism professed and inculcated by
the publicists of the seventeenth century were negated
as a philosophical doctrine ; and a nation without God
seemed to Hegel, as it did to Vico, a phenomenon not to
be found in history and existing only in the gossip of
travellers in unknown or little-known lands.' Carrying
on the work of the Reformation, which Vico could neither
grasp nor truly appreciate, the idealistic philosophy of
Germany aimed not at exterminating religion, but at
refining it, and at giving philosophy itself the spiritual
value of religion. The certitude, the hard certitude
which Vico distinguished from truth in the sphere of
law, formed the subject of thought from Thomasius to
Kant and Fichte and so on to the most recent writers,
who have sought even if they have never found the distinctive criterion of the two forms ; all or nearly all show
a vivid consciousness of what is called " constraint" or
" compulsion," a fact which had been almost forgotten
in the old superficial and rhetorical moral theory. The
historical school of law, in its reaction against the abstract
revolutionary and reformatory tendencies of the eighteenth
century, was bound to recall Vico's polemic against the
Platonic or Grotian theory of an ideal republic or a natural
law above and outside history and serving as a standard
for history, and to recognise with Vico that law is correlative to the whole social life of a people at a given moment
of its history and capable of being judged only in relation
to it ; a living and plastic reality, in a continual process
of change like that of language. Finally, Vico's providence, the rationality and objectivity of history, which
obeys a logic different from that attributed to it by the
fancies and illusions of the individual, acquires a more
prosaic name, but without changing its nature, in the
" cunning of the reason " formulated by Hegel : it appeared

again, ingeniously but perversely treated, in Schopen-
hauer's "cunning of the species," and again, treated
with little ingenuity on a purely psychological method, in
Wundt's so-called law of the "heterogenesis of ends."

Almost all the leading doctrines of nineteenth-century
idealism, we have seen, may be regarded as refluxes of
Vician doctrines. Almost all ; for there is one of which
we find in Vico not the premonition but the necessity,
not a temporary filling but a gap to be filled. Here the
nineteenth century is no longer a reflux of, but an advance
upon Vico ; and discordant voices of warning or reproach
rise up against him. His distinction of the two worlds
of mind and nature, to both of which the criterion of
his theory of knowledge, the conversion of the truth with
the thing created, was applicable, but applicable to the
former by man himself because that world is a world
created by man, and therefore knowable by him, to the
second by God the Creator, so that this world is unknowable by man ; this distinction was not accepted by
the new philosophy, which, more Vician than Vico,
made the demigod Man into a God, lifted human thought
to the level of universal mind or the idea, spiritualised
or idealised nature, and tried to understand it specula-
tively in the "Philosophy of Nature" as itself a product
of mind. As soon as the last remnant of transcendence
was in this way destroyed, the concept of progress overlooked by Vico and grasped and affirmed to some extent
by the Cartesians and their eighteenth-century followers
in their superficial and rationalistic manner shone out in
its full splendour.

But if in this point Vico cannot stand the comparison
with later philosophy, the failure is amply atoned by the
full agreement between his historical discoveries and the
criticism and research of the nineteenth century. Above
all, he agrees with his successors in his rules of method,
his scepticism as regards the narrative of ancient historians,

his recognition of the superiority of documents and monuments over narrative, his investigation of language as a store-house of primitive beliefs and customs, his social interpretation of mythology, his emphasis on spontaneous development rather than external communication of civilisation, his care not to interpret primitive psychology in the light of modern psychology ; and so on. In his actual solutions of historical problems he also agrees with later historians. These restated the archaic and barbaric character of primitive Greek and Roman civilisation, and the aristocratic and feudal tendency of its political constitution : they took up the view of ancient legal ceremonial as a dramatic poem containing allusions to the actions of fighting : the transformation of the Roman heroes into heroes of democracy came to an end with the Jacobins in France and their imitators in Italy and elsewhere ; Homer was considered great in proportion to his ruggedness; the history of Rome was reconstructed chiefly on the basis of Roman law, and the names of the seven kings appeared as symbols of institutions and the traditional origin of Rome as a late invention derived from Greece or from Greek models : the substance of this history was seen to consist in the economic and juridical struggle between patriciate and plebs, and the plebs was derived from the *famuli* or clients : the struggle of the classes, which Vico was the first to illuminate clearly, was recognised as a criterion of wide application to the history of all time and serving as an explanation of the most sweeping social revolutions : the Middle Ages, especially during the Restoration which followed the Napoleonic period, exercised a powerful appeal to sentiment and influence on thought, being admired and regretted as the antithesis of the rationalistic bourgeois society, and understood in consequence as the religious, aristocratic and poetical period discovered by Vico, the youth of modern Europe. Thus Italy rediscovered the greatness of her own Dante, and the criticism of that poet which Vico had initiated was carried to completion by De Sanctis. In the same way, Niebuhr and Mommsen brought to maturity his view of Roman history ; Wolf, his theory of Homer ; Heyne, Müller and Bachhofen, his interpretation of mythology ; Grimm and other philologists his projected reconstruction of ancient life by means of etymology ; Savigny and the historical school, his study of the spontaneous development of law, and his preference for custom rather than statute and code : Thierry and Fustel de Coulanges in France, Troya in Italy and a host of scholars in Germany his conception of the Middle Ages and of feudalism : Marx and Sorel his idea of the struggle of classes and the rejuvenation of society by a return to a primitive state of mind and a new barbarism : and lastly the superman of Nietzsche recalls in some degree Vico's hero. These are merely a few names picked without care and almost at random ; for to mention all, and each in his right place, would mean writing the whole history of the latest phase of European thought, a history which is not yet finished, though it has undergone, under the name of " positivism," a parenthetical recurrence of the abstract and materialistic thought of the eighteenth century, a parenthesis which now however seems to be at an end.

These innumerable reappearances of the work of an individual in the work of several generations, this parallelism between a man and a century, justify a fanciful phrase with which we might draw from the later developments in order to describe Vico ; namely that he is neither more nor less than the nineteenth century in germ. The description may serve to summarise our reconstruction and exposition of his doctrines, and to contribute towards a right understanding of his place in the history of modern philosophy. He may rightly be placed side by side with Leibniz, with whom he has so often been compared ;

but not, as has been believed, because of any resemblance
(the comparisons made in this belief have been shown to
be false or superficial) but precisely because he is unlike
him and in fact his very opposite.   Leibniz is Cartesianism
raised to its highest power ; an intellectualist, in spite of
the *petites perceptions* and the confused knowledge ; a
mechanicist, in spite of his dynamism, which perhaps
exists in his fancy rather than in his actual thought ;
hostile to history, in spite of his immense historical
erudition ; blind to any knowledge of the true nature of
language, though deeply interested in language all his life ;
devoid of dialectic, in spite of his attempt to explain the
evil in the universe.   In relation to later idealism, the
Leibnitian philosophy stands as the most complete expression of the old metaphysic which had to be transcended : that of Vico is the sketch of the new metaphysic,
only needing further development and determination.
The one spoke to his own century, and his century crowded
round him and echoed his words far and wide.   The
other spoke to a century yet to come ; and the place in
which he cried was a wilderness that gave no answer.
But the crowd and the wilderness add nothing to and take
nothing from the intrinsic character of a thought.

APPENDICES

APPENDIX I

ON THE LIFE AND CHARACTER OF G. B. VICO [1]

I

THE transformation, half rhetorical, half mythical, which the heat of the national reawakening effected in poets, philosophers, and almost every character of any importance in Italian history, representing them as patriots, liberals, and in open rebellion or secret revolt against the throne and the altar, tried for a time to touch with its magic wand and to work its will upon Giambattista Vico. It was said, among other things, that Vico, conscious of the severe blow dealt by his thought to the traditional beliefs of religion, and warned by his friends, took pains to plunge the New Science into such obscurity that only the finest intellects could perceive its tendencies. But though this legend, energetically spread as it was by the patriots and republicans of 1799, was believed here and there, it could not long stand out against criticism or even against common sense; and Cataldo Iannelli was right to pass over it with a few words of contemptuous irony.[2]

It is certain from an objective point of view that Vico's doctrines implicitly contained a criticism of Christian tran-

[1] Since the preceding portions of this work are strictly confined to the analysis of Vico's philosophy and give no information as to his life and personal character, the reader will not be displeased to find in this appendix a lecture delivered by myself upon the latter subject before the Neapolitan *Società di storia patria* on April 14, 1909, and later written down and published in the Florence *Voce* (1st year, No. 43, October 7, 1909). I add for convenience of memory that Vico was born at Naples on June 23, 1668 (not 1670 as he says in his autobiography), and died on January 23 (not 20 as all his biographers say), 1744: cf. the new edition of the *Autobiografia, carteggio e poesie varie* (Bari, Laterza, 1911), pp. 101, 123, 124.

[2] See for the whole question Croce, *Bibliografia vichiana*, pp. 91-5.

247

scendence and theology as well as of the history of Christianity. From the subjective point of view it may be that Vico during his youth (of which we know very little) was the victim of religious doubts. Such doubts may have been suggested to him not only by his reading, but by the society of young men of his own age, among whom " libertines," or as contemporary literature still called them " epicureans " or " atheists," were not uncommon.[1] In a letter of 1720 to Father Giacchi, he says that at Naples the " weaknesses and errors dating from his early youth " are remembered against him, and that these, fixed in the memory, became as often happens " eternal criteria for the judgment of everything beautiful and complete which he subsequently succeeded in doing." [2] What can these errors and weaknesses have been ?

Again when the *De universi iuris uno principio et fine uno* appeared, or rather the " Synopsis " which announced its programme, " the first voices " which Vico heard raised against him " were tinged with an assumed piety." He found protection and consolation in the face of such criticism in religion itself, that is to say in the approval of Giacchi, " the leading light of the strictest and most holy order of religious." [3] But just as we possess no detailed information as to the criticisms levelled against him on this head, so we have no certain knowledge even of the most general kind as to the religious doubts that may have troubled him. All Vico's writings show the Catholic religion established in his heart, grave, solid and immovable as a pillar of adamant ; so solid and so strong that it remained absolutely untouched by the criticism of mythology inaugurated by himself. Nor was Vico an irreproachable Catholic in external demonstration only. He not only submitted every word he ever printed to the double censorship, public and private, of ecclesiastical

---

[1] In the *Giornali* of Confuorto (MSS. in the library of the Neapolitan Historical Soc. xx. c. 22, vol. iii. f. 111) under August 1692, we find " certain civil persons were imprisoned in the prisons of St. Dominic by the tribunal of the Holy Office ; among them the doctor Giacinto de Cristofaro, son of the doctor Bernardo ; many others escaped, members of the Epicurean or Atheist sect, who believe the soul to perish with the body." This De Cristofaro is the famous Neapolitan mathematician and juriconsult, for whom see F. Amodeo, *Vita matematica napoletana*, part iii. (Naples, Giannini, 1905), pp. 31-44 ; he was Vico's friend. For other notices of the " Epicureans " at Naples at this time see Carducci, *Opere*, vol. ii. pp. 235-6.
[2] Letter of October 12, 1720.   [3] *Ibid.*

friends, and led his life as a philosopher and writer among priestly vestments and monastic cowls no less than among legal gowns ; he was even scrupulous enough to desist from his commentary on Grotius, thinking it unseemly that a Catholic should annotate a Protestant writer ; [1] and so delicate was his sense of Catholic honour that he refused to admit polemic upon matters of religious feeling. " As to this difficulty," he says to his critics of the *Giornale dei letterati*, " like that which you propound to me concerning the immortality of the soul, where it appears that you have in hand seven distinct arguments, if they had not been prepared for me by you, I should judge that they go deeper and penetrate to a region which is not only protected and secured by my life and conduct, but which to defend is to outrage. But let us return to our subject." [2] His Catholicism was untainted by the superstition so general and so deeply rooted at the time, especially at Naples, where St. Januarius intervened as an actor and director in every event of public and private life. It was the Catholicism of a lofty soul and mind, not the faith of a charcoal-burner. But Vico never assumed the part of censor of superstitions. He was content with not speaking of them, as one keeps silence concerning the failings of persons or institutions which command one's respect.

II

Vico's attitude towards social and political life resembles in more than one respect his attitude towards religion. There is in him no trace of the missionary, the propagandist, the agitator or the conspirator as there was in some of the Renaissance philosophers, notably Giordano Bruno and Campanella, whom although—perhaps because—a Neapolitan, Vico never mentions. Certainly, his age and his country were not the time or place for heroes ; there was none of that rapid social change and revolution from which heroes spring. Political parties however were active in favour of Austria and France, and men were arising who devoted their labours and their lives to one or other of these parties, or were persecuted and fled into exile : and above all this was the period in which

[1] *Autobiografia*, in *Opere*, ed. Ferrari, 2nd ed. iv. p. 367.
[2] The " subject " is therefore not the religious objections, which he regarded as a personal insult (*Riposta al Giornale dei letterati*, in *Opp.* ii. p. 160).

culminated the struggle between Church and State, between Naples and Rome, in the person of Pietro Giannone, a man of whom Vico never speaks, just as he never mentions and in fact seems to ignore the entire movement. Political life rolled past over his head, like the sky and its stars, and he never wasted his strength in a vain attempt to reach it. Political and social controversy, like religious, was outside the sphere of his activity. He was indeed a non-political person. We cannot describe it as a fault or a weakness, for every one has his limitations ; one struggle excludes another, and one labour makes others impossible.

Not that he avoided all contact with political life and its representatives. Only too often he was compelled to pay his respects to both, in the form of histories, speeches, verses and epigrams in Latin and Italian ; and these alone would be sufficient material for the reconstruction of Neapolitan history in all its vicissitudes from the end of the seventeenth century to the middle of the eighteenth : the Spanish viceregency, the conspiracy and revolution attempted by the partisans of Austria, the reaction and re-establishment of the Spanish viceregency, the Austrian conquest, the Austrian viceregency, the Spanish reconquest and the reign of Charles Bourbon. But Vico, " very pliant because of his necessity " [1] and as professor of eloquence in the royal university, was compelled to supply the literary compositions required by the solemnities of the day, just as the draper supplied hangings and the plasterer volutes and arabesques. And what hangings and arabesques he produced ! The Spanish style of the seventeenth century was still predominant in literature ; and this fact is alone almost enough to explain the extravagance and ornateness, as it seems to us, of Vico's flood of panegyrics. The indifference and innocence of his own attitude may be illustrated by the passage in his autobiography where after mentioning the *Panegyricus Philippo V inscriptus* composed by himself to the order of the Spanish viceroy, the Duke of Ascalona, he goes on as if it was a mere nothing, with no connexion but a simple " soon after " : " soon after, this kingdom having passed under the rule of Austria, the lord Count Wirrigo of Daun, at that time governor of the imperial armies in this country, *ordered me* " to compose inscriptions for the expiatory monuments to Guiseppe Capece and Carlo di Sangro,[2] the two rebels against Philip V. executed by the

[1] *Opp.* vi. p. 20.   [2] *Autob.* in *Opp.* iv. p. 394.

previous government some years before in the suppression of the conspiracy of Macchia described by Vico from the Bourbon point of view in his *De Parthenopea coniuratione*.

But this implies no baseness of character on Vico's part. It must be said that in these writings of his, orator and panegyrist though he is, he can never be called a flatterer. The flatterer, the man without a conscience, reviles and calumniates the enemies of the man he is praising, or even strikes the conquered : and this is servility. But Vico, who though he knew who the Italian or Neapolitan was that sent to the *Acta Lipsiensia* the note injurious to himself, and might easily have ruined him, since the note was anti-Catholic in tendency, generously refused to reveal his name,[1] gave no doubt his services as professor of eloquence but refrained from trafficking in the interests of the patrons whom he praised. Of the *Life of Antonio Carafa* which he composed for a commission and married one of his daughters on the proceeds, he says that the work was " tempered by honour towards the subject, reverence towards princes and the just claims of truth." [2] And to return to the case of Capece and Sangro mentioned above, when he spoke in the *De Parthenopea coniuratione* of the death of these two enemies to the triumphant party, he shows here too in various details the nobility of his spirit : of Capece, who refused to surrender to the Spanish soldiers, he writes " exposing his breast to death, and demanding death with his warlike arms, he fell unrepentant, a most valiant manner of death, were it only honoured in its cause " (*ostentans pectus neci eamque infensis armis efflagitans, inexoratus occubuit, fortissimum mortis genus si causa cohonestasset*). Of Sangro too, having reported the rumour that Louis XIV. sent him a reprieve which arrived too late, he adds : " whence the condemned man, who had already suffered the penalty, is the more to be pitied " (*unde maior damnati qui iam poenas persolverat, miseratio*).[3]

He must have known, and doubtless did know, that most of the persons whose praises he composed were of very little worth. To read his panegyrics, one would suppose that Naples was adorned with a nobility resplendent in its virtue, cultivation and learning : and yet, in giving Father De Vitry the information he desired upon the condition of studies in

---

[1] Letter of December 4, 1729 : in *Opp.* vi. p. 32.
[2] *Autob.* in *Opp.* iv. p. 366.   [3] *Opp.* i. pp. 367, 368.

Naples, Vico did not conceal the facts : " the nobles slumber amid the enjoyments of a life of pleasure." [1] His pupil Antonio Genovesi has preserved to us one of his satirical expressions upon this nobility, often in extreme poverty but always proud and ready to go hungry at home in order to drive abroad in coaches sumptuously dressed.[2] With reference to the literary duke of Laurenzano, he formulated the theory that " noble " writers could not fail of excellence : [3] and yet I have discovered among his papers the manuscript of a book by this duke, rewritten from end to end by the same Vico.[4] Such are the contradictions and the transactions into which a poor man falls when the pressure of want has made him timid and cautious ; so that it is not easy to determine how far his admiration was merely assumed at command or by complaisance, or how far his feeling of social inferiority developed into a real admiration for those above him in the scale, who possessed riches and dignity and everything he lacked and were the " seigneurs."

III

For, as is well known, his financial state was always of the gloomiest. The son of a small Neapolitan bookseller, he was at first compelled to go as a private tutor to a wild town of the Cilento ; later, returning to Naples, he tried in vain to obtain the position of secretary of the city, and having in 1699 been elected to the chair of rhetoric, he held that position for thirty-six years at an annual stipend of a hundred ducats (£17). His attempt to pass to a chair of greater importance in 1723 failed, whether owing to ill-luck or to inability—he recognised that he was a " man of little spirit in matters of utility," [5]—he was compelled to give up hopes of academic advancement. He was therefore obliged to eke out his resources by literary work such as we have mentioned, and still more by private lessons ; he not only kept school at his own house as well as at the university, but he went up and down other men's steps to teach grammar to youths or even to children. His family life was not a happy one. His wife was illiterate, and had not the qualities with which her sex

---

[1] *Opp.* vi. p. 9.
[2] He said that many of them " dragged their carriages with their own guts " (*Suppl. alla Bibl. vich.* p. 10).
[3] *Opp.* vi. p. 95.   [4] *Bibl. vich.* pp. 27-8.
[5] *Autob.* in *Opp.* iv. p. 349.

sometimes compensates the defect ; she was incapable of any
domestic employment whatever, so that her husband had to
take her place. Of his children, one girl died after a long
illness and the heavy expenses which embitter the diseases
of the poor ; one boy showed such strong vicious tendencies
that the father was compelled to seek the intervention of the
police and place him in a house of correction. So sublimely
irrational was his fatherly affection that upon this occasion
when he saw from the window the police officers he had called
in, coming to take his miserable and beloved son away, he ran
to him crying, " my son, flee ! " [1]

He was indeed of an extremely affectionate disposition ;
a fact which may be gathered for instance from the noble and
touching speech he composed on the death of his friend Donna
Angela Cimini, from the tone of pity and indignation with
which in the *Scienza Nuova* he spoke of the oppressed plebeians
whose history he is investigating or of the tragic figures of
Priam and Polyxena, the romance of which he feels keenly ;
and finally, from certain stylistic details scattered here and
there, such as the aphorism (no. xl.) where he says that witches
in order to solemnise their rites " slay without pity and cut
in pieces most lovely and innocent children," quite upset, in
the most inopportune but significant fashion, by the fate
of these little persons, whom his excited imagination adorns
with a superlative loveliness. His greatest domestic happiness
came from his daughter Luisa, a cultured and poetical soul,
and his son Gennaro, who shared with him and ultimately
succeeded to his chair. When, in his panegyric on the Countess
of Althann, he calls ironically upon the philosophers who
dispute as they walk in pleasant gardens or beneath painted
porticoes, free from the agony and weariness of " wives in
travail " and " children wasting away with disease," [2] we
feel that he is speaking from his own experience and smarting
under the memory of domestic troubles.

We often meet, especially in these days, with men of some
talent who consider themselves freed from this or that humble
duty : and we ought the more to admire this man of genius
who on the contrary accepted them every one, and (to use a
phrase of Flaubert's) while thinking the thought of a demigod
lived the life of a townsman or even that of a man of the people.
He had acquired the habit of reading, writing, thinking and

[1] Villarosa in the additions to the *Autobiography* (*Opp.* iv. p. 420).
[2] *Opp.* vi. p. 235.

composing his works " while discussing matters with his friends amid the uproar of his children." [1]

His health was never very good : his friends called him " Mastro Tisicuzzo " : [2] very weak in youth, he was in his old age afflicted with ulcers in the throat and pains in his thighs and legs. In a word, the repose, the peace, the tranquillity which other philosophers enjoy all their life or for long periods together was always lacking to Vico. He was forced to play both Martha and Mary : working at every moment for his own and his family's practical needs and working at the same time to fulfil the mission to which he was devoted from his birth and to give concrete form to the spiritual world that moved within him.

IV

Thus we need not invent or demand a heroic Vico, looking for him in the life of religion, society or politics. The true hero is the Vico who stands before us, the hero of the philosophic life. Others beside ourselves have noticed his love for the word " hero " and all its derivatives, " heroism," " heroic," and so on : and the continual use and varied application he makes of it. Heroism was for him the mighty virgin force which appears in the beginning and reappears in the reflux of history. This force he must surely have felt in himself as he laboured for the truth and, overthrowing obstacles of every kind, opened up new paths of science. It was this force that enabled him to overcome the youthful uncertainties, fears and defeats which sometimes plunged him in a profound individual and cosmic pessimism, visible in the poem entitled " Feelings of One in Despair," to rise to the certainty of scientific method enunciated in the *De nostri temporis studiorum ratione* and his first attempt at philosophico-historical research represented by the *De antiquissima Italorum sapientia* ; and from this point, abandoning in part his own thought and weaving a new tissue of what remained, led him to the *De uno universi iuris principio et fine uno* and to the *Scienza Nuova* " after twenty-five years," as he says of the discoveries contained in that work, " of unremitting and toilsome thought."

The work completed by this poor teacher of grammar and rhetoric, by this pedagogue whom a contemporary satirist

---

[1] *Autob.* in *Opp.* iv. p. 366.
[2] " Mr. Skin-and-bones " : cf. *Bibl. vich.* p. 87.

saw " lean, with a rolling eye, ferule in hand," [1] by this un-happy *paterfamilias*, is amazing and almost terrifying ; such is the mass of mental power compressed into it. It is a work at once reactionary and revolutionary : reactionary in relation to the present, by its attachment to the traditions of the ancient world and the Renaissance ; revolutionary as against the present and the past in laying the foundations of that future later to be known as the Nineteenth century.

Within the domain of science, this humble man of the people became an aristocrat : and the " lordly style " [2] which he falsely ascribed to the wretched writings of the proud nobles and pompous prelates of his day was in reality his own. He loathed the polite and social literature which was gradually spreading in France and Italy and other European countries, the " ladies' books." [3] But he avoided no less that other class of treatise which we nowadays call " handbooks," which explain in detail elementary definitions and facts ascertained by others ; books useless except to the young.[4] Vico, who suffered quite enough from the young within the circle of his school, saw no need to sacrifice to them any part of his own inviolable life of science. The public towards which he looked was not composed of boys, lords and ladies. When he wrote, his first practical thought was, " what would a Plato, a Varro or a Quintus Mucius Scaevola think of the fruits of his thought ? " and secondly, " what will posterity think ? " [5] Among his contemporaries he looked only at the republic of letters, the brotherhood of scholars, the Academies of Europe : a public which did not require him to repeat what had been already discovered and stated in the course of the history of science, and was perfectly familiar to him, but only demanded the exposition of such thoughts as constituted a real advance of knowledge : not voluminous works, but " little books, all full of original things." [6] His public was an ideal one, which sometimes in his simplicity he confused with the actual professional scholars and the critics of literary reviews : and the mistake often caused him surprise. Short books on metaphysical subjects seemed to him to have a peculiar power, as in fact they have ; he compares them very justly with religious meditations " which briefly set forth a small number of points " and are more valuable for the development of the

[1] *Bibl. vich.* p. 82.   [2] *Opp.* vi. p. 93.
[3] *Ibid.* vi. p. 5.   [4] *Ibid.* ii. p. 123.
[5] *Ibid.* v. p. 50 (note).   [6] *Ibid.* ii. p. 148.

Christian spirit than " the most eloquent and lucid sermons of the most gifted preachers." [1]   This love of brevity inspires his refusal to burden with many books the republic of letters, which, he says, is already sinking beneath the weight.   He left his discourses unpublished, only printed his *De ratione* out of a sense of duty, and often expressed a desire that the *Scienza Nuova* alone should survive him, as the work which summed up in itself the concentrated and perfected fruits of all his earlier efforts.

His aristocratic ideal was accompanied by the loftiest dignity and the profoundest loyalty in his conception of the life of science.   From his polemics we might compile a whole catechism on the right method of conducting literary controversy.   We must aim at victory, he says, not in the controversy but in the truth ; hence he desires that it should be conducted " in the calmest manner of reasoning," because " he who is strong does not threaten, and he who is right does not use insults " ; the dispute must at any rate be interspersed with peaceful words " showing that the minds of the disputants are placid and tranquil, not excited and perturbed." To opponents whose objections are vague he replies, " the judgment is in too general terms : and serious men never deign to reply except to particular and determinate criticisms made upon them."   When these same opponents appeal to the " refined taste of the age, which has banished," etc., etc., he replies contemptuously, " a grave criticism this, in truth : it is no criticism at all.   In thus taking refuge from one's opponents before the tribunal of one's own judgment, by saying that what they say is a thing of which one has no idea, from an opponent one becomes the judge."   He refused to rely upon his authorities, but yet did not undervalue them ; authority ought to " make us attentive to seek the causes which could have induced authors, especially the most weighty, to adopt such and such opinions."   Again, accused of attributing errors to philosophers so as to be able to refute them with ease, like Aristotle, he protests with dignity : " I would rather enjoy my own small and simple stock of knowledge than be compared in bad faith with a great philosopher."   His moderation may be illustrated by his splendid eulogy of Descartes, though he spent the best part of his mental powers in opposing him.   His loyalty is shown by his prompt recogni-

[1] For instance in his letter to Saliani, November 18, 1725, published in *Bibl. vich.* pp. 97-8, the autograph being in my possession.

tion of his own errors : " I admit," he says at one point to the critics of the *Giornale dei letterati*, " that my distinction is faulty." [1] " The reader must not think it ostentatious in us " (he writes in the second *Scienza Nuova*), " that not satisfied with the favourable judgments of such men as these upon our works, we yet disapprove and reject these works. On the contrary, it is a proof of the high veneration and respect in which we hold these men. For rude and haughty writers uphold their works even against the just accusations and reasonable corrections of others : some, who by chance are of a small spirit, sate themselves with the favourable judgments they receive and because of these go no further towards perfection : but in our case the praise of great minds has increased our courage to amend, to complete, and even to recast in a better form this work of ours." [2]

His scientific life was upright, worthy of a serious searcher after truth ; his emotional life disturbed and restless, worthy of one who sees face to face the truth he has long sought and desired, and rejoices in the power of laying it before mankind. Hence his lofty poetry, expressed not in verse but in prose, and especially in the *Scienza Nuova*. " Vico is a poet," writes Tommaseo : " he brings fire from smoke, and lively images from metaphysical abstractions : he reasons as he narrates and depicts while he reasons : over the mountain-tops of thought he does not walk, he flies ; and in one sentence he often compresses more lyrical feeling than may be found in many an ode." [3] De Sanctis saw in the *Scienza Nuova* the progress of a poem, almost a new *Divina commedia*. Sublime like Dante, he was more severe than Dante himself ; if the lips of the Ghibelline show at times the flicker of " a passing smile," Vico looks at history with a face " that never smiles." Moreover, the man whose style has been so often criticised is not a commonplace writer ; he was as careful a student of pure Tuscan [4] as he was a fine connoisseur, according to Capasso, of Latin phraseology. [5] But he was faulty in the arrangement of his books, because his mind did not master all the philosophical and historical material it had accumu-

[1] See the *Riposte* in *Opp.* ii. *passim.*

[2] *Opp.* v. p. 10.

[3] *G. B. Vico e il suo secolo* in the volume *La Storia civile nella letteratura* (Turin, Loescher, 1872), p. 104 : cf. a judgment on Vico as a writer, *ibid.* pp. 9-10.

[4] *Opp.* iv. pp. 333-4 ; vi. pp. 41, 140.

[5] *Bibl. vich.* p. 87.

lated ; he wrote carelessly because wildly and as if possessed by a demon : and hence arise the lack of proportion and the confusion in the various parts of his work, within single pages and single paragraphs. He often gives the impression of a bottle of water quickly inverted, in which the liquid trying to issue forth so presses against the narrow opening " that it comes out painfully, drop by drop." Painfully, by fragments, and disjointedly. One idea while he is expressing it recalls another, that a fact, and that another fact : he tries to say everything at once, and parenthesis branches off into parenthesis in a manner to make one's brain reel. But these chaotic periods, weighted as they are with original thoughts, are no less woven of striking phrases, statuesque words, phrases full of emotion, and picturesque images. A bad writer, if you will, but his is the kind of bad writing of which only great writers possess the secret.

V

The philosophical heroism of Vico asserts itself not only in the internal struggle with himself for the elaboration of his science. It was exposed to other and sterner trials. The position reached by his thought, opposed as it was to the present, and while apparently reactionary turned in reality towards the future, inevitably prevented him from being understood. No doubt this is the fate of every man of genius : his inmost thought is never understood, even when social fortune seems to favour him, even when he arouses enthusiasm and finds a host of disciples and imitators. The words which Hegel is said to have uttered on his deathbed—" one only of my pupils understood me, and he misunderstood me "— admirably express this historical necessity : the man whom his age fully understands dies with his age. And yet the disproportion between the value of a man's thought and his contemporaries' failure to understand it has seldom if ever been greater than in Vico's case. If he had been free from other causes of discontent, this alone would have been sufficient. The " desire for praise," which in other than commonplace minds is a desire to see what they think true and good shared, approved and universalised among other minds, was always with him a " vain desire."

He was the more afflicted by this misunderstanding and indifference because, as we may well suppose, he was fully conscious of the importance of his own discoveries. He knew that Providence had entrusted to him a lofty mission : he knew himself to be " born for the glory of his country, and therefore in Italy ; since, being born there and not in Morocco, he became a scholar." [1] When he published the *Scienza Nuova*, he believed that he had fired a mine whose loud explosion he expected every minute. Nothing happened : nobody mentioned it to him : so that he wrote some days later, to a friend : " In publishing my work in this city I seem to have launched it upon a desert. I avoid all public places, so as not to meet the persons to whom I have sent it, and if by chance I do meet them, I greet them without stopping ; for when this happens, these people give me not the faintest sign that they have received my book, and so confirm my impression of having published it in a wilderness." [2] He had frankly expected a swift and immediate effect : he had hoped to find, among his contemporaries and acquaintances at Naples, minds ready and intellects open to receive and bear fruit of his thoughts : and he hoped this of monks engaged in composing and learning by rote wordy sermons, poetasters rhyming in sonnets and advocates compiling second-hand speeches !

Instead of this, he found many sceptical and indifferent, and several inclined to laugh. His *Diritto universale* had been as Metastasio informs us [3] generally " blamed for obscurity " on its publication ; it was not widely read and was hastily criticised for the extravagances which an inattentive and superficial reading revealed at every point.[4] Father Paoli, to whom the author had given a copy, wrote in it a couplet making a joke of its unintelligibility.[5] The *Scienza Nuova* was in an even worse case. We know that Nicola Capasso, a scholar and well disposed towards Vico, on trying to read it fancied he had lost his wits, and by way of a joke hurried off to his doctor Cirillo, to have his pulse felt.[6] A Neapolitan nobleman when asked by Finetti at Venice what opinion was held of Vico at Naples, said that for a time he had passed for a really learned man, but that later his strange opinions had won him the reputation of an eccentric. " And when he published the *Scienza Nuova* ? " insisted Finetti. " Oh, by

---

[1] *Autob.* in *Opp.* iv. p. 385.
[2] Letter to Giacchi, November 25, 1725, in *Opp.* vi. p. 28.
[3] *Bibl. vich.* p. 40.   [4] *Opp.* vi. p. 20.
[5] *Bibl. vich.* p. 26.   [6] *Ibid.* p. 87.

then," replied the other, "he was quite mad!"[1] His detractors even attacked him in the modest profession by which he earned his living ; they said he was " good at teaching youths who had completed their course, that is to say when they already knew all they needed," or again, more insidiously, that he was fitted less for teaching than for " giving good advice to the teachers themselves ; "[2] so that they recognised his superiority only to use it in damaging his private interests.

VI

The indifference of the public and the insincerity or malignity of critics could not for Vico be compensated by the friends and appreciative readers of whom Vico had a certain number. How indeed could it have been otherwise, when he cultivated them artificially with such care and anxiety ? Consider for instance the way in which he cultivated the friendship of Giacchi the Capucin. He praised his " admirable works," his " most divine talents," the " rare sublimity " of his " marvellous and divine ideas." He tells him that he has given to the scholars of the city the eulogistic letter sent to him by Giacchi and that they all admire " the sublime workmanship of the conception " ; and yet he himself used to rewrite in scholar's Latin the inscriptions Giacchi composed in monk's Latin ![3] On another occasion he wrote that the praises of a Giacchi had excited envy and had in certain quarters been described as flatteries. He took no less pains to propitiate the Archbishop of Bari, Muzio di Gaeta, a conceited creature full of his own merits and incapable of speaking except about himself. Muzio wrote a panegyric on Pope Benedict XIII., a work of which, though Vico praised it again and again, he had never heard enough, and was always covertly or openly demanding new praises. So Vico used to besprinkle him patiently with the desired fluid : " the marvellous work of Your Excellency " ; his " lordly diction " ; his " Demosthenic digressions " ; his eloquence, that philosophic speech employed in Greece by the Academic school, in Rome by Cicero, and " among the Italians by none but Your Excellency ! " To the advocate Francesco Solla, who had been his pupil and had

---

[1] *Bibl. vich.* p. 86 : cf. *Autob.* in *Opp.* iv. p. 416.

[2] *Autob.* in *Opp.* iv. p. 416.

[3] Published by me in *Napoli nobilis*, xiii. (1904), f. i., and again in *Secondo suppl. alla Bibl. vich.* pp. 70-2.

subsequently retired into the country, he hinted that the *Scienza Nuova* looked towards him as one of the few men in the world possessed of a mind penetrating enough to receive it unhampered by any prejudices concerning the origin of mankind.[1] Such were the guileless artifices and the pitiful little schemes by which he contrived to give an illusory satisfaction to his thirst for recognition and praise, and a narcotic to his overwrought nerves. But the final results were miserable enough. Giacchi's letters contain not a word to show that he had ever grasped one of Vico's doctrines or even that he had examined them with any serious interest. Monsignor di Gaeta, after a labyrinth of circumlocutions, admits that he " admired more than he understood " of Vico's works ;[2] and possibly he was so much occupied in admiring his own prose that he never read them at all. Solla, in whom Vico placed such hopes, thought the discourse on the death of Angela Cimini superior to all the author's other works, including the *Scienza Nuova* itself. Vico received a no less incautious compliment from another admirer ; though a warm and affectionate one,—Esteban.[3] Compliments of a vague and unintelligent kind sometimes reached him in return for the copies of his works which he sent not only to Neapolitan scholars but to those of Rome, Pisa, Padua and even Germany, Holland and England : he sent a copy to Isaac Newton.[4] Generally, however, these gifts were received in contemptuous silence. At most, Vico acquired the reputation of a scholar among hundreds of scholars, a man of letters among thousands of similar men ; a learned man, but nothing more.

Among the modest, the insignificant, and the young, Vico no doubt had strong admirers. Among these were the poet, later a sacred orator, Gherardo de Angelis, Solla and Esteban whom we have mentioned, the monk Nicola Concina of Padua, and some more. But though their affection was strong their intelligence was weak. Even Concina admitted while rhapsodising his enthusiasm that he did not very clearly comprehend his master : " Oh, what fruitful and sublime lights are here ! If only I had the talent to make use of them, to comprehend their depth and the wonderful art of which I seem to catch a glimpse ! "[5] The best service that these friends could do him was to soothe with kindly words Vico's embittered spirit,

[1] *Opp.* vi. p. 17.
[2] *Ibid.* p. 110.
[3] *Bibl. vich.* pp. 103-5.
[4] *Opusc.*, ed. Villarosa, ii. p. 277.
[5] *Opp.* vi. p. 145.

262 THE PHILOSOPHY OF GIAMBATTISTA VICO

if they could not do so by following his inmost thoughts. This is what Esteban does at the close of the letter in which he excuses himself for his foolish remark on the funeral speech of Angela Cimini in phrases he must have gathered from the master's lips : " Be confident, Sir, that Providence, through channels unimagined by yourself, will cause to spring up for you a perennial fountain of immortal glory ! " [1] The Jesuit Father Domenico Lodovico, who wrote the couplet inscribed beneath Vico's portrait, on receiving the *Scienza Nuova* sent to the author with much sound sense a little wine from the cellar and a little bread from the oven of the Jesuit house of the Nunziatella, together with a graceful letter begging the author to accept " these trifles, simple as they are, since the infant Jesus himself did not refuse the rude offerings of pastoral peasants." He suggested too that at the side of the alphabet in the symbolic frontispiece to the work a little dwarf should be added in the posture of one dumb with astonishment like Dante's mountaineer, and that beneath him should be written, " with a significant diaeresis," the name Lodo-vico ! [2] Among the young men of his school there were some who, nourished upon his doctrines, were ready to defend their master with their swords ; [3] but we all know the value of these youthful enthusiasms. If these scholars had really assimilated Vico's doctrines or any part of them, we should have found traces of it in the literature or culture of the next generation after Vico ; but such traces are entirely absent. Hardly a single one of his formulae, his historical statements, or conceptions even superficially understood is to be found in Conti at Venice, Concina at Padua, Ignazio Luzan in Spain—though the last named was living at Naples when the *Scienza Nuova* was published ; [4] or even, within the author's own neighbourhood, in Genovesi or Galiani.

Envy, insincerity, gossip, calumny and stupidity provoked violent outbursts of anger on Vico's part. He confesses this fault in his autobiography where he says that he inveighed in too severe a manner against the errors of conception or doctrine or the incivility of his literary rivals, when in Christian charity and as a true philosopher he ought to have ignored or pardoned them. [5] But as a matter of fact this fault did not

[1] *Bibl. vich.* p. 105.
[2] " I praise Vico." Letter published by me in *Bibl. vich.* p. 107.
[3] *Bibl. vich.* pp. 87-8.   [4] *Ibid.* p. 44.
[5] *Autob.* in *Opp.* iv. p. 416 : cf. the evidence of a pupil in *Bibl. vich.* p. 89.

greatly distress him : he thought it rather an ornament. The funeral speech for Angela Cimini contained a kind of hymn to anger, the " heroic wrath which in noble spirits disturbs and shakes to the depths by its boiling all those evil thoughts of the mind, which beget the vile swarm of fraud, deceit and falsehood, and renders the hero frank, truthful and loyal ; and thus making him a partisan of truth, arms him as the valiant knight of reason to do battle with wrong and offence." [1]

Although in his writings he guards " with all his power " against falling into this passion [2] we feel a scarcely repressed torrent of wrath in his private letters whenever he denounces the " miserable pedants " who " love learning more than truth," or the common tendency of man to be " all memory and imagination," and so forth. In conversation also, it seems, he could be very violent. When in 1736 Damiano Romano published a work controverting his theory of the Twelve Tables, Vico, although according to Romano himself he had been spoken of as " most learned " and " most famous," together with other titles of respect, " tore the book to pieces with his teeth in a way that made every one present tremble with horror," finding a sign of the deepest malignity in the fact that " a lad like myself should join issue with him." [3] But his outbursts of wrath were succeeded by fits of the deepest dejection. In a sonnet he speaks of himself as overwhelmed by that fate " which the unjust hate of others often creates," and says that for this reason he has separated himself from human society to live with himself alone. Sometimes he shakes off this torpor for a moment : then, he says :

> I draw within myself again, and pressed
> By heavy cares, return to where I stood : [4]
> My fate and not my fault I do lament.

VII

But among all these troubles, obstacles and disappointments, in the midst of this sadness which often draped his life in black, Vico enjoyed one of the loftiest joys accessible to man ; the " life of meditation " freed and purified from

[1] *Opp.* vi. p. 254.   [2] *Autob.* in *Opp.* iv. p. 416.
[3] *Bibl. vich.* p. 88.
[4] Sonnet published by G. Gentile, *Il Figlio di G. B. Vico* (Naples, Pierro, 1905), p. 173.

passion, lived by man in solitude without the turbulent and
grievous company of the body " : the life of security, because
it is " made one with the soul always ready and present which
shows man his being rooted in the Eternal that measures all
times and walking in the Infinite that comprehends all finite
things ; it crowns him with an eternal and immeasurable joy
not restricted invidiously to certain places nor grudgingly to
certain times ; but it can grow up within himself only if
without envy of rivalry or fear of diminution it spreads and
communicates itself unceasingly to more and more human
minds." [1] That he has attained truth he never doubts,
though he never ceases to elaborate it further ; with the
system presented in the work on *Universal Law*, his mind, he
says, " rested content." [2] The weariness and even the pain
he had suffered were dear to him, because through them he
arrived at his discoveries : " I bless the twenty-five full years
I have spent in meditation upon this subject, in the midst
of the adversities of fortune and the checks I have often
received from the unhappy example of great thinkers who
have attempted new and weighty discoveries." [3] How could
he have done anything but bless these fatigues, pains and
adversities, if, whenever he rose above the passionate per-
turbations of the empirical man and the struggles of the
practical man, his mind showed him the inevitable necessity
of his toil and of his sufferings, two necessities fused into one
another so as to become one and indivisible ?

His own philosophical doctrine then brought him the
remedy for his ills, and worked in his spirit the *catharsis* of
liberation ; the doctrine of the immanent Providence, or as
it was later called, historical necessity, which was his central
thought. " Praise be to Providence for ever, which, when the
weak sight of mortals sees in it nothing but stern justice,
then most of all is at work on a crowning mercy ! For by this
task I see that I am clothed upon with a new man ; I feel
that everything that goaded me to bewail my hard lot and to
denounce the corruption of literature that has caused that
lot, has vanished ; for this corruption and this lot have
strengthened me and enabled me to perfect my task. And
more, it may perhaps not be true, but it would please me,
were it true, that this labour has filled me with a certain
spirit of heroism, through which no fear of death any longer

[1] *Opp.* vi. p. 287.   [2] *Ibid.* p. 18.
[3] *Ibid.* pp. 153-4.

disturbs me and my mind feels no disquietude at the words of my rivals. Lastly, it has established me as upon a mighty rock of adamant before the judgment of God, who rewards the work of creation by the approval of the wise, who are always and everywhere few in numbers . . . men of the loftiest intellect, of a learning all their own, generous and great-hearted, whose only labour is to enrich with deathless works the commonwealth of letters." [1] Thus Providence showed him the necessity of all that had befallen or should befall him in his life, taught him resignation and promised him glory.

VIII

So the hot-tempered man became at last tolerant : tolerant with that tolerance, that lofty indulgence which must not be confused with common toleration. The University, in which he had hoped for advancement and towards which he directed the thought of his earlier works, would have none of him ; he retired within himself to think out the *Scienza Nuova.* Now, says he with a smile in which we may still see a trace of bitterness, I owe this work to the University, which, by judging me unworthy of the chair and not wishing me to be " occupied in treating paragraphs," gave me leisure for meditation : " what greater obligation could I have ? " [2] A friend, Sostegni the Florentine, in a sonnet to Vico, let slip some words in condemnation of the city of Naples for making so little of her distinguished son. Vico in his reply justifies his native place in noble words, as being stern towards him because she expected and desired much of him :

> Stern mother, she caresses not her son,
> Lest so she fall into obscurity,
> But gravely listens, watching as he speaks. [3]

This was the spirit that found expression in the Auto-biography, a work which has been misjudged and in fact entirely misunderstood by Ferrari, who censures its prevailing teleological tendency and laments the absence of a " psychological " explanation of Vico's life ; [4] as if Vico had not himself explained that he was writing it from a " philosophical "

[1] *Opp.* vi. pp. 29-30.
[2] *Ibid.* p. 29.   [3] *Ibid.* p. 446.
[4] In the Introduction to vol. iv. of the *Opere.*

point of view.[1] And what is the meaning of a philosophical treatment of a philosopher's life but an understanding of the objective necessity of his thought and a perception of the scaffolding it involves even where the author at the moment of thinking did not clearly perceive it ? Vico " meditates upon the causes, natural and moral, and upon the occasions of his fortunes ; he meditates upon the inclinations or aversions he felt from childhood towards this or that branch of study ; he meditates upon the opportunities or hindrances which assisted or retarded his progress ; he meditates, lastly, upon certain efforts of his own in right directions which bore fruit in the reflections upon which he built his final work, the *Scienza Nuova,* which work was to demonstrate that his literary life was bound to have been what it was and not different." [2] Vico's *Autobiography* is, in a word, the application of the *Scienza Nuova* to the life of its author, the course of his own individual history : and its method is as just and true as it is original. Vico succeeded in part only of his attempt, and could not form a criticism and history of himself to the same extent to which a modern critic and historian is in a position to do—whose efforts will again be improved upon by those of the future—is too obvious to need emphasising. The *Autobiography* itself concludes with a blessing upon the author's hardships, a profession of faith in Providence and a sure expectation of fame and glory.

IX

In the last years of his life Vico, enfeebled by age, domestic trouble and illness, " entirely gave up his studies " : [3]

> My pen is slipping from my palsied grasp ;
> The door of my thought's treasury is closed,[4]

he cries in two mournful lines of a sonnet in 1735. He prepared at this time additions and corrections for a possible reprint of the second *Scienza Nuova,* and incorporated them in the final manuscript of the work ; he thought for a time of printing his small work " on the Equilibrium of the Living Body " (*De aequilibrio corporis animantis*) composed many years earlier and now lost ; [5] he still discharged some of the duties

[1] *Autob.* in *Opp.* iv. p. 402.   [2] *Ibid.*   [3] *Ibid.* p. 415.
[4] *Opp.* vi. p. 425 (Sonnet on the marriage of Raimondo di Sangro, 1735).   [5] *Bibl. vich.* pp. 38-9.

of his office, such as the speech on the marriage of the king, Charles Bourbon, in 1738. But from 1736 or 1737 his son began to assist him in his professional work, and in January 1741 he was definitely appointed to the chair on his father's resignation.[1] Vico henceforth lived among his family like an old soldier *exacta militia*, thinking over his past battles and conscious of having done his life's work. His good son read to him for some hours every day out of the Latin classics he had once loved and studied so well. And in this evening of his life he was at least spared the crowning agony suffered in his last years by a philosopher more fortunate than himself, Immanuel Kant ; the agony of continuing and completing his system of philosophy, and wearing himself out in a fruitless struggle with thoughts that eluded his grasp and words that no longer obeyed him. Vico had said all he had to say ; a great historian of his own life, he knew the moment at which Providence had finished its work in him, closed the door of thought it had so freely opened, and ordered him to lay down his pen.[2]

[1] Gentile, *Il Figlio di G. B. Vico*, pp. 30-48.
[2] The documents and the scattered notes used in this lecture and quoted from the contents of my *Bibliografia vichiana* are now all collected in my edition of the *Autobiografia, carteggio e poesie varie* : cf. the present vol. *infra*, p. 308.

APPENDIX II

THE LATER HISTORY OF VICO'S THOUGHT [1]

THE history of the vicissitudes of Vico's reputation must not be allowed to replace or be confused with the exposition and valuation of his thought, by losing sight of the history of philosophy properly so called or confusing it with the history of culture.[2] But even when we pass to this second history, we must guard against another kind of error, namely the pretence of determining by its means whether Vico's work was or was not of use in the advancement of culture, and what degree of utility we should grant it. The inquiry is meaningless, and the degree cannot be measured : for rightly considered one disciple may be worth tens or hundreds, one effect produced after centuries may compensate its age-long delay, one point undeservedly forgotten may become as notable and instructive as the best-deserved reputation, and one single truth twice discovered independently may from this re-discovery and seeming superfluity receive a confirmation of its inevitable necessity. The work of Vico—such is the usual verdict—was 'entirely useless, because it appeared out of its due time and prematurely, and remained unknown or was known only because it could convey nothing new. Such language is a blasphemy against history, which allows nothing to be useless and is always and throughout the work of Providence, whose vast utilities must not be measured by the pettiness of the human span.

Was Vico appreciated in the course of the eighteenth

[1] This appendix briefly recapitulates the chief results of my researches into the subject set forth in the *Bibliografia vichiana* and its two supplements (cf. the present volume, *infra*, p. 310), to which work I refer for fuller details and for the evidence for the facts here laid down.

[2] See above, pp. 236, 237.

century ? Did any one read him, understand him and follow
his lead ? The question has been answered with equal
decision in the affirmative and the negative. The affirmative
answer has been supported by a diligent collection of scattered
passages up and down the writers of the century mentioning
his name and doctrines and an accumulation of possible or
apparent traces of his thoughts visible though unacknow-
ledged in Italian and foreign literature. But a thinker like
Vico can only be said to be known when his fundamental
thought has been grasped and the spirit that animated him
has been felt. Now the majority of the facts alleged as proof
of the efficacy of his work concerns particular doctrines
detached from the whole and accepted or contested just like
those of any other scholar and critic or any paradox-monger
of his time. This is true in the first place of his theory on the
origin of the Twelve Tables, discussed in the controversy
between Bernardo Tanucci and Guido Grandi from 1728 to
1731, contested in 1736 by Damiano Romano, accepted in
France by Bonamy in 1735 and recalled in 1750 by Terrasson ;
of the views on the history and primitive government of
Rome, mentioned by Chastellux, adopted and expanded by
Duni, and used by Du Bignon who learnt them from Duni ;
of the hypotheses as to the prehistoric period and the origins
of humanity, employed and modified by Boulanger in France
and Mario Pagano in Italy ; and lastly, of some conceptions
upon poetry and language which reappear in Pagano,
Cesarotti and some others.

A more essential question was that of the method of
studying and judging political institutions and laws ; a question
upon which Montesquieu has been compared with Vico and
accused of freely using the *Scienza Nuova* without acknowledg-
ing his debt. It is now established through Montesquieu's
journal that in 1728 Antonio Conti at Venice advised the future
author of the *Esprit des Lois* to buy Vico's book at Naples ;
and Montesquieu must have followed this advice on reaching
Naples in the following year ; for a copy of the 1725 edition
of the *Scienza Nuova* is still preserved in the library at the
château of La Brède. But the mind of the French writer
was too different from and inferior to that of Vico to draw
vital nourishment from a work such as the *Scienza Nuova* ;
and the traces of imitation alleged to have been discovered in
the *Esprit des Lois* are very doubtful and in any case of minor
importance. It must be said on the other hand that the

merit generally attributed to Montesquieu of having introduced the historical element into positive laws and thus
considering legislation in a truly philosophical manner (as
Hegel said later), that is, as a moment depending upon a
totality relative to all the other determinations which go to
form the character of a people or a period ; this merit, in
order both of time and of excellence, belongs in reality to
Vico.

Like Montesquieu in the science of legislation, so Wolf in
the Homeric question has been suspected of tacitly deriving
help from Vico's speculations. But at the time when he
published the *Prolegomena ad Homerum* in 1795 Wolf did not
know the *Scienza Nuova* ; which he knew in name only in
1801 and in fact the year after, when Cesarotti presented him
with the book. We must observe that Vico's judgment as
to the barbaric nature of the Homeric epos and the absence in
it of esoteric wisdom had been published in 1765 by the
Gazette littéraire de l'Europe ; and further, that the *Scienza
Nuova* was known and used by the Danish philologist and
archaeologist Zoega, who quotes it in an essay on Homer
composed in 1788 though not published till long afterwards ;
and that Zoega corresponded with Heyne, who afterwards
accused Wolf of having derived from his own lectures the
theory set forth in the *Prolegomena*. Heyne had in fact
expressed the idea of a gradual genesis of the Homeric poems
in 1790. In a word we may say that Vico's views had to some
extent penetrated into the atmosphere of German philology :
in which case Wolf may have originally had a certain indirect
knowledge of them. Even apart from this indirect communication the fact remains, and is recognised by all students
of the question, that the Homeric theory conceived by Wolf
must really be called not Wolfian but Vician, since such it truly
is in its fundamental characteristics. Moreover, Wolf, as a
philologist far superior to Vico but much less great as a
thinker, was not in a position to understand the ideas which
had led his predecessor to the doctrine he held concerning
Homer : a fact which is clear from the somewhat superficial
article he wrote on the subject in 1807.

There was certainly at Naples during the eighteenth
century a vague consciousness in many minds of the greatness
of Vico's work ; but in what precisely this greatness consisted
nobody could determine, owing to the lack of adequate
experience and preparation. Outside Italy, especially in

Germany, where this preparation existed or at least was much greater, Vico's work remained generally unknown, partly through the discredit into which Italian books had fallen since the end of the seventeenth century, and partly through the difficulties which Vico's style presented to a foreign reader. When the *Scienza Nuova* did fall into the hands of men competent to understand it, a series of insignificant accidents interposed to prevent such an understanding. Hamann procured the *Scienza Nuova* from Florence in 1777, at which time he was engaged upon economics and physiocracy, fancying that it dealt with these subjects ; and the delusion was not dispelled when in glancing over it he found himself faced by a collection of philological studies and studies carried out with considerable carelessness. Goethe received it at Naples in 1787 from Filangieri, who warmly recommended it, took it back to Germany and lent it in 1792 to Jacobi ; but it was a happy coincidence rather than a true knowledge or a clear intuition that led him to couple Vico's name with that of Hamann. Herder, who may also have known Vico's work less through his correspondence with Hamann in 1777 than by his travels in Italy in 1789, speaks of it in 1797 in quite general terms, without noticing one of the many connexions between Vico and himself, especially as regards the theory of language and poetry.

The only men in the eighteenth century who really to some extent penetrated into the fundamental thought of Vico and proclaimed though unwillingly his genuine greatness were— and this is another proof of the solid mental fibre of Catholicism—his Catholic opponents, of whom there were plenty : Romano, Lami, Rogadei, and above all Finetti. They saw that in spite of his stubborn protestations of religious orthodoxy Vico held a conception of Providence very different from that of Christian theology ; and that though he continually used the name of God he never allowed him to operate effectively in history as a personal God ; that he made so sharp a distinction between sacred and profane history as to reach a purely natural and human theory of the origin of civilisation, by means of the state of nature, and of the origin of religion, by means of fear, shame and the imaginative universal ; while the traditional Catholic doctrine admitted a certain communication between sacred and profane history, and recognised in pagan religion and civilisation the leaven of some kind of vague recollection of the primitive revealed truth ;

that though protesting that he accepted and reinforced the authority of the Bible, he threatened and shook it on many points ; and that his criticism of profane historical tradition, conducted in a haughty spirit of rebellion against the past, might open the road to the most dangerous abuses, since it provoked the application of the same spirit and method to sacred history, which happened in the case of Boulanger.[1] In this accusation are faithfully indicated all the points destined later to enter into the nineteenth century's solemn eulogy of Vico. Thus churchmen began to be suspicious of him ; and this bore fruit later in the restoration period, in the anti-Vician polemic of Bishop Colangelo, and somewhat earlier in a verdict of the royal censor Lorenzo Giustiniani, who pronounced the *Scienza Nuova* " a work marking a most unfortunate crisis in European history."

This tendency was opposed by the enthusiastic young students of social and political matters at Naples at the end of the eighteenth century, preparing themselves for an active part in the imminent revolution. Among them Vico came to be considered as an anti-clerical and anti-Catholic, and the legend arose, mentioned elsewhere in this volume, that Vico purposely and deliberately made his work obscure in order to escape ecclesiastical censure. These young men applied themselves to the study and praise of the *Scienza Nuova* ; they proposed to reprint it, since it had become rare, together with the other works and unpublished manuscripts of the author ; they prepared expositions and criticisms of Vico's philosophical and historical system ; some like Pagano tried to work it up afresh by adding to it the ideas of French sensationalism, others like Filangieri did not let their admiration of it dispel their rosy dreams of reform. In 1797 the German Gerning on coming to Naples noted the zeal with which Vico was studied, and projected a translation or at least a summary of the *Scienza Nuova* in German. When the fall of the Neapolitan Republic in 1799 drove these young men, or rather those of them who escaped the massacres and the gallows of the Bourbon reaction, into exile in Northern Italy and especially in Lombardy, the cult of Vico was for the first time ardently propagated. Vincenzo Cuoco, Francesco Lomonaco, Francesco Salfi and other southern patriots passed the knowledge of the *Scienza Nuova* to Monti, who mentioned

[1] Labanca has devoted a highly instructive volume to the Catholic criticisms of Vico : see the present volume, *infra*, p. 309.

it in his inaugural lecture at Pavia in 1803, to Ugo Foscolo, who absorbed many of its ideas into his poem the *Sepolcri* and his critical essays : to Alessandro Manzoni, who was later to institute in his *Discorso sulla storia longobarda* a famous comparison between Vico and Muratori : and to others of less importance. Cuoco introduced Vico's work to Degérando, then at work on his *Histoire comparée des systèmes philosophiques* ; another exile, De Angelis, put the *Scienza Nuova* into the hands of Jules Michelet ; Salfi mentioned Vico in articles in the *Revue Encyclopédique* and in books and minor works in French. It was also through the suggestion of these Neapolitans that the *Scienza Nuova* was reprinted at Milan in 1801 ; and other editions and collections of Vico's smaller works were not long in appearing. Thus in the first decade of the nineteenth century Vico's reputation, which had till then been merely local to Naples, spread over the whole of Italy.

But, suitably to their personal disposition and to the spirit of the times, the first and chief debt which the patriotic students of Vico owed to his thought was political in character or rather belonging to political philosophy ; and consisted in a criticism of that Jacobinism and philo-Gallicism of which they had had such unhappy experience in the events of 1799.[1] Vico's thought led them to more concrete concepts ; and this is particularly visible in Vincenzo Cuoco's admirable *Saggio storico sulla rivoluzione napoletana* (1800). Similarly Ballanche some decades later in his *Essais de palingénésie sociale* (1827) wrote that if Vico had been known in France in the eighteenth century he would have exercised a beneficial influence on the subsequent social revolutions. Another particular aspect of Vico's work, the reform undertaken by him of historical methodology and social science as an aid to history, was observed and emphasised by the archaeologist Cataldo Iannelli in his work *Sulla natura e necessità della scienza delle cose e delle storie umane* (1818). Foscolo and those who drew their inspiration from him chiefly introduced into literary criticism and history something of Vico's conceptions on the historical interpretation of poetry.

In Germany on the other hand Jacobi, who had read the *De antiquissima*, immediately placed himself in the centre of the Vician philosophy by discovering and pointing out in 1811, in his work *Über den göttlichen Dingen und ihrer Offenbarung*, the close connexion between the principle of the con-

---

[1] See above, pp. 247-9.

vertibility of the true and the created and the Kantian theory that one can perfectly conceive and understand only what one is able to construct : a single step from which position leads, as he observes, to the system of identity. The same fact was recognised by Baader, who found in this system the confirmation and foundation of the principle enunciated by Vico. But the translation of the *Scienza Nuova* made by Weber in 1822 seems to have been unsuccessful ; and it does not appear that Vico was known to Hegel, with whom he has so many substantial and formal affinities, especially in the *Phenomenology* ; and whose mania for triads might be blamed just as the Catholic Finetti had blamed Vico for always standing " upon rule of three." The resemblances again of Vico's theories to the new German philological doctrines of Niebuhr, Müller, Böckh and many others were not at all willingly admitted. The attitude of Niebuhr is characteristic. Whether he knew Vico's work or not when he published the first edition of his *Römische Geschichte*, he certainly knew it later through Savigny and through the article entitled *Vico und Niebuhr* published in 1816 by the Swiss Orelli ; and yet he continued to ignore him, through some kind of contempt or depreciation ; an attitude hardly praiseworthy but imitated by Mommsen.

In France, the spread of knowledge concerning Vico's thought was due to Michelet, who translated his works and in his last years described Italy as " the second mother and nurse who in my youth suckled me upon Virgil, and in my maturity nourished me with Vico ; potent cordials that have many times renewed my heart." Michelet was the first or one of the first to proclaim, in his introduction, that Vico was not understood in the eighteenth century because he wrote for the nineteenth. Michelet was joined by Ballanche, of whom we spoke above, and also by Jouffroy, Lerminier, Chateaubriand, and Cousin, some of whom grasped the connexion between Vico and the German philosophy that Cousin was at this time propagating in France ; and later by Laurent, Vacherot, De Ferron, Franck, Cournot and many others. Vico was read and admired by Comte, who mentioned him in a letter to John Stuart Mill in 1844, and lastly Léon Gambetta conceived in his youth a general history of commerce upon the scheme of the Vician " reflux." The popularity of Vico's name in France at this period was so great that it is several times mentioned in joke in passages of Balzac's novels and in Flaubert's *Bouvard et Pécuchet*. But thought of the quality of Vico's could never have a very deep or lasting influence in the persistently intellectualistic and spiritualistic atmosphere of France. Perhaps the most conspicuous results it produced were the theories of Fustel de Coulanges on the ancient city and the origin of feudalism.

But, to return to Italy, if the aspirations towards a national uprising, which tended to vindicate and glorify all the ornaments Italy could boast, raised Vico's name almost to a level with that of Dante, the simultaneous renaissance of philosophy, which was shaking off the sensationalism and materialism of the eighteenth century, was bound to attach itself to the last great idealistic philosopher, to use his thoughts and to shelter itself behind his authority. Vico's complete works were now collected and editions of the single treatises multiplied. And since in the national uprising two currents could be distinguished, partly successive and partly fused, the neo-Guelphian and the radical, and since this distinction was represented in the philosophical awakening by that between Catholic idealism and rationalistic idealism, the schools of Rosmini and Gioberti on the one hand and Bruno and Hegel on the other ; Vico, at once a Catholic and a free philosopher, lent himself admirably, as is easy to understand, to the contrary sympathies and interpretations of the two schools. Thus originated two different pictures of him, both historically justified, though the one painted him as he would have wished to be, the other as he was. The Vico of the liberal Catholics was above all the Vico of the metaphysical points, the Platonist, the mystic of the unknowable God, the traditionalist of the prologues to the *Diritto universale*, and hence the strictly Italian philosopher as opposed to those of the rest of Europe, sons of the Reformation : whereas the Vico of the rationalists, the bold and heretical author of the *Scienza Nuova*, is a European philosopher to be set side by side with Descartes and Spinoza, Kant and Hegel. The former picture may be seen in the works of Rosmini, Gioberti, Tommaseo and many others, among which we must not forget those of a Neapolitan writer of lofty spirit, Enrico Cenni, perhaps the best of all, who draws a loving picture of the Vico of the Catholics. The latter portrait is found in the philosophers and critics who from 1840 onwards acquired their education in the school of German idealism ; especially Bertrando Spaventa and Francesco de Sanctis, who were the first to see clearly Vico's relations to earlier and later European thought and to substitute for mere observations and vague impressions on the subject a scientific interpretation and a determinate judgment. That the second school of interpreters and critics were in the right, and that the liberal or idealistic Catholics had taken up an untenable position and reproduced in their irresolution and incoherence the irresolution and incoherence of Vico himself, was proved by the fact, among others, that less liberal but more consistent Catholics like the Spaniard Jaime Balmes show an inflexible distrust and hostility towards the author of the *Scienza Nuova.*

The study of history in Italy during this period was less deeply modified by Vico's influence ; chiefly perhaps because the impulse of the national uprising led to the neglect of primitive and Roman history and the devotion of all its best energies to research into the origin and vicissitudes of the Italian republics, a subject Vico had entirely ignored. On the other hand, jurisprudence especially in the south was dominated by his thought ; and though it produced in this field no great scientific results, it gave to the jurists a loftiness and breadth of judgment and a concreteness of view which were long remembered and regretted.

After 1870, with the decay of philosophy in Italy and elsewhere, the study of Vico also decayed : and for more than forty years there was no demand for a reprint of his works. The monograph by Cantoni in the year 1867, in spite of some valuable passages, already shows unmistakable signs of the decadence, founded as it is upon the idea that Vico's value is greater according as he is less of a metaphysician and more of a psychologist and historian : a position due not so much to the intrinsic weakness ascribed to him by Cantoni in philosophical matters as to the implicit conviction on the critic's part that metaphysic in general is a valueless thing, useful only for rousing enthusiasm in the addled heads of southern Italians. The great idealist of the New Science was subjected, as a final insult, to the praises of the positivists, who in their astonishing ignorance almost amounting to innocence did not—and still do not—hesitate to allege as a confirmation of their formal profession of faith the words " verum ipsum factum," which according to them means that the truth is the fact which we see and touch. Writings making any serious contribution to the knowledge of any particular point on Vico's doctrines were rare. Interest in Vico only reawoke within the last decade with the general reawakening of philosophical studies.

Of the two best comprehensive works on Vico published towards the end of last century one is due to the German Catholic Karl Werner (1881) who expounds his philosophical and historical doctrines with great care, judging them from the point of view of speculative theism, a theory evolved under the influence of Baader and the second philosophy of Schelling, and tending much more to the comprehension of Vico than the psychology of Cantoni. The other is the work of an Englishman, Robert Flint (1884), who wrote for the collection of Philosophical Classics a brief monograph upon the subject, accurate in detail, and if not profound at least guided by clear and sound sense. Recently Sorel in France has shown the fruitfulness of certain views of Vico's, especially that of the reflux, by applying them to the history of primitive Christianity and the theory of the modern proletarian movement, while in Germany Biese and Mauthner have brought his conceptions of metaphor and language once more into favour.

But in spite of all this Vico has never had justice done him in works devoted to the history of modern philosophy. These, in the case both of Höffding's book and of the greatly superior work of Windelband, and in fact of all others, either pass over the Italian philosopher in complete silence or else merely mention him as an experimenter, later than Bossuet and earlier than Herder, in the dubious science of the " philosophy of history." This lack of attention arises partly from an insufficient knowledge of Vico's real nature ; his fertile activities in the theory of knowledge, in ethics, in aesthetic, in law and in religion are all hidden behind that one label " philosopher of history." Partly however it is due to the reaction of the history of politics and culture on the history of philosophy ; which produces the effect that thinkers whose social influence came to an end with the fall of the peoples or states to which they belonged, or who for some reason or other had no considerable influence on European civilisation, are sacrificed to others much less important from a philosophical point of view but more influential or better known as exponents of social life and representatives of cultural tendencies ; so that where it would be thought impossible to ignore, for example, Paley or d'Holbach or Mendelssohn, it seems natural to pass over Giambattista Vico, though in such company he is a giant among pigmies. The historical injustice of this course has been already shown theoretically by the distinction we have emphasised between the history of philosophy and the history of culture ; and in Vico's special case by our whole work, which clearly shows the lacuna left by the omission of Vico in the general history of European thought at the beginning of the eighteenth century.

APPENDIX III

THE SOURCES OF VICO'S THEORY OF KNOWLEDGE[1]

My statement, that the criterion of knowledge contained in Vico's formula of the conversion of the true with the created is an original and modern principle, has been contradicted by certain Catholic editors ; who state that this doctrine, however true, is not original to Vico, and is indeed far from modern, being a purely Scholastic doctrine. If I thought otherwise, this was only due to my insufficient knowledge of Scholasticism.

I might indeed ask at the outset how such complete ignorance of scholasticism were possible : an ignorance not of its manifold varieties and the tangled forest of its distinctions— that would be comprehensible : but of no less a matter than the fundamental criterion of its theory of knowledge, the starting-point of modern thought and as such, it would seem, inevitably familiar to every student of the elements of philosophy. But since it is always useful to suspect oneself of ignorance, or even to believe oneself more ignorant than one really is, I will make so far as concerns myself a voluntary display of humility. I find it less easy, I confess, to extend the accusation of ignorance to all who, like myself, have failed to run Vico's criterion to earth in the scholastic lumber-room : Jacobi for instance, who on reading it as expressed in the *De antiquissima*, sees in it the first manifestation of Kantianism and absolute idealism : [2] or the Catholic theologian Baader, who finds its later development in Schelling's philo-

---

[1] A lecture delivered before the *Accademia pontaniana* on March 10, 1912, and here reprinted from the *Atti* of that society, vol. xlii.
[2] *Von den göttlichen Dingen und ihrer Offenbarung* (1811), W.W. iii. 351-354.

sophy of identity : [1] or the learned and subtle Spanish Thomist, Jaime Balmes, who treats it as a unique idea and attacks it from the scholastic point of view : [2] or the equally learned Catholic Bertini, who accepts and develops Jacobi's observation : [3] or the eminent historian of philosophy Wilhelm Windelband, who, while unacquainted with Vico's doctrines, on coming across indications of a similar thought in Sanchez's *Quod nihil scitur* was greatly struck by it and endorsed its value by the assertion that it was to bear fruit at a later date and in the hands of a greater philosopher, Immanuel Kant : [4] or again the specialist in the history of scholasticism, Karl Werner, the author of a careful monograph on Vico,[5] who nowhere notices the alleged scholastic character of Vico's theory of knowledge. Scholasticism must indeed be a difficult and mysterious doctrine, if it is inaccessible to all these students, qualified and bound though they are to understand it.

But we cannot pause on the threshold to speculate : we must plunge straight into the argument. In what part of scholasticism can we find Vico's criterion converting knowledge with creation ?

The Thomistic saying, " truth and reality are convertible," *ens et verum convertuntur*, has been quoted : [6] but quotations of this kind are perhaps more calculated to confuse by words than to convince by facts. The same value attaches to the statement that Vico himself confessed the scholastic origin of his principle, since the very first chapter of the *De antiquissima* begins with the words " in Latin, the truth and the fact reciprocate, or, as the scholastic mob says, convert," " *Latinis verum et factum reciprocantur, seu, ut scholarum vulgus loquitur, convertuntur.*" Here it is perfectly clear to any one on a moment's thought that Vico, Latinist as he was, meant

[1] *Vorlesungen über religiöse Philosophie*, W.W. i. 195, and *Vorles. über spekul. Dogmatik, ib.* ix. 106 (passages quoted by K. Werner, G. B. Bico, p. 324).
[2] *La Filosofia fondamentale*, translated from the Spanish, Naples, 1851, bk. i. ch. 30-31.
[3] *Storia critica delle prove metafisiche di una realtà sovrasensibile* (*Atti dell' Accademia di Torino*, i. 1866), pp. 640-41.
[4] *Geschichte der neueren Philosophie* (1878), 5th edition, i. 23.
[5] *G.B. Vico als Philosoph und gelehrter Forscher* (Wien, 1881). It is well known that Werner has written upon St. Thomas, Duns Scotus, late Scholasticism, Suarez, Augustinianism, nominalism, etc.
[6] Th. Neal (A. Cecconi), *Vico e l'immanenza*, in the Roman *Cultura contemporanea*, iii. (1911) parts 7-8, pp. 1-24,

simply to substitute the Ciceronian " *reciprocari* " for the barbarous " *converti*."

St. Thomas explained the meaning of his formula quite clearly, especially in the Summa Theologica, Part I. question xvi. art. 3. Here he asks whether the truth and the reality are convertible, *utrum verum et ens convertantur*; to which he replies as follows : " that as the good is of the nature of the desirable, so the truth has the nature of knowledge. But in so far as a thing has existence in itself, thus far it is knowable. And for this reason it is said in *De anima*, Bk. III. text. 37 (431 b 21) that " the soul is in a sense all things " according to sense and intellect. And hence as the good is convertible with the existent, so is the true. But yet as the good adds to existence the nature of the desirable, so also the truth adds a reference to the intellect." (*Quod sicut bonum habet rationem appetibilis, ita verum habet ordinem cognitionis. Unumquodque autem in quantum habet de esse, in tantum est cognoscibile. Et propter hoc dicitur in 3 de Anima, text. 37, quod ' anima est quodammodo omnia ' secundum sensum et intellectum. Et ideo sicut bonum convertitur cum ente, ita et verum. Sed tamen sicut bonum addit rationem appetibilis supra ens, ita et verum comparationem ad intellectum.*) Nothing then can be known except what exists, and nothing can exist but what is good : existence, truth and goodness are all convertible. Thus, too, things are called good in so far as they correspond to the idea in their Creator's mind. " Each single thing partakes of the truth of its own nature in so far as it imitates the knowledge of God, like an artefact in so far as it agrees with the art " : " the knowledge of God is the cause of things " : " the knowledge of God is the measure of things." (*Unumquodque in tantum habet de veritate suae natura, in quantum imitatur Dei scientiam sicut artificiatum in quantum concordat arti* I. xiv. 12. *Scientia Dei est causa rerum* I. xiv. 12. *Scientia Dei est mensura rerum* I. xiv. 12.) But truth and goodness, the objects of intellect and will respectively, if on the one hand they are " convertible in reality," *convertentur secundum rem*, on the other they are " distinguishable in thought," *diversificantur secundum rationem* (I. lix. 2). What have these thoughts in common with Vico's idea that the condition of knowing a truth is to create it ? In fact, what is here stated is that the condition of making a thing is to know it, or as St. Thomas says in the same place (I. xiv. 8) in St. Augustine's words (*De Trinitate* xv. 13) "*Universas creaturas et spirituales et corporales non quia sunt ideo novit Deus, sed ideo sunt quia novit.*" (God does not know all His creatures corporeal and spiritual because they exist : but they exist because He knows them.)

Vico makes no kind of mention of the formula *ens et verum convertuntur*, though he knows and quotes—a fact which has escaped my critics—the analogous phrase " the true and the good are convertible," *verum et bonum convertuntur :* [1] a formula which he diverts to his own purposes, or rather unites it with his own. " In the first place," he writes, " I establish a truth which is convertible with the created, and in this sense I understand the good of the schools, convertible with existence : and hence I infer that the one and only truth is in God, since in Him is contained all Creation." [2] This union is reached quite openly by identifying *verum* with *factum*, then *factum* with *ens*, and finally the *verum-factum-ens* with the *bonum* : by substituting the doctrine of Vico for that of the schools. By such a method of interpretation one could reduce all doctrines to a single one, a *perennis philosophia*. I do not say that it would be a method entirely devoid of truth ; but it is certainly not a historical method.

That Vico's criterion is not only different from but inconsistent with Thomism was shown, as I have already said, by Balmes ; who pronounced it " specious but devoid of solid foundation." He uses St. Thomas's statements to controvert Vico's theological doctrine that God understands because He creates, opposing to it the Scholastic view that He creates because He understands. He denies that the Word was conceived by the mere knowledge of what is contained in the divine omnipotence, for it is conceived not simply by creatures but also and chiefly by the cognition of the divine essence (" for the Father by understanding himself and the Son and the Holy Ghost and all other things embraced by His knowledge conceives the Word, so that thus the whole Trinity is implied in the Word, and also every creature " : *Pater enim intellegendo se et Filium et Spiritum sanctum et omnia alia quae ejus scientia continentur concipit Verbum, ut sic tota Trinitas Verbo dicatur, et etiam omnis creatura*) ; he objects that, granting this criterion, God could never know himself, because He is not His own cause. He denies that

[1] Cf. *Summa Theol.* i. q. v. a. 1 : q. xxi. a. 1-2.
[2] *Prima risposta al Giornale dei letterati* (*Opere,* ed. Ferrari, ii. 117).

intelligence is only possible through causality, inasmuch as it is also possible through identity. He accuses Vico's criterion of involving scepticism : in a word he maintains that the facts of knowledge are known by reason, even if they are not the products of reason.[1] I am not concerned to ask whether Balmes is right, or whether Vico's criterion can be reconciled with Christian theology. I am concerned merely with establishing, not only by quotation from St. Thomas but also by the help of the judgment of an authoritative interpreter of his system that this doctrine is not Thomistic.

Even granting that the criterion in question is irreconcilable with Thomism but not with an improved Christian theology, it is certainly irreconcilable with both in the form it adopts in what I have called " Vico's second theory of knowledge," in the *Scienza Nuova*, which Balmes either did not know or omitted to mention, and is passed over by my critics with a light-heartedness that is not particularly enviable. One of them asserts that " the alleged distinction " (the distinction that is drawn by myself) " between Vico's first and second theories of knowledge does not in point of fact exist, and produces no effects of any kind." What ? Has it no effects, when those historical studies and sciences of mind, which in the *De antiquissima* occupied the lowest position among mere probabilities became in the *Scienza Nuova* the truest of all—true even in a higher degree than mathematics itself as dealing with the human world which " is man's creation ? " when their form is found " in the modifications of the actual human mind itself ? " when they have " a reality as much greater, as the reality of the laws of human affairs is greater than that of points, lines, areas and figures ? "[2] Is there no distinction, when we pass from the scepticism of the *De antiquissima* to the rationalism of the statement that these " proofs are of a divine nature," and must produce " a divine pleasure, since in God to know and to create are one and the same " ?[3]

It is true that upon this point my attention has been recalled to a well-known passage of Galileo (*Dialogo dei massimi sistemi*), an especial favourite of our own Spaventa,[4]

---

[1] Balmes, *loc. cit.*
[2] *Scienza Nuova*, ed. Nicolini, i. 187-8.
[3] *Ibid.* p. 188.
[4] *Scritti filosofici*, ed. Gentile, pp. 383-7, and *Esperienza e metafisica*, p. 218 *sqq.*

where we find the thought that the human intellect differs from the divine *extensivè* but not *intensivè*, and that if the divine intellect knows infinitely more about mathematical propositions because it knows them all, yet " of these few facts known by the human intellect, its knowledge is equal to that of the divine in objective certainty, since it attains comprehension of the necessity than which no greater certainty, it seems, can exist." But in any case Galileo was not a Schoolman, and moreover this pronouncement of his seemed so dangerous to the Christian theory of ideas, that he himself was obliged to alter it by admitting that while " so far as the truth of which mathematical proof gives no knowledge is concerned, this is identical with that which the divine wisdom knows," yet " the manner, in which God knows the infinitely numerous propositions of which we know a few, is immensely superior to our own, which proceeds discursively from one conclusion to another, while His is simple intuition." It is important too not to forget that this very statement figures among the heads of the accusation in Galileo's trial.[1]

If the formula of the conversion of the true with the created is not found in Thomism, it may perhaps be found, at least in its original, sceptical or mystical, intention, in other tendencies of scholasticism or mediaeval philosophy generally. With Thomism Vico seems to have had neither acquaintance nor sympathy : but from his autobiography it is plain that he studied nominalism and the summaries of Petrus Hispanus and Paulus Venetus, though with little profit,[2] and later also, much more profitably, the Scotist philosophy ; which he considered the most Platonic of the Scholastic systems.[3] Traces of this appear in several views expressed in the *De antiquissima*, especially in those dealing with universals and ideas. In this direction, the direction that is to say of the Scotist system and the closely allied system of Occamism, I have attempted various researches, without attaining any remarkable results : further, I have applied for assistance to various specialists in Scholasticism, but in vain ; they would

[1] See Gentile's note, *loc. cit.*

[2] *L'Autobiografia, il carteggio e le poesie varie,* ed. Croce, pp. 4-5. Mauthner's assertion (*Beiträge zu einer Kritik der Sprache,* Berlin, 1901, ii. 497-8) that Vico was a nominalist and that the great discoveries of the *Scienza Nuova* were due to his nominalism, is quite arbitrary and not founded correctly on his autobiography.

[3] *Autobiography,* ed. cit. pp. 5-6. Pietro Giannone was also studying Scotism about 1690 (*Vita scritta da lui medesimo,* ed. Nicolini, pp. 6-7).

do nothing but express their own superficial impressions or lose themselves in idle disputation. In general it seems possible to say that Duns Scotus's theory of knowledge presents points of affinity to that of Vico : for example, in the polemic against the Thomistic doctrine of the *adaequatio intellectus et rei*, which he refutes by applying it to the divine knowledge, since God knows objects as willed by Him, and they exist because He wills their existence without His being necessitated by them.[1] For Occam again the thought of objects has no reality and objectivity (or subjectivity according to the usage of Scholastic terminology, which is the reverse of modern) in God, and is nothing else than the objects themselves, known by God according to the possibility of creating them, in virtue of which they are thinkable to the divine mind.[2] But the question for Vico is not merely the priority of creation to knowledge or knowledge to creation, but the convertibility or identity of knowledge and creation.

In certain recently published philosophical observations by Paolo Sarpi,[3] a nominalist of Occam's school,[4] the following statements are to be found. They are the more notable because standing as they do without any results in Sarpi's thought and being undeveloped in subsequent philosophy, they seem to be not his own invention but a mere repetition of scholastic dicta. " We have certain knowledge both of the existence and of the cause of those things which we understand fully how to create : of those which we know by experience, we know the existence, but not the cause. We can however guess at it, and look simply for a possible cause : but out of many found to be possible we cannot be certain which is the true one. This fact may be seen in descriptions of astronomical theories, and would also be true in the case of a man who saw a clock for the first time. Of the various guesses, that of a man who knew how to make similar objects would be nearest the truth, *e.g.* one who understood the construction of machinery when he saw a different kind of machine : but none the less he will never on that account [5] know for certain. There are then three kinds of knowledge :

[1] Werner, *Johannes Duns Scotus* (Wien, 1881), p. 76.
[2] Werner, *Die nachscotistische Scholastik* (Wien, 1883), p. 82.
[3] *Scritti filosofici inediti*, ed. Papini (Lanciano, Carabba, 1910).
[4] See Gentile's observations on Papini's edition, in the *Critica*, review viii. 62-5.
[5] Papini's edition has " po' " (little) : but his source, the Marcian MS., has an abbreviation to be read as " però " (therefore).

first, knowledge how to make the object : secondly, experience of it : and thirdly, guessing at possibilities." This thought, then, namely that objects are known by their creator, and that God knows objects because He creates them, seems to have been current in the schools : and this explains the fact of its reappearing in an incidental manner and as an obvious truth in Francesco Sanchez's *Quod nihil scitur* (1581) where it is declared impossible "*perfecte cognoscere quis quae non creavit ; nec Deus creare potuisset nec creata regere quae non perfecte precognovisset*[1] (that one should know perfectly things which he has not created : nor could God have been able to create nor after creating them to control things which He had not perfectly foreknown).

But need we continue to look for it in the guise of a casual remark or an isolated proposition, devoid of philosophical connexion, in the works of philosophers or the lecture-rooms of the schools ? Did it not simply form a part of the common thought which daily declares that the man who has made a thing knows it better than he who has not made it ? Probably a little attention would reveal it in many and dissimilar treatises ; and for my own part, while reading the *Chronicon* of Otto of Freising the other day, I came across it in the introduction to the third book, where the chronicler, writing as is well known under the influence of St. Augustine's *Civitas Dei*, is arrested by the objection that God's designs in history are inscrutable, and delivers himself of the following reflections : " What then shall we do ? If we cannot understand, shall we hold our peace ? Then who will reply to those who flatter, repel those who attack, and by the reason and might of his words confute those who would destroy the faith that is in us ? So we cannot understand the secret counsels of God, and yet we are often compelled to give a reasonable account of these things. What ? Shall we reason about things which we do not understand ? We can give reasons, but human reasons, when yet we cannot understand the divine reasons. And thus it happens that when we speak of theological matters, lacking the right words for them, we being men use our own words ; and in speaking of so great a God in human language, we use our words the more boldly *quo ipsum figmentum nostrum cognoscere non dubitamus*, because we never doubt that we know the thing we have ourselves formed : *quis enim melius cognoscit quam qui creavit ?* for who knows

[1] Appendix to his *Opera medica* (Tolosae Tectasogum, 1636), p. 10.

a thing better than he who has created it ? " [1] The logic of the Abbot of Freising at this point may be thought a trifle sophistical : but the fact remains that he refers to a common opinion that he knows things who has made them.

But probably Vico was stimulated to the establishment of his criterion less by certain tendencies of Scotism or by current opinions than by the philosophers of the Renaissance, which he considered the golden age of metaphysical study, when shone, as he says, " Marsilio Ficino, Pico della Mirandola, Augustino Nifo and Augustino Steuco, Jacopo Mazzoni, Alessandro Piccolomini, Matteo Acquaviva and Francesco Patrizio." [2] In Ficino, whose name he couples with those of Plato and Plotinus,[3] and especially in his *Theologia Platonica*, Vico could read a magnificent description of the productive character of the divine wisdom and its parallelism with that of the geometrician. Nature, says Ficino, which is divine art, differs from human art in that it produces its creations from within, by living reasons : and " it does not touch the surface of matter by means of a hand or any other external instrument, as the soul of a geometer touches the dust when he describes figures upon the earth, but *perinde ut geometrica mens materiam intrinsecus phantasticam fabricat*, it operates like the mind of a geometer creating an imaginary matter from within itself. For as the geometer's mind, while it considers within itself the nature of figures, forms internally by pictures the image of figures, and by means of this image forms an imaginary spirit without any toil or design, so in the divine art of nature a wisdom of some kind by means of intellectual processes endows with natural seeds the life-giving and motive force itself which is its companion." [4] Vico must have recalled this passage in Ficino when in his inaugural lecture of 1699 he compared God, " the artist of nature," to the human mind which " we may without impiety call the God of art," just as he must have remembered it in the *De*

[1] *Ottonis Episcopi Frisigensis Opera*, ex recens. R. Wilmans, i. *Chronicon* (Hannoveriae, 1867), pp. 118-19.

[2] *Autob.* ed. cit. p. 21.

[3] *Ibid.* p. 25.

[4] *Theologia Platonica* (Bâle, 1561), i. 123. This passage of Ficino has been quoted and commented on by my friend Gentile, in a highly important monograph on *La prima fase della filosofia di G. B. Vico* (viz. the " inaugural lectures "), published in the miscellany in honour of Francesco Torraca (1912, see *infra*, p. 310) and read in MS. by myself, thanks to the courtesy of the author.

antiquissima where he compares God to the geometrician.[1]
Vico might however have found thoughts of this kind in
various Renaissance philosophers, not only in Ficino : among
others, in Girolamo Cardano, who contrasts divine and human
knowledge, though with a different conclusion ; and restricts
the one to finite objects (" for understanding is brought about
by a kind of proportion, *proportione quadam fit*, and there is
no proportion between the infinite and the finite "), denying
that man can know God, for as Vico said later in almost the
same words, " if I knew God, I should be God," *si scirem Deus
essem.* Thus he postulated " other sciences, and other modes
of understanding, entirely different from this of ours ; more
true, more solid, more firm, as a body is than its shadow : and
again other principles which we can by no reason apprehend."
And not only did he postulate them, but among the human
sciences he observed one which as opposed to the natural
sciences reached not merely the surfaces of things but almost
the things themselves, namely mathematics. " The human
soul, situated in the body, cannot attain to the substances of
things, but wanders about upon their surfaces by the help of
the senses, examining measurements, actions, resemblances
and doctrines. But the knowledge of the mind, which creates
the fact, is in a sense itself the fact, just as even among human
sciences the knowledge of a triangle, that it has three angles
equal to two right angles, is practically identical with the
truth itself (*scientia vero mentis, quae res facit, est quasi ipsa
res, veluti etiam in humanis scientia trigoni, quod habeat tres
angulos duobus rectis aequales, eadem ferme est ipsi veritati*),
whence it is clear that there is in us a natural science of a
different kind from true science."[2] Here, in the definition of
divine knowledge and of the procedure of human knowledge
in the case of mathematics, as opposed to that of physical
science, is implicit the principle that true knowledge consists
in the identity of thought with its object.

The idea of the opposition of mathematics to physical
science, in the certainty of the one and the uncertainty of the
other, persisted in the Neapolitan philosophers and scientists

[1] See Gentile's monograph, mentioned above.
[2] These passages of the *Tractatus de arcanis aeternitatis*, ch. iv., and
of the *De subtilitate*, bks. xi. and xxi. are quoted and commented on
by Fiorentino, *Bernardino Telesio ossia studî storici su l' idea della natura
nel risorgimento italiano* (Florence, Le Monnier, 1872), i. 212-13, who
does not fail to observe the relations with Vico's criterion.

of Vico's youth, even if they lost sight of the reason of this opposition. Tommaso Cornelio in his " progymnasma " *De ratione philosophandi* (1661) after reviewing the errors produced by the illusions of sense in physical science, says, " the contemplations of mathematics are not subjected to errors of this kind, dealing as they do with things whose images are not introduced into the mind by the senses ; for the mind can by itself adequately conceive figures and numbers, whose properties and analogies are examined by mathematicians, without aid from sense." [1] This ought to be emphasised, since it seems highly probable that Vico was stimulated to the establishment of his general theory of knowledge by reflection upon mathematics and the contrast between it and physical science. In fact the Latin speeches, our earliest documents for his studies, though they show the influence of Ficino and a certain amount of Cartesianism,[2] are never dominated by this general criterion. It is only in the last of these speeches, that of 1707, that the distinction between mathematics and natural science begins to appear ; in the next year it is clearly stated in the *De ratione studiorum*, where it takes the form of a general criterion. " We demonstrate geometry because we make it : if we could demonstrate physical facts, we should be creating them. For the true forms of things exist only in God the greatest and best, and to these the nature of them conforms " (*geometrica demonstramus quia facimus : si physica demonstrare possemus, faceremus. In uno enim Deo Opt. Max. sunt verae rerum formae, quibus earundem est conformata natura*). And this theory attained its full development in 1710 in the *De antiquissima*.

Such are the probable precedents, or as the common but inaccurate metaphor expresses it, " sources " of Vico's theory of knowledge. I do not think that the formation of this theory can have been influenced by the propositions of Geulinx and Malebranche which have been pointed out to me,[3] namely that " no one can make that which he does not know," and that " God alone knows his works, because he foreknows his action." In these propositions the old Thomistic doctrine is

---

[1] Thomae Cornelii consentini *Progymnasmata physica* (Naples, MDCLXXXVIII.), p. 70 : cf. also p. 64.

[2] See Gentile's monograph, mentioned above.

[3] By A. Pastore in a review of my monograph on Vico in the *Giorn. stor. d. lett. ital.* lviii., cf. pp. 400-402.

290 THE PHILOSOPHY OF GIAMBATTISTA VICO

substantially summarised. Much more tenable would be a
connexion or at least a comparison with Spinoza; we may
recall the Spinozistic identification of the *ordo et connexio
idearum* and the *ordo et connexio rerum*. Another ingenious,
but I think, inaccurate view is that " the analytic geometry
of Descartes was the introduction of the genetic principle into
the study of geometrical objects," so that the principle *verum
ipsum factum* " before being formulated by Vico had been
practised by Descartes "; and Vico in the *De antiquissima*
" adopted the scientific method of Descartes, which he stated
as the convertibility of the true with the created," raising it
" from a certitude to a criterion." [1] We are dealing here not
with practice, but simply with the theory of method : for
this method, conceived in its universality, just so far as it is
practical has always been practised ; not by Descartes alone,
and not only by analytic geometry.

We should certainly be better informed as to the precedents
of Vico's criterion if we knew more of his studies preparatory
to the *De antiquissima*, and if in general we had more literary
evidence about his youth. Perhaps even the precedents I
have indicated, which I only called probable, are not quite
free from an element of chance ; they may be connexions
only imagined by myself and non-existent for Vico's mind,
while others not accidental may perhaps be still unknown,
or await discovery by a student more fortunate than myself.
But it may not be out of place to remark that the search for
" precedents " does nothing to explain the new thought that
followed them ; much less does it detract from the value of
that thought. Such information, though on the one hand it
enriches our knowledge of the history of philosophy, on the
other hand has absolutely no effect upon the determinate
thought under examination. It is valuable in the biography
of a philosopher, but valueless for the comprehension of the
proper meaning of the new theory, which must be sought
essentially in the new problem which it faces and attempts to
solve. In the history of philosophy the same principles hold
good as in that of literature. Take for example the episode
of Argante and Tancred in canto xix. of " Jerusalem Delivered " ; Argante, while taking up his position for the fight
with his adversary, turns " as if in doubt " to the " afflicted
city," towards Jerusalem attacked by the crusaders ; and

[1] A. A. Zottoli, *G. B. Vico*, in *Cultura*, Rome, xxx. (1911) pp.
422-3.

when Tancred brutally mocks him, asking whether he does this out of fear, he replies :—

> I was but thinking how this city,
> The immemorial green of Juda's realm,
> Is falling, vanquished ; whose unhappy fate
> I have in vain endeavoured to repel.

Here the precedents are easily found ; Hector parting from Andromache and foreseeing the unhappy fate of Ilion, Priam and all his people (ἔσσεται ἦμαρ, etc., *Il.* vi. 448-9) ; or Aeneas as he gazes upon its downfall (*ruit alto a culmine Troia :* . . . *si Pergama dextra*, etc., *Aen.* ii. 290-92). And yet the tragic melancholy of Argante is an entirely new creation, and altogether original to Tasso.

Ficino, Cardano, Tommaso Cornelio, Scotus and Occam, and any others who have been or shall be added to the list, have or may have anticipated this or that element of Vico's formula : and yet when we turn from their statements to the *De antiquissima* and the polemics that follow it, and read the definition of science, of true science, as the conversion of the true with the created, it strikes us as an entirely original theory. The fact is that Vico had not to face the same opponents and to solve the same problems that were faced and solved by the schoolmen, nominalists and mystics of the Middle Ages or by the Platonists and naturalists of the Renaissance, nor yet those of Descartes in his *Discours sur la méthode* ; and the saying that " he alone knows things who creates them " acquires a new value, a new meaning (and this is its proper meaning) from its being used to refute the Cartesian *cogito* and the doctrine of immediate knowledge. Vico takes an old rusty sword and makes of it at least a glittering and trenchant weapon. For the same reason the phrase is no longer a mere accident or incident, but the starting-point of a special study, the foundation of a new philosophy, and Vico could quite well describe it as something not learnt from another but thought out and established by himself. And when he wants to find some original for it, he invents a history which is really a fiction or a myth ; namely the history of ancient Italian wisdom which used this criterion as its supreme guide and left a trace of it in the Latin language in the synonymity of the words *verum* and *factum*.

The refutation of the Cartesian criterion (which De Sanctis thought " complete," the " last word of criticism " [1]) is the

---

[1] *Opp.* ed. Ferrari, ii. 166.

negative aspect of Vico's theory of knowledge. Its positive side, absent in the *De antiquissima,* is developed as we have said in the *Scienza Nuova,* where the human knowledge of the mind and of history is raised to the level of divine knowledge. And since some critics have not only chosen to ignore the obvious difference between these two phases of Vico's thought but have spoken of a too easy transition from the one to the other, it will be well to observe that this transition was for Vico if not entirely conscious at least very slow and very difficult. He must at one time have shared Descartes' and Malebranche's contempt for history ; in the speech of 1701 he even echoed a saying of Descartes against philologists :— " You, Philologist, boast of knowing everything about the furniture and clothing of the Romans and of being more intimate with the quarters, tribes and streets of Rome than with those of your own city. Why this pride ? You know no more than did the potter, the cook, the cobbler, the summoner, the auctioneer of Rome." [1] But eleven years later, in the second reply to the *Giornale dei letterati,* Vico refers to the same phrase with the contrary conclusion, and deplores that " the study of languages is to-day considered profitless, thanks to the authority of Descartes, who says that to know Latin is to know no more than did Cicero's servant-girl." [2] Vico had in the meantime become conscious of the importance of the " probable " knowledge of history and politics. He refers to his former anti-historical Cartesianism in a passage of the *De constantia philologiae* which has generally escaped notice. Speaking of philology he says : " I, who have all my life delighted in the use of reason more than in memoiy, seem to myself the more ignorant the more facts I know in philology. Whence René Descartes and Malebranche were not far wrong when they said that it was alien to the philosopher to work much and for long at philology." But he adds that later he perceived that " these two most notable philosophers ought, it they had been zealous for the common glory of Christendom, not for the private glory of philosophers, so to have pressed forward the study of philology as to see whether philology could be attached to the principles of philosophy (*ut viderent philosophi an philologiam ad philosophiae principia revocare possent*)." [3] The elevation of philology

[1] *Orazioni latine,* ed. Galasso, p. 28.
[2] *Opp.* ed. Ferrari, ii. 166.
[3] *Ibid.* 232.

to the rank of philosophy, of the knowledge of the world of man
to the level of divine knowledge, is the positive aspect of Vico's
theory of knowledge. It is this that is developed in the
Scienza Nuova, towards which the *De antiquissima*, with the
indication of the historical sciences as against Cartesianism,
only prepared the way.

Thus of the three points in which I placed the originality
and value of Vico's first theory of knowledge, two, namely
the criterion of knowledge opposed to that of Descartes and the
defence of concrete as opposed to abstract sciences, are not
only left intact by the inquiries into their sources which I
have just described, but are actually reinforced.

There remains the third of my points : the Vician theory of
the arbitrary nature of mathematics, the originality of which
has also been impugned by arguments which seem to me to
have even less foundation than those I have examined
above.

Do we find the doctrine that the fundamental objects of
mathematics, the unit of arithmetic and the point of geometry,
are unreal or fictitious, propounded before Vico's time ? Do
we find it—this is the chief point—propounded not as a casual
remark or an intuition of a truth, but as a consciously reasoned
concept from which legitimate consequences are drawn as
to the limitations of mathematics and its inability to furnish
real knowledge of mind, nature and history ?

All through the Middle Ages the Aristotelian theory of
mathematics is continually enunciated. According to this
theory mathematics is the most certain of the sciences because
the simplest ; it abstracts from all sensible matter, but not
from intelligible matter (ὕλη νοητή) which exists in sensible
objects but not qua sensible (ἐν τοῖς αἰσθητοῖς ὑπάρχουσα
μὴ ᾗ αἰσθητά).[1] According to Cassiodorus it constituted
the body of *doctrinalis* as opposed to *naturalis* (physical)
science and *divina*. Albertus Magnus followed Aristotle in
defining mathematical entities as separable " in imagination,"
" in thought " but not " in reality " (*in phantasmate, secundum
rationem, non secundum esse*) from the sensible matter to which
" they are conjoined by existence " (*per esse sunt coniunctae*) ;
and St. Thomas said that mathematics " though the objects
it considers are not separate, yet considers them in so far as
they are separate " (*etsi sunt non separata ea quae considerat,*

[1] *Metaphys.* vi. 1036 a.

tamen considerat ea in quantum sunt separata).[1] The arbitrary character of its foundations was never suspected. Dante, when he wished to indicate " the things which not being subject to our power we can only contemplate and not create," enumerated " the objects of mathematics, physical science and divinity " (*mathematica, physica et divina*).[2]

Just as mathematics was not always equally valued in antiquity, so, and much more so, after the Renaissance of learning, it was variously exalted or despised. Giordano Bruno satirised the abuse of it, and said that without physical science " to be able to calculate and measure, to understand geometry and perspective, is but a pastime of ingenious fools," and warned his readers against confusing mathematical " signs " and real " causes " : " a reflected or direct ray, an acute or obtuse angle, a perpendicular, incident or straight line, a greater or smaller arc of a circle, such and such an aspect, are mathematical circumstances and not natural causes. To play with geometry is one thing, to prove by means of nature is another. It is not lines and angles that make the fire more or less hot, but near and far situations, short and long spaces of time." [3] Campanella flatly denied Aristotle's assertion of the superiority of mathematics to physical science, declaring that its alleged purity was really weakness (*debilitas*), its simplicity was inability to include more things (*plura accipere*), its universality a contradiction against the nature of true science which is always of particulars (*de singularibus*), its demonstrative method by signs not by causes (*per signa, non per causas*) ; and finally that it is not a science investigated for its own sake and is valueless unless it is applied to physical matters (*nisi applicentur physicis rebus*).[4] Bacon is of the same opinion, that mathematics taken by itself is useless, and is useful only as an " auxiliary science," a " great appendix " to the physical sciences.[5] These definitions and restrictions, and others like them, might have yielded as a conclusion the entirely instrumental

[1] The passages of Cassiodorus, Albertus and St. Thomas may be found collected in Mariétan, *Problème de la classification des sciences d'Aristote à saint Thomas* (Paris, 1901), see pp. 80, 168-9, 182-3, 185-6.

[2] *De monarchia*, i. c. 3.

[3] *La Cena delle ceneri* (1584) in his *Opere italiane*, ed. Gentile, i. 62, 107-8.

[4] *Logicorum libri tres*, bk. ii. art. 7-10 (in the *Philosophiae rationalis pars secunda*, Parisiis, 1637, pp. 433-7).

[5] *De dignitate et augmentis scientiarum*, bk. iii. c. 6.

and practical character of mathematical science : but the conclusion was not drawn, so far as I know ; and Bacon himself considered mathematics as in itself too exclusively and uselessly theoretical. " For since," he goes on in the passage above quoted, " it is a fact of human nature, no doubt to the great detriment of science, that it rejoices in the open plains of generalities, so to speak, rather than in the forests and closes of the particular, no discovery is more pleasant and gratifying than mathematics wherewith to sate this love of wandering and of meditation."

The " creation " of mathematics spoken of by Ficino, Cardano and others signified a mental production entirely free from material presuppositions, and for that reason not less true but true in a higher sense. It is almost the same sense as that found in Descartes and his followers. Locke asserts the reality of mathematical truths, though he admits that there are in nature no figures corresponding to the archetypes existing in the mind of the geometrician ;[1] and Leibnitz, commenting on this passage, says that " the ideas of justice and temperance are no more our own invention than those of the circle and the square."[2] Tommaso Cornelio, whom we have quoted on the contrast between physical science and mathematics, also believed that mathematics rested on " certain notions and understandings which nature has put into the minds of men as foundations of science."[3]

Another kind of " creation," and one which seems to have more connexion with Vico's " *fingere*," is discussed in a passage of Aristotle's *Metaphysics* which has had a good deal of influence. " We find also," Aristotle says, " geometrical figures by actualising them (ἐνεργείᾳ), because they are found by being divided : if they *were* divided, they would be obvious, but in reality they exist potentially. Why has the triangle two right angles ? Because the angles round one point are equal to two right angles. If then we construct the angle along one side, it would become plain to any one looking at it. Why is the angle in the semicircle equal to a right angle ? Because if there are three equal lines, two in the base and one drawn perpendicular to it, it is plain to any one who sees it and knows that. Whence it is evident that we discover things that exist potentially by reducing them to actuality.

[1] *Essay*, iv. ch. 4, § 6.
[2] *Nouveaux essais*, iv. ch. 4.
[3] *Op. cit.* p. 64.

This is because the actuality is understanding, and the potentiality proceeds from the actuality; so we know by making (καὶ διὰ τοῦτο ποιοῦντες γιγνώσκουσιν)." [1] But these observations belong to the explanations given by Aristotle in this passage of the conceptions of potentiality and actuality; they are not at all opposed to his theory of mathematics as studying the intelligible matter which subsists in sensible matter, and they only explain the difference between potential and actual truth. In the same way we sometimes find in later philosophers the assertion that mathematical truths are demonstrated and problems resolved " by making them." Thus Sarpi writes in the passage mentioned above: " in mathematics, he who constructs knows because he makes, and he who analyses learns because he seeks how the thing is made. The mode of composition then belongs to the inventive faculty and that of analysis to the discursive: the former is that of problems, the latter of theorems; the latter are demonstrated by analysis, the former by composition." [2]

It has also been recently asserted that the Vician philosophy of mathematics reappears bodily in Galileo and his school; [3] an astounding fact when baldly stated, since even

---

[1] *Metaphys.* viii. 1051 b. I append the passage: εὑρίσκεται δὲ καὶ τὰ διαγράμματα ἐνεργείᾳ· διαιροῦντες γὰρ εὑρίσκουσιν. εἰ δ᾽ ἦν διῃρημένα φανερὰ ἂν ἦν· νῦν δ᾽ ἐνυπάρχει δυνάμει. διὰ τί δύο ὀρθαὶ τὸ τρίγωνον; ὅτι αἱ περὶ μίαν στιγμὴν γωνίαι ἴσαι δύο ὀρθαῖς. εἰ οὖν ἀνῆκτο ἡ παρὰ τὴν πλευρὰν ἰδόντι ἂν ἦν εὐθὺς δῆλον. διὰ τί ἡ ἐν ἡμικυκλίῳ ὀρθὴ καθόλου; διότι ἐὰν ἴσαι τρεῖς, ἥ τε βάσις δύο καὶ ἡ ἐκ μέσου ἐπισταθεῖσα ὀρθή, ἰδόντι δῆλον τῷ ἐκεῖνο εἰδότι. ὥστε φανερὸν ὅτι τὰ δυνάμει ὄντα εἰς ἐνέργειαν ἀναγόμενα εὑρίσκεται. αἴτιον δ᾽ ὅτι νόησις ἡ ἐνέργεια· ὥστ᾽ ἐξ ἐνεργείας ἡ δύναμις. καὶ διὰ τοῦτο ποιοῦντες γιγνώσκουσιν.

[2] *Scritti filosofici*, ed. Papini, p. 7. In a passage of the *Arte di ben pensare* (*Scritti*, p. 72) Sarpi returns to mathematics and, while agreeing that it is less uncertain than the other sciences because in it " the mode and the proposition " are more clearly shown, goes on to say " it is also made in the same manner (as the others): it is not free from the suspicion of being not quite true." But clearly he is here speaking of the application of mathematics, of the act of counting and measuring physical objects: " this alone is certain: I count and reason in this manner, just as in eating honey I feel the effect which I call sweet; where I may be in error is the question whether this effect comes from the object or from the disposition of my taste: and there is no science where there are number and measurement, for all we can know is that we measure or count like this, and that the measure comes in or is used as many times as the thing seems to be equal to one such part and that equality is a concept of ours by which we express what then seems to happen."

[3] G. Papini, *La Novità di Vico* in *L' Anima*, Florence, September 1911, pp. 264-6; cf. on this article, *Critica*, x. 56-8.

though Vico opposes and prefers the great Pisan to Descartes for the moderate use he makes of mathematics in physical science, it is certain that for Galileo as for Leonardo da Vinci mathematics had an objective validity, and the book of nature is written in mathematical characters and geometrical figures. In any case, the passage of Galileo which has been quoted in this reference, on the intensive identity of human with divine knowledge, has nothing to do with the present question, and another passage which asserts that the explanations of terms are free, and it is in the power of every workman to circumscribe and define in his own way the things he is dealing with, without ever being led by this into error or falsehood, and that for instance one may call the bow the stern and the stern the bow, says nothing but a platitude hardly worth saying except by way of adorning a page of controversial rhetoric.[1] In controversy one is often obliged to insist upon platitudes, and the controversy upon which I am now engaged itself presents too many examples.

A passage from the *Lezioni accademiche* of Galileo's pupil Evangelista Torricelli in which he speaks of the difference between physical and mathematical definitions seems at first sight more convincing. But the critic who has called attention to this passage[2] says too much when he asserts that " it is beyond doubt that Vico had read it," since it is unquestionable that Vico had *not* read it. The *Lezioni accademiche* were published first posthumously in 1715[3] and Vico's theory of mathematics is expounded in the *De ratione* in 1708 and the *De antiquissima*, 1710. This, it is true, is of secondary importance, for Vico may have known Torricelli's doctrine through indirect channels, through other books or even orally through some Neapolitan friend or pupil of Torricelli ; in any case, if the latter's theory though unknown to Vico was really identical with his own, the similarity of ideas between the two would be of the greatest interest. Unfortunately the

---

[1] Papini probably owes this passage to a small anthology of Galileo by Favaro (Florence, Barbèra, 1910), p. 303, which refers to the national edition of his *Opere*, iv. 631 ; here the passage occurs in the *Considerazioni sopra il discorso di Colombo* (1615).

[2] G. Papini, *loc. cit.* pp. 265-6.

[3] *Lezioni accademiche di Evangelista Torricelli, mathematico e filosofo del serenissimo Ferdinando II Granduca di Toscana, lettore delle matematiche nello studio di Firenze e accademico della Crusca* (Florence, MDCCXV.). The editor's preface shows that the work had not been previously published.

critic has been too hasty, as it seems to me, even in his study and interpretation of the pages of Torricelli.

In the passage in question, a lecture *Della leggerezza*, read to the Accademia della Crusca, Torricelli controverts, as based on mere appearances and not confirmed by facts and reasoning, Aristotle's definition in the *De coelo* : " heavy is that which has a natural property of going towards the centre." He remarks upon this : " The definitions of Physics differ from those of Mathematics in that the former are obliged to adapt and adjust themselves to the object defined, while the latter mathematical definitions are free and can be formed at the will of the geometrician who is defining. The reason is perfectly plain : the things defined in Physics do not come into being with the definition, they exist already by themselves and are found in nature previously. But the things defined by geometry, that is by the science of abstraction, have no existence in the universe of the world other than that which definition gives to them in the universe of intelligence. Thus whatever objects of Mathematics are defined, the same objects will come into existence simultaneously with the definition." [1]

The arbitrary character of mathematics seems here to be clearly stated. But let us reserve our judgment and read on. " If I were to say, the circle is a plane figure with four equal sides and four right angles, this is not at all a false definition ; but for the rest of my book I should have to mean, whenever I spoke of a circle, a certain figure which others have called a square. But if a man should say in Physics, ' the horse is a rational animal,' should we not be justified in calling him the horse ? We must first look very carefully to see whether the horse is a rational animal or not and then define it as it is, in order that the physical definition may conform to the object and not be counted defective." Here we see that what appeared to be a profound thought has turned out to be a platitude ; it is indifferent whether we call the bow the stern or the stern the bow, said Galileo, or, says Torricelli in his turn, whether we call a square a circle or a circle a square ; while it does not seem to him an indifferent matter whether we call a horse a rational animal. But even this does not prevent him from admitting later some degree of arbitrariness in physical terminology, when he says, " since then it is not demonstrated that the intrinsic principle of downward motion

[1] *Op. cit.* pp. 31-2.

exists upon the earth, I will accept this definition, if the tests will allow me, as the simple imposition of a name, and, replacing the verb ' to be ' by the verb ' to be called,' I will adapt the definition to my own requirements thus : That is called heavy which descends to the centre.   Whenever any one says, the earth is heavy, I will agree, but always with the interpretation that the word ' heavy ' only signifies descending in a lighter medium." [1]

It seems to me then that the difference which he begins by laying down between mathematics and physical science is considerably obscured in the sequel.   And indeed how could Torricelli have seriously thought that the foundation of mathematics was a " fiction," when among his lectures one heard the title " in Praise of Mathematics " ?   In this lecture he says, quite in the Galilean style : " That to read the great Book of the Universe, the book on whose pages may be found the true philosophy written by God, mathematics are indispensable, will be seen by any one who with noble thoughts aspires to the science of the integral parts and greatest members of this huge body we call the World.   The one alphabet, the only characters with which we can read the great manuscript of the divine philosophy in the book of the Universe are those poor figures you see in the text-books of geometry." [2] The most we can see in these statements is a vague and hazy presentment of the profound difference between physical truths and the so-called truths of mathematics.

In conclusion, until for the third of my three points we can discover much more obvious " sources " than those suggested up till now, I shall see no cause to modify my verdict upon the originality of Vico's conception of mathematics. This originality is further proved by the important consequences drawn by Vico from his theory of mathematics for his philosophical method ; for every one knows that a thought taken over bodily from another remains inert and sterile, while an original idea is always active and fruitful.

Note.—I have selected, of the various criticisms directed against my book on Vico, that concerning his " originality," because this gave me opportunities for researches and explanations of some value.   But my book has been subjected to two general criticisms which do not lend themselves to the same treatment.

It has been said that in my exposition of Vico's philosophy

[1] *Op. cit.* p. 33. [2] *Op. cit.* p. 66.

I have followed my personal philosophical convictions : and
sermons and epistles have been showered upon me preaching
the duty of casting off prejudices, etc., and narrating the
history of philosophy in an objective manner, etc. But I
should like my critics to believe that my " convictions "
cannot have, to my mind, the character of prejudices, but
precisely that of liberation from prejudice, which is what
they demand : that detachment and purity of understanding
which is necessary for the comprehension of historical facts,
and is not, as some fancy, a primeval innocence, but the fruit
of laborious cultivation. To grasp Vico historically in his
strict reality I have been compelled to undergo a *catharsis*
of prejudices, consisting in my case of the philosophy to which
my own efforts had led me. My ideas may be untrue, but
that is another question ; and that means that if their falsity
is proved I am bound to clear and purify my mind by means
of less false ideas ; but these in their turn must always be ideas
and become convictions. In point of abstract method, no
objection at all can be made to any one who looks at Vico
through the spectacles of scholasticism if he thinks they make
his sight more distinct and penetrating ; the most we can do
is to try and persuade him that there are better spectacles
on the market. But we certainly have the right to smile if
this same scholastic goes on to warn us that " in studying a
philosopher, in investigating and reconstructing his thought,
it is absolutely necessary to bring to the task a mind free from
preconceptions and hostile to prejudices " ; while all the
time he is trying to pass off his scholastic opinions and religious
beliefs under the banner of objectivity, sincerity and freedom
from prejudice. " Philosophers "—I have seen this assertion
too—" are unfitted for writing the history of philosophy,
because they have ideas of their own." And who is fitted for
it ? People who are not philosophers ? Does not Vico teach
us precisely this, that where he who makes the facts (as
the philosopher makes philosophy) himself narrates them,
there history reaches its highest certainty ?

The other criticism concerns the idealistic interpretation
which I have given to some of Vico's doctrines. It is con-
tended that Vico was a Catholic, and that fact is supposed to
prove that he could not have entertained the ideas which I
find in his works. But that Vico professed himself an entirely
orthodox Catholic, and that he clung to Catholicism with all
the strength and zeal of his mind I have myself said again and

again : I have even defended him against the accusations or praises dealt out to him by other critics for deceit or prudence in his attitude to the Church.   But is it really so amazing, so unheard-of a thing, to find heterodox ideas in an orthodox writer ?   Are they not found in the Early Fathers and the Schoolmen, in mediaeval and modern theologians and mystics ? To take an example of the many that occur, an example for a double reason above suspicion : Nicholas of Cusa was a Catholic and in fact a Cardinal of Holy Church, and in his lifetime the intimate friend of three popes.   And yet the Catholic historian of Scholasticism, De Wulf, wrote of him " Le Cardinal catholique est-il donc panthéiste ? . . . Il s'en défend vivement dans son *Apologia doctae ignorantiae*, mais on peut dire de lui comme d'Eckehart : ' il fait fléchir la logique au profit de son orthodoxie et retient de force les conséquences de ses prémisses ' " (*Hist. de la philos. médiévale*, p. 389).   If this happened to the Cardinal of Cusa or the Franciscan Master Eckehart, could it not happen to the Catholic Vico ?   M. de Wulf the Catholic historian is allowed to use this admirable method of criticism and to distinguish intention and action, will and logic.   Why should it be denied to me ?

But enough.

APPENDIX IV

BIBLIOGRAPHICAL NOTES

I. WORKS OF VICO

VICO's earliest extant work is the poem entitled *Feelings of one in despair*, composed certainly before the author's twenty-fifth year at Vatolla in the Cilento, where he lived for nine years as a tutor at the Casa Rocca, printed by Gonzatti at Venice and dated 1693. This was followed by verses and speeches of a merely rhetorical character.

The philosophical characteristics are accentuated in the six speeches read by Vico at Naples University, 1699–1707, not printed by him, and rediscovered and published by Galasso (Naples, Morano, 1869). In these speeches, though some tendencies of his thought show themselves, his philosophy is still the traditional system, not without some traces of Cartesianism. Vico's opposition to Cartesianism and formal adoption of his own views are announced for the first time in the inaugural lecture for the year 1708, entitled *De nostri temporis studiorum ratione*, published next year by the author himself (Naples, Mosca, 1709). A long digression (§§ 12-15) contains a sketch of the history of Roman jurisprudence, his first essay in the historical studies which led later on to the *Diritto universale* and the two *Scienze Nuove*.

The following year appeared Vico's first constructively philosophical and historical work: the *De antiquissima Italorum sapientia ex linguae Latinae originibus eruenda*, or rather the first book of that work (Naples, Mosca, 1710): the other two were never written, but we can form an idea of their intended contents from what is said in the Autobiography. Beside Vico's theory of knowledge in its first form and the metaphysic which he always maintained in its entirety, the *De antiquissima* contained an attempt to reconstitute for the

302

first time primitive wisdom, or rather one particular instance of primitive wisdom, that of Italy ; but as we have already said in the text of our exposition the attempt was founded on the idea that this wisdom was philosophical, and conducted according to the criterion of the transmission of culture which Vico subsequently rejected, as he rejected the traditional opinion, accepted in this work, of the Athenian origin of the laws of the Twelve Tables. We must accordingly refuse to accept Cantoni's verdict (*G. B. Vico*, p. 38) that the *De antiquissima* forms " a strange anomaly in the history of Vico's thought, being contrary to his whole scientific life, his tendencies, his principles, and the method which later he almost universally applies in his historical researches." The reverse is in fact the case : namely that this work is the starting-point of his future developments and that without it we cannot understand his later thought.

The criticisms directed by the *Giornale dei letterati d' Italia* (1711, vols. v. and viii.) against the historical and some of the philosophical positions of the *De antiquissima* evoked Vico's two important *Replies* (Naples, Mosca, 1711 and 1712) in which he defends and elucidates his views on the theory of knowledge and metaphysics. The part of the *De antiquissima* that never went to the press included his meditations on the philosophy of medicine, from which he extracted an essay *De aequilibrio corporis animantis :* this he thought of publishing many years later, but it is now lost. Of these studies, therefore, as of his speculations upon physics intended to constitute a *Liber physicus*, we know only what he tells us in his autobiography.

Setting aside his rhetorical and occasional compositions, the largest of which is the *De rebus gestis Antonii Caraphaei* (Naples, Mosca, 1716), the continuation of his thought, now concentrating upon moral and historical problems, is sketched in a lecture of 1719 (of which an abstract is included in the autobiography) and developed first in 1720 in a printed prospectus of four double-columned pages known as the *Sinopsi del diritto universale*, and secondly in the vast treatise, *De universi iuris uno principio et fine uno liber unus* (Naples, Mosca, 1720) completed next year with the *Liber alter qui est de constantia iurisprudentis*, and supplemented in 1722 by the *Notae in duos libros*, etc. (same publisher) ; a work which is usually referred to briefly following the author's example as the *Diritto universale*.

This book, according to Cantoni (*op. cit.* p. 243) represents the culminating point of Vico's scientific activity. The verdict is no more acceptable than that quoted above. The author (*Opp.* v. 10-11) rejected the *Diritto universale* because he seemed to find persisting there the prejudice and the pretence of " descending " from the thought of Plato and other philosophers to that of primitive man, a tendency which led him astray " in certain matters " ; but he also calls it, and rightly, a " sketch for the *Scienza Nuova,*" which it really is. The ideas about poetry are here still confused, Homer is not yet a myth, the mythological canons have less unity than they acquired later, the theory of reflux is only faintly adumbrated, and in a word both the ideal eternal history and the theory of knowledge upon which it is founded are as yet immature. The book is all contained, under a new form, in his later work, except the general ethical and juridical philosophy, which is not highly original, and some historical developments which are merely alluded to in the later writings.

The MS. of an Italian work in two books, in which Vico expounded his doctrines " by a negative method," has been lost. But he expounds them positively and at less length in the *Principî di una Scienza Nuova intorno alla comune natura delle nazioni, per la quale si ritrovano i principî di altro sistema del diritto naturale delle genti* (Naples, Mosca, 1725) which is known by the title (again authorised by himself) of First *Scienza Nuova.*

In 1725, the year of the publication of the first *Scienza Nuova,* Vico related the history of his studies : *Vita di G. B. Vico scritta da se medesimo,* which was inserted in Calogerà's *Raccolta di opuscoli scientifici e filologici* (Venice, Zani, 1728, vol. i. pp. 145-256). Among the minor writings of this period may be noted the two speeches on the death of the Countess of Althann (1724) and the Marchesana della Petrella Angiola Cimini (1727) ; the little volume *Vici vindiciae* (Naples, Mosca, 1729) containing a personal defence (together with an important theoretical digression on " laughter ") against a malevolent notice inserted in the *Acta Lipsiensia* of 1727, about the *Scienza Nuova* ; and some fine letters to Giacchi, Degli Angioli, Esperti, De Vitry and Solla on the contrast between his works and the state of learning at this time.

To the first *Scienza Nuova* Vico thought of adding a long series of *Annotations* in a reprint of it which he was preparing at Venice between 1728 and 1730. But since this scheme was not carried out, and on the other hand he was dissatisfied with the book not so much on account of the matter, he says, as on account of the arrangement (*Opp.* vi. 11), he resolved to publish an entirely new exposition of his doctrines in the *Cinque libri de' principî di una Scienza Nuova d' intorno alla comune natura delle nazioni, in questa seconda impressione con più propia maniera condotti e di molto accresciuti* (Naples, Mosca, 1730), which form the second *Scienza Nuova*. While Cantoni (*op. cit.* pp. 238-9) considers this work the dotage of Vico's thought, it is really the necessary result and perfect form in which his previous attempts issued ; it is the book which with the *De antiquissima* and the autobiography supplies all the necessary material for a knowledge of his thought. In the *Diritto universale* and the first *Scienza Nuova* we can find a few details omitted in the later work ; but those treatises display the same doctrines as the second *Scienza Nuova* in a manner much less profound and solid, and certainly less characteristic of the author. The detailed comparison of these three works has been made with great care in the short summaries added by Ferrari to his editions of the first and second *Scienza Nuova*.

Even the 1730 edition was increased by the author from 1731 to about 1740 by many variations and additions, though without changing the arrangement or the substance of the work. These additions were taken for the most part incorporated in a final MS. on which was based the edition of the *Principî di una Scienza Nuova intorno alla comune natura delle nazioni*, published the very year of Vico's death (Naples, Stamperia Muziana, 1744). In the National Library at Naples are preserved the autographs both of this MS. and of two earlier MSS. of additions and corrections, unpublished fragments of which have been published by Giordano (Naples, 1818) and Del Giudice (Naples, 1862). All the unpublished fragments and variants have been now collected by Nicolini in the edition hereafter mentioned (p. 307).

After the second *Scienza Nuova* Vico wrote hardly anything. We may note among these few productions the speech *De mente heroica* (Naples, 1732), the addition to the autobiography (1731), and a few sonnets in which, composed though they were, like almost all his verses, by request and as occasional pieces, a personal note may at times be felt.

II. REPRINTS, COLLECTIONS, AND TRANSLATIONS

Two collections of Vico's minor works have been made, one of the *Latinae orationes* alone by F. Daniele (Naples, 1766), and the other, rich in unpublished matter, of the Italian and Latin *Opuscoli*, in four volumes, by C. A. de Rosa, Marchese di Villarosa (Naples, 1818–23). Vico's son Gennaro furnished Villarosa with all his father's extant papers ; and these priceless autographs are still preserved at Naples in the house of my intimate friends the engineers Tommaso and Vincenzo de Rosa di Villarosa.

The first and only edition as it may be called, since all others are merely reproductions of it, of Vico's complete works is that of Giuseppe Ferrari, in six volumes (Milan, *Classici italiani*, 1835–37) reprinted with improvements in 1852–54. The *Opere* edited by N. M. Corcia (Naples, Tipografia della Sibilla, 1834, 2 vols.) are only a selection ; and the *Opere* edited by F. Predari (Milan, Bravetta, 1835) never went beyond one ill-arranged volume. The edition which followed that of Ferrari (Naples, Iovane, 1840–41) is also incomplete and ill-arranged, but contains some small unpublished works. The Neapolitan edition of the *Opere* in eight volumes (i.-ii. 1858, iii. 1861, iv. 1859, v.-vi. 1860, vii. 1865, viii. 1869, the earlier volumes at the Tipografia dei Classici Italiani, the others by the publisher Morano) is based mainly upon Ferrari, but somewhat incorrect ; it is however the most complete of all, as containing the *Sinopsi*, the *Istituzioni oratorie*, and the *Orazioni latine* published by Galasso subsequently to Ferrari's edition, as well as the Italian translations by the advocate F. S. Pomodoro of the *De ratione*, *De antiquissima*, and *Diritto universale*.

Unpublished or scattered works of Vico not appearing in any of these editions have been collected by Croce, *Bibliografia vichiana* and *Primo* and *Secondo supplemento* : see below.

A critical edition of the second *Scienza Nuova* is now being printed in the *Collezione dei classici della filosofia moderna diretta da B. Croce e G. Gentile* (Bari, Laterza) : the first volume is to be published at the same time as the present monograph.[1] It is being edited by Dr. Fausto Nicolini, who by using the autograph MSS. has enriched Ferrari's edition, which contained the fragments suppressed in the 1730 issue, by all the frag-

[1] By now (1913) the second volume has appeared : the third will appear next year.

ments of the intermediate redactions down to the 1744 text ; Vico's quotations have been checked and references given in notes to the passages of classical and modern authors to which he refers ; and, finally, in deference to a wish often expressed by men of letters as authoritative as Tommaseo, the orthography and punctuation have been corrected. Ferrari's valuable summaries are reproduced, with a few emendations, in Nicolini's edition.

Nicolini is also at work on a new edition of the complete works, to form part of Laterza's collection of *Scrittori d' Italia*, the scheme and detailed index of which may be seen in Croce, *Secondo supplemento alla Bibliografia vichiana* (pp. 102-13). The fifth volume of this collection, edited by Croce, is also to appear with the present monograph.

Vico's Latin works have frequently been translated into Italian : the *De antiquissima* anonymously, perhaps by Vincenzo Monti (1816), and later by Sarchi (1870) : the first book of the *Diritto naturale* by Corcia (1839), Amante (1841), Giani (1855), and Sarchi (1866), and both books, with the *De ratione* and *De antiquissima*, as we have said, by Pomodoro.

The second *Scienza Nuova* was translated into French, much abbreviated, by Jules Michelet, under the title of *Principes de la philosophie de l'histoire* (Paris, Renouard, 1827) and frequently reprinted ; and again, in full, by an anonymous translator described as " l'Auteur de l'Essai sur la formation du dogme catholique," in reality Cristina Trivulzi, Princess of Belgioioso (Paris, Renouard, 1844). Michelet also translated some of Vico's minor works, published with the *Scienza Nuova* in the edition of the *Œuvres choisies de Vico* (Paris, Hachette, 1835) and frequently reprinted.

In German there is a translation in full with good notes by W. E. Weber (Leipzig, Brockhaus, 1844). There is also a summary of the first book of the *Diritto universale* by K. H. Müller, forming the first volume of a series of Vico's *Kleine Schriften* which was not continued (Neubrandenburg, Brünslow, 1854).

The only English translation is a version of the book on Homer based on Michelet's French translation and inserted in H. Nelson Coleridge's *Introduction to the Study of the Greek Classic Poets* (3rd ed., London, Murray, 1846).

III. BIOGRAPHY OF VICO

By way of supplement to the autobiography, Villarosa collected information on Vico's last years and published it as a continuation of that work in his edition of the *Opuscoli*, vol. i. (1818).

This supplement, together with everything else that has been published in the way of documents or contemporary records of Vico, may be found collected in the fifth volume of the new edition of his works above mentioned (p. 307) and entitled : *L' Autobiografia, il carteggio e le poesie varie*, ed. B. Croce (Bari, Laterza, 1911).

IV. LITERATURE ON VICO

There are only three monographs on Vico which may still be read with profit (that of Ferrari, *La Mente del Vico*, admirable editor though he was, may best be consigned to merciful oblivion) ; they are as follows :—

1. Carlo Cantoni, *G.B.V., studî critici e comparativi* (Turin, Civelli, 1867). Cf. for certain reservations A. Faggi, in *Rivista filosofica italiana*, vol. ix., 1906, pp. 593-606, and G. Gentile, in *Critica*, vol. v., 1907, pp. 197-201.

2. Karl Werner, *G.B.V. als Philosoph und gelehrter Forscher*, (Wien, Braumüller, 1881). Cf. *Zeitschrift für Philosophie und philos. Kritik*, vol. lxxii., 1883, pp. 139-52.

3. Robert Flint, *Vico* (Edinburgh and London, 1884). Italian translation by F. Finocchietti, Florence, 1888).

See what has been said of these above, p. 277. Of short and general studies the following are the best :—

1. B. Spaventa, *G.B.V.*, in *Prolusione e introduzione alle lezioni di filosofia* (Naples, Vitale, 1862), pp. 83-102, reprinted under the title *La Filosofia italiana nelle sue relazioni con la filosofia europea*, ed. G. Gentile (Bari, Laterza, 1908) ; see pp. 111-35 of this reprint.

2. F. de Sanctis, *Storia della letteratura italiana* (Naples, Morano, 1870 ; new ed. Croce, Bari, Laterza, 1912), vol. ii. pp. 342-62.

3. F. Fiorentino, *Lettere sopra la " Scienza Nuova "* (Florence, 1865), reprinted in *Scritti varî* (Naples, Morano, 1871), pp. 161-211.

4. E. Cauer, *G.B.V. und seine Stellung zur modernen Wissenschaft* (in *Deutsches Museum*, edited by R. Prutz and W. Woelfsohn, Leipzig, Hinrichs, year 1, 1851, vol. i. pp. 249-65).

For special points the following may be consulted :—

1. F. A. Wolf, *G.B.V. über den Homer* (in *Museum der Alterthumswissenschaft*, Berlin, 1807, vol. ii. pp. 555-70).

2. J. K. von Orelli, *Vico und Niebuhr* (in *Schweizerisches Museum*, Aarau, vol. i. p. 184 *sqq.*).

3. C. Iannelli, *Sulla natura e necessità della scienza delle cose e delle storie umane* (Naples, Porcelli, 1818, and Milan, Fontana, 1832).

4. Emerico Amari, *Critica di una scienza della legislazione comparata* (Genoa, Istituto dei Sordomuti, 1857). Cf. on this book K. Werner, *E.A. in seinem Verhältnis zu G.B.V.* (Wien, 1880 ; from the *Sitzungsberichte der phil.-histor. Klasse* of the Imperial Academy of Vienna, vol. xcvi.).

5. F. Acri, *Teoria del V. intorno alle idee o paradimmi* (in *Abbozzo di una teoria delle idee*, Palermo, Lao, 1870 ; and with modifications in the volume *Videbimus in aenigmate*, Bologna, Mareggiani, 1907, pp. 287-313).

6. E. Cenni, an exposition of Vico's metaphysic in the volume entitled *Considerazioni sull' Italia ad occasione del traforo del Gottardo* (Florence, Cellini, 1884), pp. 109-82.

7. E. Bouvy, *De V. Cartesii adversario* (Paris, Hachette, 1889).

8. E. Bouvy, *La Critique dantesque au dix-huitième siècle : Dante et V.* (Paris, Leroux, 1892).

9. G. Sorel, *Étude sur V.* (in *Devenir social*, Paris, vol. ii., 1896) and see esp. the same author's *Le Système historique de Renan* (Paris, Jacques, 1905), *passim*.

10. B. Labanca, *G.B.V. e i suoi critici cattolici* (Naples, Pierro, 1898).

11. G. Rossi, *V. nei tempi di V.* (in *Rivista filosofica italiana*, vol. ii., 1899, pp. 294-319, and part 2, *ibid.* vol. x., 1907, pp. 602-34).

12. A. Olivieri, *Gli studî omerici di G.B.V.* (in *Atti della r. Accad. di archeologia, lettere e belle arti*, Naples, vol. xxiv., 1905).

13. C. Trabalza, *Storia della grammatica italiana* (Milan, Hoepli, 1908), ch. xii. pp. 364-76.

14. P. Garofalo, *Acrisia vichiana nella " Scienza Nuova,"* critical annotations (Naples, Detken, 1909) : cf. F. Nicolini, in *Critica*, vol. viii., 1910, pp. 374-8.

15. G. Maugain, *Étude sur l'évolution intellectuelle de l'Italie de 1657 à 1750 environ* (Paris, Hachette, 1909).

16. On my own previous work upon Vico, it should be

observed that the materials of the chapter on Vico's aesthetic doctrine in Croce, *Estetica* (4th ed., Bari, Laterza, 1912, ch. v. pp. 255-71), have been worked up in a more mature form into ch. iv. of the present monograph : the essay on Vico's Ethics (in *Critica*, vi., 1908, pp. 71-7) has been absorbed into chaps. vi.-viii. ; and similarly that on the *Lineamenti di storia letteraria in G.B.V.* (*ibid.* pp. 460-80) into chaps. xvi. and xviii. ; my other scattered writings have in general been only of technical, philological, or polemical interest. In the miscellaneous *Studî in onore di F. Torraca* (Naples, Perrella, 1912) is a short essay by me upon *La Dottrina del riso e dell' ironia in G.B.V.*

The whole of the literature on Vico, together with extracts from rare books, minor works, and articles, and with unpublished documents together with fully detailed notes on the editions of Vico's writings, is collected in the three works to which I have frequently referred, namely : B. Croce, *Bibliografia vichiana contenente nella parte I il catalogo delle edizioni, traduzioni e manoscritti delle opere di G.B.V. ; nella parte II, quello dei giudizî e lavori storico-critici intorno al V. sino al- l' anno corrente ; nella parte III lettere inedite del V. e al V., documenti e altri scritti inediti o rari, e varie appendici illustrative* (Naples, 1904 : reprinted from *Atti dell' Accademia pontaniana*, Naples, vol. xxxiv. ; pp. xii. 127, 4to) ; — *Supplemento alla Bibliografia vichiana* (Naples, 1907 ; reprinted from *Atti*, vol. xxxvii. pp. 34, 4to)—and *Secondo Supplemento* (Naples, 1911, reprinted from *Atti*, vol. xl. pp. 116, 4to) ; the whole collected in one volume under the title : *Bibliografia vichiana ; raccolta di tre memorie presentate all' Accademia pontaniana di Napoli nel 1903, 1907 e 1910*, with an appendix by F. Nicolini (Bari, Laterza, 1911).[1]

---

[1] Since the publication of the Italian edition of this work in 1911 several studies of Vico have appeared. The following may be noted :—

G. Gentile, *La Prima Fase della filosofia di G.B.V.*, Naples, 1912 (in the *Studî in onore di F. Torraca*), quoted *supra*, p. 287 n.

F. Pessico, *Ripensando la Scienza Nuova* (in *Rassegna nazionale*, November 1, 1912).

G. Folchieri, *Il Carattere dell' opera di G.B.V.* (Perugia, Bartelli, 1913).

F. Nicolini, *Spigolature vichiane ; sul testo delle Vindiciae* (in *Scritti varî in onore di R. Renier*, Turin, 1912).

B. Croce, *Il V. e la critica omerica* (in the volume *Saggio sullo Hegel e altri scritti di storia della filosofia*, Bari, Laterza, 1913, pp. 269-282).

Cf. also W. Windelband, *Die Geschichte der neueren Philosophie*, 5th ed. Leipzig, 1911, vol. i. pp. 597-8.

NOTE

CHAPTER I.—For this chapter see the *De ratione*, the *De antiquissima*, the two *Riposte al Giornale dei letterati*, and the first part of the Autobiography. For the note (p. 8) on the spirit of the Reformation, see *Opere*, ed. Ferrari, 2nd ed. vi. 5.

Chapter II.—*Opp.* v. 147, 239, 136-7, 51 ; iv. 33 ; v. 50-51, 147 ; iv. 33, 63-4 ; iii. 200 ; v. 17, 97, 103, 149-50, 174 ; iv. 20, 248 ; iii. 232 ; iv. 20 ; v. 562.

Chapter III.—*Opp.* v. 147, 162, 99, 42 ; iv. 73, 81, 174-5 ; v. 91, 145.

Chapter IV.—*Opp.* v. 141, 166, 42 ; iii. 232, 272-3 ; iv. 20 ; v. 175, 259, 107 ; iv. 22, 33 ; v. 180, 441, 209-10, 201 ; iv. 205, 206 ; iii. 274, 275 ; v. 230, 211, 169 ; iv. 201, 233, 365 ; v. 55, 82, 187, 196-7 ; iv. 224 ; v. 110, 112, 168, 212, 237, 217, 379, 440, 212, 238 ; iv. 24.

Chapter V.—*Opp.* v. 80-81 ; iv. 20, 21, 74 ; v. 169 ; v. 161-7 ; iv. 191-3, 168-9 ; v. 18 ; iv. 169, 50-51 ; iii. 26, 110 ; ii. 96-7 ; v. 166, 43, 169, 420-21, 387, 192, 379, 108.

Chapter VI.—*Opp.* v. 437, 18 ; iv. 165 ; v. 109, 110, 534 ; vi. 15 ; v. 532 ; iii. 12 ; v. 106 ; v. 49 ; iii. 343 ; vi. 127 ; iii. 30 ; iv. 87 ; iii. 57 ; v. 490 ; iv. 40-41 ; iii. 30 ; iv. 334 ; iv. 35 ; iii. 12, 30 ; v. 97 ; iii. 234-40 ; iv. 49 ; v. 98, 131 ; iv. 42-3.

Chapter VII.—*Opp.* v. 142, 168, 173, 248, 250 ; iv. 291 ; v. 106, 242, 142, 137-8, 290 ; iv. 175-7, 42-3 ; v. 153, 241 ; iv. 9 ; v. 96, 242, 574 ; iv. 332 ; v. 97 ; iv. 176-7, 43 ; v. 176, 131.

Chapter VIII.—*Opp.* iv. 309-13 ; v. 185 ; iii. 55, 28, 43-4 ; v. 97 ; iii. 47-52, 52-3 ; iv. 14, 45, 57 ; v. 148, 133 ; iii. 53, 85-7, 58 ; v. 240-41, 484 ; iv. 170-71, 180, 351.

Chapter IX.—*Opp.* v. 462-3, 544 ; iv. 43-4, 46 ; iii. 94, 192-3, 85, 87 ; iv. 18, 335, 15 ; v. 129-30, 563, 564 ; iii. 55 ; v. 571 ; iv. 245, 13, 159-60 ; *Scritti inediti*, Del Giudice, pp. 11-14.

Chapter X.—*Opp.* v. 13-14, 128, 143-4, 172, 570 ; iii. 22 ; iv. 42 ; v. 97, 572, 45-6, 463.

Chapter XI.—*Opp.* iv. 62 ; v. 116, 183, 558, 559, 561, 570 ; vi. 127 ; iii. 95 ; iv. 249.

Chapter XII.—Same sources as for Ch. I. and also vi. 105-6 ; v. 524-5.

Chapter XIII.—*Opp.* v. 60 ; iii. 249 ; v. 157, 167-70, 108 ; iii. 251-61 ; iv. 17, 253 ; v. 103, 217-18, 562 ; *Scritti inediti,* p. 9.

Chapter XIV.—*Opp.* v. 94-6, 58, 79, 321, 63-4, 84-5, 96, 93, 100 ; iv. 2 7-8, 29-30, 97, 169, 200, 271 ; v. 182-3, 61-4 ; iii. 230 ; iv. 236-43, 184 ; iii. 450-59 ; v. 113, 115, 149, 211, 59, 74, 100, 183 ; iv. 75-6, 89 ; v. 206 ; iv. 99 ; iii. 273 ; v. 260 ; iii. 280 ; v. 430-31, 202-3, 98-9.

Chapter XV.—*Opp.* v. 356, 357, 255, 355, 121, 361-3, 363-365, 340, 341, 253, 251-3, 259, 132, 118, 278, 311, 309, 307, 118-19, 120, 121, 481, 484-6, 293-4, 246, 526, 528, 530-31, 223-5, 444, 43, 114-15, 222-3, 460, 220, 194, 191-3, 186, 249, 369, 371, 372, 375, 382, 403, 69 ; iv. 54, 83-4, 225-6.

Chapter XVI.—*Opp.* v. 380-81, 422-5, 452, 277, 360-61, 381, 426, 435-6, 465, 425, 427, 442, 427-32, 440-41, 445, 448-9, 451, 455, 428-9, 445, 449-56, 445-6, 448, 452, 378-81, 441-2, 453-4, 78, 446-7, 458-60, 433-4, 439 ; iv. 178 ; vi. 46 ; v. 100-101, 467-80, 381, 223-4, 457, 100, 102, 226, 438 ; iv. 163, 25, 63, 200, 128 ; iii. 295.

Chapter XVII.—*Opp.* iv. 249-50, 228 ; v. 183, 188 ; iii. 306-10 ; iv. 93, 34, 155 ; v. 86, 277, 322-3, 416, 129, 413-416, 81, 326, 86 ; iii. 473 ; v. 509-10, 102 ; iii. 469-75, 87, 122-3 ; iv. 67-71 ; v. 123-4, 191, 85, 100, 88, 290-91, 310, 496, 88-92, 123, 495-505, 502, 327, 525-30, 531, 534, 506, 474-476, 401, 551, 555, 514, 476, 515, 537-8, 122, 503, 521, 508, 523, 503, 514.

Chapter XVIII.—*Opp.* v. 550, 537, 259, 540-41, 546, 555-556 ; iv. 101, 545, 347-8, 552, 555, 544, 554, 537, 539, 538, 551, 328, 547, 552, 512, 553, 550, 508-9, 68, 488, 547, 538-9, 231, 233, 204, 222, 226, 361, 425, 428-39, 457 ; iii. 357 ; vi. 37, 45-6 ; iii. 270 ; vi. 35, 37-8, 42, 48 ; v. 429, 439 ; iv. 198-200 ; vi. 38 ; v. 43, 226, 555, 544, 508-9, 557-8 ; iv. 235-6, 71.

Chapter XIX.—For this chapter see the *De ratione,* the first pages of the Autobiography and the letters to Esperti, De Vitry, and Solla.   On wisdom see also *Opp.* v. 153.

INDEX OF NAMES

Comte, A., 274
Concina, N., 261
Confucius, 180
Confuorto, 248
Conrad III., 221
Constantine, 211
Conti, A., 269
Conti, N., 62
Corcia, N. M., 306-7
Corneille, 232
Cornelio, T., 289, 291, 295
Coulanges, Fustel de, 243, 275
Cournot, 274
Cousin, 274
Cristofaro (G. de), 248
Croce, B., 306 *seqq.*
Cujas, 216
Cuoco, V., 130, 272
Curiatii, 174
Curius, 168
Curtius, 168
Cusa (N. of), 301
Cyclic poets, 192

Dale (van), 71
Daniele, F., 306
Dante, 150, 223-5, 242, 257, 275
Darius, 51
Decius, 168
Degérando, 273
Descartes, 1-35, 80, 137, 232, 238, 256, 275, 290 *seqq.*
Dio Cassius, 202
Diodorus Siculus, 156, 202
Dion of Syracuse, 226
Dionysius of Halicarnassus, 201
Domitian, 125
Draco, 176, 180
Dubois, Cardinal, 233
Duni, 269

Eckehart, 301
Eling, Ingewald, 52
Ennius, 194
Epicureans, 87, 97
Epicurus, 82, 101, 137
Esperti, 304, 312
Esteban, E., 261
Euclid, 28
Eusebius, 176
Ezekiel, 92

Fabius Maximus, 205
Fabricius, 168
Faggi, A., 308
Ferrari, G., 265, 305 *seqq.*
Ferron (de), 274

Fichte, 240
Ficino, M., 138, 287, 291, 295
Filangieri, 271, 272
Finetti, 259, 271, 274
Finocchietti, F., 308
Fiorentino, F., 288, 308
Flaubert, 253, 275
Flint, R., 277, 308
Folchieri, G., 310
Fontenelle, 71, 154
Foscolo, 170, 273
Franck, A., 274

Gaeta (di), M., 260
Galasso, A., 302, 306
Galiani, 262
Galen, 50
Galileo, 14, 15, 138, 141, 283, 296-7
Gambetta, 274
Garofalo, P., 309
Gassendi, 138
Genovesi, A., 252, 262
Gentile, G., 263 *n.*, 267, 287 *n.*, 306 *seqq.*
Gerning, 272
Geulinx, 289
Giacchi, 248, 260, 304
Giani, C., 307
Giannone, P., 121, 250, 284 *n.*
Gioberti, 275
Giordano, 165, 305
Giudice (del), G., 305, 311
Giustiniani, L., 272
Goethe, *viii*, 271
Gorgias, 177
Gracchi, 205
Grandi, 269
Gravina, 31
Grimm, 243
Grotius, 22, 31, 46, 74, 82 *seqq.*, 249
Gunther, 223

Hadrian, 212
Hamann, 239, 271
Hannibal, 158
Hecataeus, 189
Hegel, 238 *seqq.*, 270, 274-5
Heraclitus, 202
Hercules, 65, 179
Herder, 145, 239, 271, 277
Hermodorus, 202
Herodotus, 73, 158, 187
Hesiod, 63
Heyne, 239, 270
Hobbes, 78, 87, 101
Höffding, H., 277
Hoffmann, 234

THE END